P9-EDM-195

Hiking and Exploring the
Paria River

Michael R. Kelsey

Including: The Story of John D. Lee and Mountain Meadows
Massacre

Kelsey Publishing
456 E. 100 N.
Provo, Utah, USA 84601
Tele. 801-373-3327

First Edition November 1987
Copyright © 1987 Michael R. Kelsey All Rights Reserved
Library of Congress Catalog Card Number 87-082452
ISBN 0-9605824-7-9

List of Distributors for Kelsey Publishing

Write to one of these companies when ordering any of Mike Kelsey's books. His books and a price list
are at the back of this book.

Alpenbooks, P.O. Box 27344, Seattle, Washington, 98125
Banana Republic, 175 Bluxome Street, San Francisco, California, 94107
Bookpeople, 2929 Fifth Street, Berkeley, California, 94710
Canyon Country Publications, P. O. Box 963, Moab, Utah, 84532
Gordon's Books, 2323 Delgany, Denver, Colorado, 80216
Many Feathers--Southwestern Books, 5738 North Central, Phoenix, Arizona, 85012
Quality Books (Library Distributor), 918 Sherwood Drive, Lake Bluff, Illinois, 60044
Mountain 'n Air Books, 3704 1/2 Foothill Blvd., La Crescenta, California, 91214
Recreational Equipment, Inc.(R.E.I.), P.O. Box C-88126, Seattle, Washington, 98188
Wasatch Publishers, Inc., 4647 Idlewild Road, Salt Lake City, Utah, 84124

For the **UK** and **Europe**, and the rest of the world contact:
CORDEE, 3a De Montfort Street, Leicester, England, UK, LE1 7HD

Printed by Press Publishing, 1600 W. 800 N., Provo, Utah.

All fotos by the author, unless otherwise stated.
All maps, charts, and cross sections drawn by the author.

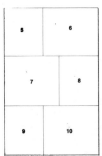

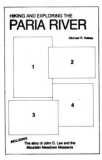

Front Cover

1. Buckskin Gulch
2. Bryce Canyon National Park
3. The Cockscomb
4. Round Valley Draw

Back Cover

5. Mollies Nipple and Nipple Lake
6. Upside Down Rock, Lower Paria River Gorge
7. Jacob Pools, Sand Hill Crack
8. Paria River Spring
9. Bull Valley Gorge Bridge
10. Starlight Canyon Narrows

Table of Contents

Acknowledgments

Many people helped with information for this book, but special thanks should go to the following people. The most important person has to be Rod Schipper, more commonly known as Skip. He's the BLM ranger who lives and works at the Paria River Ranger Station. He has had this same job since 1980, and knows the lower Paria better than anyone. Skip spent hours proof reading the hiking section of this book.

Besides Skip, the BLM geologist in Kanab, Pete Kilborne also contributed in his specialty field. Other residence of Kanab the author interviewed were: Calvin C. Johnson, Jeff Johnson, Leola Scheonfeld, Merrill MacDonald, Mason Meeks, Merrill and Ramona Johnson and Dunk Findlay. Also Mel Schoppman and Bill Leach of Page, Arizona, and George Fisher, now of Las Vegas. Also Bryce Canyon ranger Nate Inouye, and St. George BLM employees Tom Folks, Mike Small and Jennifer Jack.

In the Bryce Valley towns, the author spoke with Kay Clark, Ken Goulding, Ralph Chynoweth, Bob Ott, George Thompson, Joe Dunham, Marian Clark, Wallace Ott, Jack Chynoweth and Herm Pollock. Nearly all of these people are in their 70's, and one, Marian Clark is in his 90's, therefore lots of good information was given about the canyons and the early day ranches.

As usual, my mother Venetta Kelsey, helped proof read the manuscript on more than one occasion. She also watches the business when the author is on the road.

The Author

The author experienced his earliest years of life in eastern Utah's Uinta Basin namely around the town of Roosevelt. Then the family moved to Provo, where he attended Provo High School, and later Brigham Young University, where he earned a B.S. degree in Sociology. Shortly thereafter he discovered that was the wrong subject, so he attended the University of Utah, where he received his Masters of Science degree in Geography, finishing in June, 1970.

It was then that real life began, for on June 9, 1970, he put a pack on his back and started traveling for the first time. Since then he has traveled to 129 countries and island groups. All this wandering has resulted in several books written and published by him: *Climbers and Hikers Guide to the Worlds Mountains(2nd Ed.); Utah Mountaineering Guide, and the best Canyon Hikes(2nd Ed.); China on Your Own and the Hiking Guide to China's Nine Sacred Mountains(3rd Ed.); Canyon Hiking Guide to the Colorado Plateau; Hiking Utah's San Rafael Swell;* and *Hiking and Exploring Utah's Henry Mountains and Robbers Roost.*

Grosvenor or Butler Valley Arch.

4

Introduction to Hiking

This book is basically a hiking guide to the Paria River of Southern Utah. The Paria begins at Bryce Canyon National Park, and flows almost due south, across the Utah-Arizona state line, and ends at the Colorado River and Lee's Ferry in northern Arizona. After the Grand Canyon, Zion Narrows and possibly the Escalante River system, this river drainage has more visitors than any other canyon on the Colorado Plateau. If you like narrow canyons, including the best slot canyon hike in the world, this is the place for you. One can take day hikes in some of the shorter tributaries, or take a week-long marathon walk in the lower end of the Paria Canyon. This area has all kinds of hikes.

The best way to describe where the Paria is, is to say it's about half way between Kanab, Utah, and Page, Arizona, and right in the middle of some of the best parts of the Colorado Plateau. You can get there from St. George and Zion N.P. to the west; from Richfield, Panguitch, and the Bryce Valley towns of Tropic, Cannonville, and Henrieville to the north; from Capitol Reef N. P., Torrey, Boulder, and Escalante to the northeast; from Flagstaff, and either Page and Lake Powell, or Jacob Lake to the south. All these approach roads are major paved highways.

Local Towns and Facilities

In these last few years, since tourism has been so important to the local economies, better accommodations have been built. Here's a run down on what's where in the immediate area.

Page, Arizona This town was built to house and accommodate the workers who built Glen Canyon Dam across the Colorado River, thus creating Lake Powell. Today it's the southern gateway to Lake Powell, and is the local headquarters for the National Park Service, which administers Glen Canyon National Recreational Area. Page has two supermarkets, and a good shopping mall. The town is full of tourists, as well as Navajos from the reservation, and seldom slows down. There are motels and other facilities which are normally found in larger towns. The population is about 6500 now, but has a disproportionately large number of churches, maybe 20-25! A good place to shop for food, sporting goods, books, about everything.

Kanab Kanab is a town a little smaller than Page, but this one is more quiet--mainly because the reservation and lake are further away. Kanab has one huge supermarket, and another smaller one, plus numerous convenient stores. Its facilities are similar to those of Page, with many motels, gas stations and restaurants. It's the county seat, and has two book stores, an airport and golf course. Kanab is the movie capital of southern Utah, and its the jumping off point to the north rim of the Grand Canyon, which is open from about mid-May until late October.

Panguitch This town is just northwest of Bryce Canyon, and is smaller than Kanab. Panguitch is a county seat, and has moderately good facilities, including one small supermarket, and many motels and restaurants. Panguitch still depends mostly on farming and ranching for support, but in summer it's busy with tourists.

Bryce Canyon Facilities Along the highway between Panguitch and Bryce Canyon National Park, are many motels, convenient stores, and independent campsites. On the Paunsaugunt Plateau, and just south of the entrance to the park, is Ruby's Inn. This is a huge complex, with gas station, store(including curios and books), restaurant, laundromat, campground, horseback rides, a rodeo three nights a week in season, and helicopter rides into the park. Inside the park are two campgrounds; one is open year-round now, the other open in summers only. Bryce also has an historic old lodge and cabins for rent.

Tropic This is the biggest town in the Bryce Valley, and that's where the high school is found. Tropic has two gas stations; one with a small supermarket, the other with a convenient store; a burger and malt shop combined with motel(it's open from about Easter until after the deer hunt, at the end of October); and one garage, the only one in the valley. It appears only the burger stand in open on Sundays, everything else is closed.

Cannonville This small town has but one store which sells about everything--a kind of general store. It used to sell gas, but no more. Closed Sundays

Kodachrome Basin State Park In 1987, Bob Ott and family from Cannonville, opened a small campers store in the state park just south of the campground. They have horse and wagon rides, and are catering to senior citizens and campers. The store is about 13 kms southeast of Cannonville, and will be open from about Easter to early November.

Henrieville Henrieville has one small gas station-convenient store, which is closed on Sundays.

Escalante A town full of ranchers, lumbermen, and several BLM, Forest Service and NPS personnel. It has a couple of gas stations, several motels, two small supermarkets(general stores), a new restaurant and one burger stand, which does a good business in the spring, summer and fall, with the hikers heading into the Escalante River country.

Road Report

For the most part access to most of these canyons is reasonably good. If you're going down the Lower Paria River Gorge, you're in luck; you only have to drive about 3 kms on a graveled, all-weather road, and you're at the White House Trailhead. At the bottom end of the river, which is Lee's Ferry, you'll be on pavement all the way. For the rest of the hikes, with the exception of those inside Bryce Canyon National Park, you'll have to do some driving on dirt or graveled roads, but as a general rule all the hikes featured in this book are easy to get to with an ordinary car in dry weather.

Skutumpah Road This is a main link between the little community of Johnson, located about 16 kms due east of Kanab, and the Bryce Valley towns of Cannonville, Henrieville, and Tropic. The Skutumpah Road part of this link begins at the head of Johnson Canyon, where the road divides; one goes northwest to Alton, the other heads northeast to Cannonville. It's 103 kms from Kanab to Cannonville along Highway 89, Johnson Canyon, and finally along the Skutumpah Road.

The road up Johnson Canyon is paved most of the way, then it's sort-of-graveled up to about the Skutumpah Ranch. After that it's maintained and graded, but made out of what ever land the road passes through. In places it's just ordinary dirt, other places it's gravely, and still other places it's made of clay beds. When it rains only lightly, it seldom effects the road. All you have to do is wait 'till the sun hits it a few minutes, and away you go. When heavy rains soak the area, it may be a one or two day wait in the warmer season, maybe a weeks wait in the winter.

For the most part, this road is closed in winter, but 4WD's do it at that time, especially during dry spells, or in morning hours when it's frozen. However, on the dugway just above Willis Creek to the south, is a seep right next to the road. This makes the road icy in winter, and 4WD's slide off it occasionally. For the most part, the Skutumpah Road is open for all traffic from about the first part of April through mid-November. Because there are a number of ranches along this road, it's well maintained, and carries half a dozen vehicles a day.

Cottonwood Wash Road The Cottonwood Wash Road runs south out of Cannonville, to and past Kodachrome Basin State Park, to Butler Valley Arch(officially known as Grosvenor Arch), and down the Cockscomb Valley(Cottonwood Wash) and eventually to Highway 89, to between mile posts 17 and 18.

This Cottonwood Wash Road was built back in about 1957, by a cooperative organized by 72 year-old Sam Pollock in the local Bryce Valley towns, and including Escalante and Antimony. These people wanted a shortcut to the Lake Powell area to increase tourism in their own little area. The $5500 for the road was raised by donations and sales of various kinds. The county loaned them one caterpillar and a road grader, and a mining company pitched in a compressor. The project took 70 days to complete.

The part of the road to Kodachrome is supposed to be paved in the late 1980's, but until that happens, it's an all-weather gravel road. East of the Kodachrome Turnoff, the road deteriorates, but is maintained regularly, and is used by maybe 20-30 cars daily in the warmer 6 months of the year. For the most part, it's a warm weather road, as there are slick spots in places, when ever it rains hard. Those spots that become slick, which is mostly in winter time, are made of the gray colored clay beds of the Tropic Shale.

Nipple Ranch Road This is a maintained county road to the Nipple Ranch just north of Mollies Nipple. It begins on Highway 89 at mile post 37, and runs to an old drill site north of the Kitchen Canyon. This is a good road for the most part, but it gradually deteriorates as you drive along it. In it's upper parts just west of Mollies Nipple, there are several big sand traps, so it's recommended you take precautions(and perhaps a shovel), and if possible a 4WD. This is one of the few roads which will be easier and safer to drive if the weather is a little wet; because sand sets up and is easier to drive in when wet.

House Rock Valley Road This road runs from Highway 89 just west of The Cockscomb(between mile posts 25-26), south to Highway 89A, where an abandoned ranch and gas station called House Rock, is located. House Rock is in the upper western part of House Rock Valley. The road is about 50 kms long, and is for seasonal use. Normally it's open almost year-round, but in winter and when it's wet because of heavy storms, it is slick in places. The bad places are a result of the road running over clay beds, most of which are just south of the state line and on the Arizona side. It's a maintained road, but the Utah side is usually in better condition than the Arizona side. Generally the northern and southern ends are in very good condition--the middle parts being a little rougher. Road crews in Utah usually work the road over in April each year. During the warmer half of the year it has moderately heavy traffic(for such an out of the way road).

Pahreah Road The road to old Pahreah ghost town begins between mile posts 30 and 31, on Highway 89, about half way between Page and Kanab. This is a good 10 km long road, which is well used in the warmer half of the year. In winter it may be slick in spots, because most of it runs along the Moenkopi clay beds. It is definitely impassable during or just after heavy rains, but ordinarily it's a road for all vehicles.

Off Road Vehicles

In the spring of 1987, the Utah State Legislature passed four bills dealing with all aspects of Off Road Vehicle(ORV's) use. These new laws are written up as the **Utah Off-Highway Vehicle Act**, Title 41, Chapter 22, Utah code anotated 1953, as amended in April 1987. To make a long story short, here's the most important part.

41-22-12. (2) states: No person may operate and no owner of an off-highway vehicle may give another person permission to operate an off-highway vehicle *on any public land which has not been designated as open to off-highway vehicles.*

In a letter to this author from Governor Norm Bangerter, he states, ..."*the statute specifies that all public land shall be presumed closed to the use of off highway vehicles unless designated as open by the agency or entity controlling said land."*

It sounds almost too good to be true. But in reality, Utah State laws do not control the Federal Agencies, which control most of the land in the state. They are the Bureau of Land Management and the Forest Service. The BLM, which administers almost all the land in the Paria drainage, continues to designate about 95% of it's land as open to Off Road Vehicles. So BLM policy is going contrary to the wishes of the Utah State lawmakers. The only areas safe from these maurading dirt bikes and three and four wheeled land molesters are areas set aside as wilderness by law. In those places under study as wilderness areas(WSA's), ORV's are allowed on existing roads only.

Now this sounds good too, but the problem is, they don't always stay on the existing roads! This all adds up to nothing and a law without teeth and full of holes. Only when the BLM decides they're going to stop allowing people to use public lands as test sites for their ORV's, will America be serious about saving what little pristine land it has left.

Climate of the Paria River Region

Below are three tables showing climatic information for three locations in the region. *Cannonville* is in the Upper Paria River Basin and in Bryce Valley; *Kanab* is just to the west of the drainage area at the bottom of the western part of the Vermilion Cliffs; and *Lee's Ferry* is at the very mouth of the Paria on the Colorado River. By viewing these table, you can understand how the altitude and other factors effect the temperatures and the amounts of precipitation. One can also understand why spring and fall are the ideal times to hike in most of the areas covered in this book.

Cannonville, Utah--Altitude 1835 meters

Fahrenheit = 9/5 x C, + 32,   Centigrade = 5/9 x (F-32), 1 inch = 2.54 cms.

Month	Precipitation(cm)	Max. Temps.(C)	Min.Temps.(C)
January	2.72	5.3	-10.2
February	2.44	7.0	-8.5
March	2.26	11.1	-4.4
April	1.78	15.6	-1.4
May	1.47	20.8	1.5
June	.97	26.9	6.0
July	3.53	29.4	9.6
August	4.29	27.7	8.8
September	3.25	24.4	4.4
October	2.06	18.8	-.8
November	1.70	12.2	-5.4
December	2.41	5.9	-9.9
Average	**28.89**	**17.1**	**- 0.8**

Kanab, Utah--Altitude 1501 meters

Month			
January	3.76	8.0	-6.2
February	3.51	10.8	-4.1
March	3.51	15.0	-1.6
April	2.41	20.1	1.8
May	1.45	25.1	5.7
June	.84	30.7	9.9
July	2.64	33.8	14.2
August	3.30	32.4	13.5
September	2.62	28.7	9.7
October	2.44	22.3	4.1
November	2.21	15.0	-1.4
December	3.12	9.0	-5.3
Average	**31.08**	**20.9**	**3.3**

Lee's Ferry, Arizona--Altitude 950 meters

Month			
January	.96	8.3	-3.9
February	1.19	13.9	-.5
March	1.24	18.9	3.9
April	.99	25.0	8.9
May	.79	30.0	13.3
June	.61	35.5	17.8
July	1.85	39.4	22.2
August	3.00	37.7	21.1
September	1.30	34.4	16.1
October	1.07	26.1	9.4
November	.99	19.4	1.7
December	1.12	9.4	-2.8
Average	**15.11**	**24.8**	**8.9**

Best Hiking Times

For those heading into the Lower Paria River Gorge, the best time in the spring is from about late March through the end of May(but late May through June for the Buckskin Gulch). For some of the canyons higher in the drainage, April through mid-June is usually the best time.

In the fall season in the lower gorge, late September through mid-November are best, but higher in the drainage, early September until early November is usually best, although snow can come during that time. For the higher country, Bryce Canyon and Table Cliff Plateau, the summer months, or from about late May through October are usually the best, but early or late season bad weather spells can shorten the season.

The time of year when the flash flood danger in the narrow slot-type canyons is highest, is from mid-July through August(the worst time) and extending to mid-September. Regardless of the time of year, one should always stay tuned to the local radio stations and have a generally good weather forecast before entering places like the Buckskin Gulch. Rod Schipper(Skip) the resident ranger at the Paria Ranger Station, always has the weather forecast posted in front of the ranger station. Always stop there and check things out before entering the narrow canyons.

Flash Flood Frequency   Measured at Lee's Ferry

January——1/5	April——— 0	July———1.9	October——3/10
February—1/10	May———1/10	August——3.0	November–1/2
March———3/10	June——— 0	September-1.4	December–3/10

A **flash flood** is defined as a rise in daily runoff of 50 CFS or more. The actual rise in runoff rate will normally occur over a short period of time and be maintained for 1 to 4 days. 200 to 400 CFS rises in river levels are periodically recorded. A frequency of 1/5 indicates a flash flood will occur during this month once in five years. 3.0 indicates an average of 3 flash floods during this month each year. O indicates there have been no flash floods during this month in the 10 year record used for computing this chart(from the USGS at Lee's Ferry). The biggest flood ever to be recorded on the Paria River at Lee's Ferry, was on September 12, 1958. That one measured 19,000 cubic feet per second.

Drinking Water

In recent years there seems to be great controversy over what is and is not suitable drinking water in the back country. The US Public Health Service requires the National Park Service to inform hikers to boil all surface water, including water coming out of springs! This seems unbelievably short sighted, and leaves little room for using common sense. The chief reason they do it, is to save themselves from possible law suits.

Since the author has never gotten ill when hiking and climbing in his life, it seem logical that he may have just the right common sense. This life time of travel includes hiking and climbing in 129 countries and island groups, since 1970. Here are some steps the author has taken to prevent getting the belly ache while hiking the Paria Country.

On day hikes he always carries a plastic bottle full of "city" water. However, if he passes a good spring which is obviously unpolluted, he usually drinks from the spring because it's often colder. An unpolluted spring is basically one which cattle cannot get into. If it is free flowing, comes right out of the ground or rock wall, and has no fresh cattle sign near, then it should be good to drink as-is.

When it comes to some of the small side canyon streams, the thing you'll have to look for are any fresh sign of cattle. If there are cattle in the area, then you'd better purify or filter any running water. Keep in mind, if there are cattle around, then risks are higher. But if it's summer, and the cattle have been taken out of the canyons to the higher summer ranges, and the water is free flowing, then the risks are almost nil. The Giardia cysts cannot swim; they can merely float down stream. If the stream has a good flow, then shortly after the cattle leave a canyon, the water should then become drinkable. This is what many old timer cowboys from the area, who have drank this Paria water all their lives, have told the author.

If you're still not convinced, in the latest catalog from R.E.I., they show water filters for $549, $165, $40 and $34. They also have small bottles of Iodine tablets for $3(containing 50 tablets-one per liter). On all overnight hikes the author carries a bottle of Iodine tablets, but has only used these tablets once in the Paria drainage, and three other times in his life while hiking or climbing.

Here's a tip for those who will spend several days in a canyon camping. Take along one or more large water jugs--3.75 liters or one US gallon. This will enable you to carry water from a spring to your campsite, which may be distant from a good water supply. The local water availability and possible hazards are discussed under each hike.

The chief reason for taking precautions is to escape the intestinal disorder called Giardiasis. This is caused by the microscopic organism, Giardia Lamblia. Giardia are carried in the feces of humans and some domestic and wild animals. The cysts of Giardia may contaminate surface water supplies. The symptoms of this stomach problem include diarrhea, increased gas, loss of appetite, abdominal cramps, and bloating. It is not life threatening, but it can slow you down and make life miserable. Some BLM and national park rangers constantly harangue hikers about its deathly possibilities, but if you take the precautions mentioned above, and under each hike, you'll surely miss out on this one.

Insect Season

The insect season seems to begin in late May, and continues to about the first part of July, in most of the Paria Country. In the wide areas of the canyons above both Lee's Ferry and Pahreah, there are small gnats which get into your hair and bite hard; and large gray horse flies which bite the back of bare legs. These horse flies are always found around areas where there's water and tamarisk(pronounced *tamarack*) bushes. The month of July isn't so bad, but it's plenty hot then. For some reason they mostly dissappear in about mid-July, or about when the first monsoon rains begin. In the fall there seems to be a general absence of these pests, especially from mid-September on. To avoid horse flies, simply wear long pants. Insect repellent can help some in detracting the gnats.

The author can't remember any of these insects in the narrow canyons, such as the Buckskin. He can't remember of any mosquitos, except in swampy places, such as around Adair Lake. Nor can he remember any mosquitos in the Lower Paria River Gorge, where he has made 7 trips over the years, and in all seasons.

Equipment for Day-Hikes

These are some of the things the author carries on day hikes. A day-pack, a bottle of water, camera and lenses, extra film, short piece of nylon parachute cord, toilet paper, pen and small notebook, map, chapstick, compass, pocket knife, a walking stick (made from an aluminum shower curtain rod, that has a clamp on top which screws into the bottom of a camera, and serves as a camera stand), a cap with "cancer curtain" around the back, and usually a lunch. If it's cool or colder weather, then gloves and an overcoat are added. In these cases, you'll want one of the larger day-packs, in order to carry it all throughout the day. In warmer weather, he wears shorts and a "T" shirt; in cooler weather, long pants and a long sleeved shirt.

Equipment for Overnight Hikes

For those with less experience, here's a list of things the author normally takes on longer hikes. A large pack, sleeping bag, thermal rest sleeping pad, tent--with rain sheet, small kerosene stove, several lighters(no matches any more!), 10 meters of nylon parachute cord, camera and lenses, walking stick, with camera stand on the top end, one large water jug, a one liter water bottle, a stitching awl and waxed thread, small plyers, cannister with odds and ends(bandaids, needle and thread, patching kit for sleeping pad, wire, pens, etc.), maps, notebook, reading book, chapstick, compass, toilet paper, pocket knife, rain cover for pack, small alarm clock, candles for light, tooth brush and tooth paste, face lotion, sunscreen, cap with cancer curtain, soap, small flashlight, and a lightweight mini-umbrella.

Food usually includes such items as oatmeal or cream of wheat cereal, coffee or chocolate drink, powdered milk, sugar, cookies, crackers, candy, oranges or apples, carrots, Ramen instant noodles, soups, macaroni, canned tuna fish or sardines, vienna sausages, peanuts, instant puddings, bread, butter, peanut butter, salt and pepper, plastic eating bowl, spoon, small cooking pot, extra fuel for stove.

Boots or Shoes

Because many of the canyons you'll be hiking in have running water, you'll surely want some kind of a boot or shoe which can be used when wet--some kind of a wading shoe. Many people just use an old pair of running or gym shoes. But here are some precautions; if the shoes are too worn out, you may lose them before the hike ends, especially if taking in the Lower Paria Gorge; if the running shoe is too old, it may lack proper support for the foot--a tip for older hikers; a shoe made of canvas and rubber will last longer in a watery situation, than one with leather parts; leather shoes should be treated with oil after a long wading hike, such as through the Upper or Lower Paria Canyon.

Hiking Rules and Regulations

Bryce Canyon National Park

There are some rules to backpacking in Bryce Canyon, as there are in any of our national parks. Here are some of them. If you're planning to camp out in the backcountry, then you'll need a free camping permit. Pick this up at the park visitor center, along with other last minute information. If you're just day-hiking, no permit is needed. You must camp in designated campsites only, and use a stove of some kind--no camp fires allowed. Camping is limited to three days in any one site. No wheeled vehicles of any kind are allowed on the backcountry trails. If you're still interested, get all the latest information at the visitor center just as you enter the park. Backcountry rangers will give you a long list of do's and don'ts.

For many reasons, there aren't too many hikers camping in the backcountry of Bryce Canyon. One big reason is the fact there is almost no live running water in the park. Largely because of this, most people do day-hikes.

Paria Canyon--Vermilion Cliffs Wilderness Area

Here's a list of regulations pertaining to the Lower Paria River Gorge between the White House Trailhead and Lee's Ferry. It also includes the popular Buckskin Gulch, main tributary to the Paria.
1. No campfires are allowed within the Lower Paria Canyon, Buckskin Gulch, and all tributary canyons in this lower canyon.
2. Group size is limited to 15 people. Large groups must contact the BLM two weeks in advance.
3. Carry out all trash. Do not burn or bury it. This includes all biodegradable material and cigarette butts.

4. Bury human waste and toilet paper in a "cat hole" type of latrine, away from springs and campsites locations. Burn the toilet paper before burial.

5. Dogs are allowed, but they must be restrained from disturbing wildlife or other hikers.

6. Don't make camp right next to any spring. Keep the site as natural as possible.

7. Don't wash dishes near springs or any drinking water supply.

9. Pick up a free camping permit in the Kanab BLM office or Paria Ranger Station, within 24 hours of departure. This inables you to get the latest weather forecast.

9. Please sign in at the register as you enter the canyon, so that counts can be made on visitation days.

10. Perhaps the most important thing to remember is, to be considerate of others who will visit this place after you.

For more detailed information contact the BLM office, Kanab, Utah. Their fone number is 801-644-2672. Their address is in the north part of town, at 318 North, First East, Kanab. Office hours are 7:45 A.M. to 4;30 P.M., M. S. T., weekdays(Utah uses Daylight Savings Time).

Rod Schipper at the Paria Ranger Station, between mile posts 20 and 21 on Highway 89, is there in his home/office from about 8:00 A.M. to 11:00 A.M., on most days throughout the year. He maintains radio contact with the Kanab office.

Car shuttle service for Paria Canyon hikers is available at Lee's Ferry and at Page, Arizona. Contact the Kanab BLM office for their latest list of shuttle people.

Visitor Use--Lower Paria Canyon

This chart shows the number of visitors to the Lower Paria River Gorge and the Buckskin Gulch in the five year period of 1982 through 1986. The figures are averages for each month. These figures may give you some ideas on when to go to avoid the biggest crowds.

Month	Average Number of Hikers
Januray	23
February	19
March	187
April	237
May	468
June	325
July	78
August	52
September	98
October	165
November	72
December	27

A canyon as popular as this one is bound to have a few rules, but they're nothing to what you find in some places. So hikers are asked to be thoughtful of those who will follow. The author was in this lower gorge 5 times during the spring and summer of 1987, and found almost no litter. Can't we all help to keep it that way, and keep the best canyon hike in the world as pristine as it is today?

Hiking Maps for the Paria River

Included here is an index map showing the USGS topographic maps of the region. Any serious hiker should get one or several of the maps shown on this index.

There are basically three sets of maps for the area. They are the newer metric maps at 1:100,000 scale, and the other standard maps at 1:62,500(15 minute) and 1:24,000(7.5 minute) scale.

The author prefers the newer metric maps, and uses these almost exclusively. If you buy the three most important maps--*Kanab, Smoky Mountain,* and *Glen Canyon Dam,* you can hike and tour almost the entire region. Other than these, you'll need the *Escalante* map for a couple of hikes, and the *Panguitch* metric covers the northern end of the Skutumpah Road and Bryce Canyon. Also the *Fredonia* map covers the House Rock Valley Road. For those people who want the Upper Paria River Gorge, Hackberry Canyon, The Cockscomb and all the tributaries, *Kanab* and *Smoky Mountain* just about cover it all. Only one small corner of the *Panguitch* map might help with the upper Paria hike.

INDEX TO TOPOGRAPHIC MAPS–PARIA RIVER

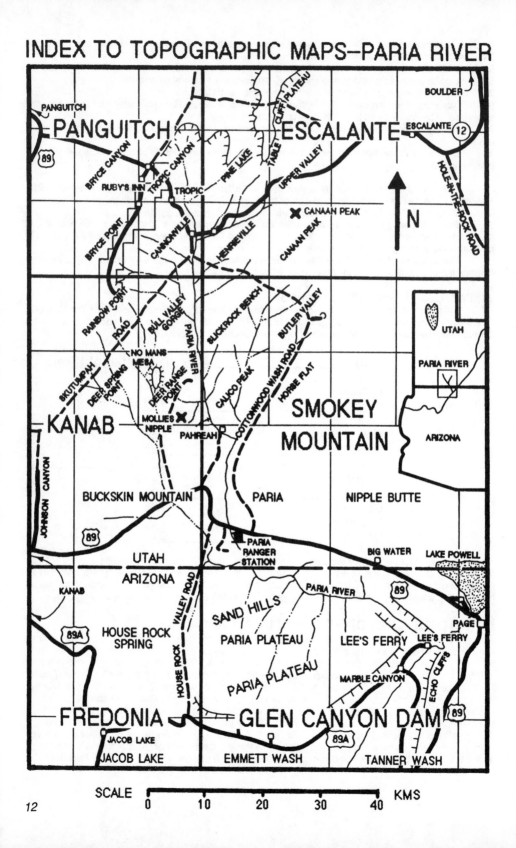

One reason the author likes the metric maps is they are all new, dating from about 1980. So virtually all roads are shown on these maps. Most other maps date from the 1950's, and lack the newer roads. Another reason, just one map may cover several hikes, whereas with the larger scale maps(1:24.000), you may have to have several maps to cover one hike. The metric maps also fold up and fit in your pocket.

Some people don't like metrics, but with the USA, Burma and Brunei being the only countries on earth still using this antiquated English System, it's something we'll all have to live with sooner or later. But even if you don't like metric and don't understand it, you can still get along with these maps because they are still laid out in one square mile sections, the same as on all USGS maps. Since all land is surveyed in these section and townships grids, it seems we will never get away from this old system entirely.

For the Lower Paria River Gorge, you could buy the three maps at 1:62,500 scale, *Paria, Paria Plateau* and *Lee's Ferry*. But you can do better than this, if you buy one or all four of the map series titled *MF-1475*. In this series, there are four maps, *A, B, C, and D*. They cover Geology, Geochemical Data, Mines and Prospects, and Mineral Resource Potential. Map C or D might be the two best for hiking the canyon. These maps are at scale 1:62,500, and are based on the regular the USGS maps at the same scale. The great thing about this one map is, it includes all the Lower Paria Canyon, the Paria Plateau and the House Rock Valley Road. All on just one map costing $1.50.

Another good map for those hiking the lower canyon, is the BLM publication, *Hikers Guide to Paria Canyon*. It is based on the 1:62,500 scale maps, but concentrates on just the lower gorge, omitting the Paria Plateau or Sand Hills. In late summer of 1987, the BLM was in the process of updating this old map, so hopefully this one will be of better quality than the first edition. You can buy this one at the BLM offices in Cedar City, St. George, Kanab and the Paria Ranger Station. It'll cost about $1.00.

Another good map to have in addition to the hiking type, is a map put out by the Utah Travel Council, entitled *Southwestern Utah*. This is a tourist map, which shows the entire area(except the Arizona part), and is at 1:250,000 scale. In the summer of 1987, a new series of maps have just been releasd. This new series covers the state of Utah with five maps, instead of with eight, in the old series.

Wilderness Areas of the Paria River Basin

As of 1987, there were two officially designated wilderness areas in the region covered by the Paria River. These are the Paria Canyon and the Vermilion Cliffs Wilderness Areas. Actually, they are combined now, to form one very long and almost circular wilderness, surrounding the Sand Hills or Paria Plateau.

In the middle and upper parts of the Paria, there are three Wilderness Study Areas, and parts of another. The smallest of the four is *The Cockscomb WSA*. It lies between Highway 89, the Cottonwood Wash Road, and The Box--where the Paria River flows through The Cockscomb. It for the most part, covers the part of The Cockscomb between The Box and Highway 89. The Hattie Green Mine is found in this section.

Between old Pahreah, and the Cottonwood Wash and Skutumpah Roads, is another very large WSA. This one is called the *Paria--Hackberry WSA*. It covers virtually all of both the Upper Paria River Gorge and Hackberry Canyon. Also included is Mollies Nipple, No Mans Mesa, Bull Valley Gorge, Upper and Lower Death Valleys, and the lower part of Round Valley Draw.

There are problems with including this vast region into Americas Wilderness System, one of which is the fact that for more than a century, early settlers(and now cattlemen) have used vehicles in the washed-out Paria River bottom. Cattlemen still take cattle into the middle parts of this Upper Paria River Gorge with the help of 4WD's. There are also recreationists in that canyon just out joy-riding! and test driving their ORV's. Some compromise will surely be worked out.

The third area under consideration for wilderness status is *The Blues WSA*. This covers the blue-gray colored clay hills to the southwest of the tip of Table Cliff Plateau, and to the west and south of Canaan Peak. The formations exposed there are: the Kaiparowits, Wahweap, Straight Cliffs and Tropic Shale. Much of the area has a resemblance to the Mancos Shale beds west of both Green River and Hanksville.

The last WSA included in the Paria Basin is the *Wahweap WSA*. It extends out of the area covered in this book and almost to Lake Powell. Part of it covers the upper parts of The Cockscomb, which is just to the east of the Cottonwood Wash Road. This is one of the more spectacular sites on the Colorado Plateau.

In Arizona, many new wilderness areas have been set aside in the last few years, but Utah is lagging behind. Most of the BLM controlled WSA's in Utah will be put to Congress for the final decision in the early 1990's.

WILDERNESS AND WILDERNESS STUDY AREAS

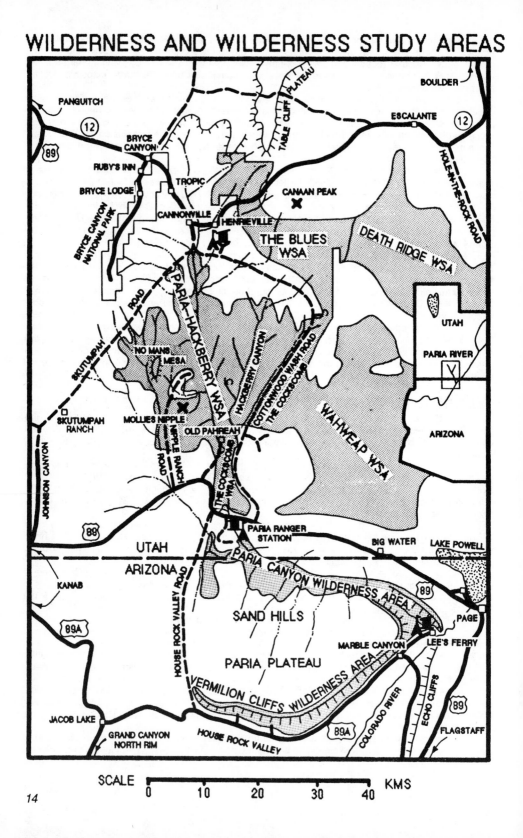

SCALE

0   10   20   30   40   KMS

Fotography in Deep, Dark Canyons

If you have talked to anyone who has tried taking fotos in some of the deep and dark canyons of the Colorado Plateau, and especially narrow canyons like the Zion Narrows and Buckskin Gulch of the Paria, they'll likely tell you the fotos just didn't turn out right. Since most of these hikers have only tried taking fotos in such places once or twice in their lives, it's easy to understand how they failed. Here are some tips on how to make your fotos better on your first trip down the Buckskin Gulch, Bull Valley Gorge, or Round Valley Draw.

Some of the more common problems are these: Maybe the worst thing that happens is that the fotos turn out far too dark, there being very little light in the narrow canyon. The obvious reason for this is the camera just doesn't have the capabilities to take a good foto in dark places.

Another common problem is that the pictures are fuzzy or blurred or seem out of focus. This is caused by a combination of low light, a slow shutter speed, and using the camera without a tripod.

Still another problem is, half of the foto may be very bright or totally washed out, while the other half is dark, sometimes black and showing nothing. This is caused by taking a picture with half of the area in bright sunshine, the other half in the shade. These are the more common problems. Below are some suggestions on how you can correct the situation.

Camera and Lens

The most common type of camera used by hikers these days is the 35 mm, with a through-the-lens metering system. Others may use the instamatic type, but these are of the poorest quality, and will produce poor quality fotos.

The recommended equipment to take is a 35 mm camera, with two lenses; one the normal 50 mm which comes with the camera, and a moderately wide angle lens, such as a 24 mm, 28 mm or 35 mm. A lens wider than about 24 mm, will distort the foto more than most people want. If only one lens could be taken, the author would likely choose a 35 mm. A serious fotographer will take at least two lenses, perhaps more.

Most of these 35 mm cameras have a shutter speed range from one full second up to 1/1000 of a second. In the darker canyons, you'll likely be using low shutter speeds, from 1/30 to 1/15 of a second, or lower, depending on your film speed.

The author now carries a Pentax K-1000, a totally mechanical camera, with a through-the-lens metering system, and a screw-on selftimer. He would prefer a built-in timer, because he uses it often. But other factors were more important when he was shopping for this camera, such as the need for a mechanical camera.

Mechanical cameras, of which there are very few on the market today, are much more sturdy and can withstand more bumps and abuse, than the newer electronic models. Mechanical cameras are also more likely to work after being wet, such as when you stumble in the river, than the electronic ones. They are also easier and less expensive to repair. With electronic cameras, you may have a developing minor short in the system, but which the repairman can't find or fix. The mechanical camera is easily diagnosed and repairs made quickly. These mechanical cameras are usually less expensive as well.

The author carries at all times a 50 mm, 28 mm, and a 70-210 mm zoom. The zoom lens is seldom used in the canyons, but was used often when fotographing more open areas in this book. In the past, zoom lenses have been pretty poor quality, but the newer ones are much improved. There are new models out now which range from 28 mm to 70 mm, or thereabouts. This would be a good lens to have, except that it would be rather slow; that is, the F stop would be no better than about 2.8, and likely closer to 3.5, which makes it difficult to take good fotos in dark places. A lens with an F stop of 1.4 or 1.7, allows much more light onto the film, than a 2.8 or 3.5 lens. Try and have at least a F 2.0 lens, or faster, if you can.

Film Type

Besides using a fast lens(F1.4 or F1.7) to get pictures in these slot canyons, you can also compensate for the darkness by using a faster film. Film speeds range from a slow 25, 50, or 64 ASA, up to faster 400 or 1000 ASA. If you're out on the ski slopes on a bright sunny day, you'd want a film with a slow speed, such as 25 or 50 ASA. But if you're in darker places such as the Buckskin, you'll want the fastest film you can get, like the 200, 400 or 1000 ASA films. The author uses 200 ASA color slide film only, and it works well in bright sunny scenes, as well as in the darkest canyons.

Another technique you can use, is to "push" the film. For example, if you use 200 ASA Ektachrome(color slide film), you can set your camera ASA setting on 400 or 800 ASA, which is one or two full stops above or ahead. This higher setting(say two full stops) will change your shutter speed from 1/15 of a second, to 1/60 of a second. In this example, instead of using a tripod, you can hand hold the camera, and still get good results.

When it comes time to develop the film, you'll have to take it to a lab which specializes in film finishing, and tell them you pushed the film either one or two stops. They will then leave it in the developer for a longer period of time, thus compensating for the adjustment you made with the ASA setting on the camera.

You can use the "pushing" technique on Ektachrome(or any color slide film which uses the E-6 processing method, such as Agfachrome 200 ASA) 200 or 400 ASA film, or B+W 400 ASA film. If using the 400 B + W film, you can push it as far as 1600 ASA, or two stops, which would virtually eliminate the need for a tripod. Lab people have also told the author this technique does not work for color print film, such as the new 1000 ASA Kodacolor print film. But that's plenty fast anyway. Before you try this method of "pushing the ASA", you might call a local lab first, to get everything straight.

Tripod or Camera Stand

Carrying a tripod or camera stand down a long canyon hike, is asking too much for most people, but it will pay off with better results. Actually, if you have a fairly fast lens(F1.4 or F1.7), a fast film(200, 400 or 1000 ASA), and compensate by pushing the film(one roll of film in the darkest narrows only) one or two full stops, you can easily get by without the tripod. But here's an alternative to a bulky tripod.

Make a walking stick out of an aluminum shower curtain rod. Cut off one end, and have someone weld it to form a "T". You can use it to probe for possible deep holes, and can stick it in the mud and with the aid of a small camera clamp, can use it as a tripod. This is what the author uses, since he is alone more than 99% of the time. One thing to remember though, when you're using it in a very dark part of the narrows, with the shutter speed at perhaps 1/15 of a second, be sure and lean it against the canyon wall. Otherwise, you'll get a swaying motion in the single leg, which will make your foto blurred.

If your camera indicates the shutter speed is below 1/60 of a second, use a stand of some kind--either a rock, tripod, or walking stick. Sometimes you can lean against a wall and get moderately good results by hand-holding it at 1/30 of a second, but rarely.

More Tips

When in a place like the Buckskin Gulch, never take a foto in an area where there's a streak of sunlight in the foto. If you do, part of the picture will be washed out and extra light, the other part will be dark or totally black. Instead, take a picture where the sunlight is being bounced off the upper walls, and diffused down into the canyon bottom.

Another way would be to wait for a cloud to cover the sun, then the light is diffused, thus eliminating the harsh contrasts between sun and shadow. Some of the best times to take fotos in the Buckskin, Bull Valley Gorge or Round Valley Draw, is in mid-morning or mid-afternoon. This way you can easily find places where the sun isn't shining down into the narrows, but instead is shining on an upper wall, and is bounced or diffused down into the dark corners.

If you should slip and fall into the water, or somehow drop your camera in the stream, here are the steps to take. Immediately, take out the camera battery. Quickly roll the film back into the cannister, and remove it. Open the camera and shake and blow out any water. Allow it to sit in the sun to dry, turning it occasionally to help evaporate any water inside. If you're near your car, start the engine, turn on the heater, and hang the camera in front of it. The warmer or hotter the camera gets, the better. This helps the water to evaporate more quickly. The quicker the water evaporates, the less corrosion there will be on the electrical system; and less rust on metal parts.

If your camera is under for just a second or less, as if you slipped down into the water and got right back up, there likely will not be any water inside the camera. In this case, by following the above steps, you will likely be fotographing again in half an hour, especially if the water is clear, no sand has gotten into the camera, and if the sun is warm. The author has had many of these little accidents, and with each of his cameras two or three times. The last several times, no repair work was needed because he did the right things to get the camera dry.

Metric Conversion Table

1 Centimeter = .39 Inch	1 Mile = 1.609 Kilometers	1 Quart (US) = .946 Liter
1 Inch = 2.54 Centimeters	100 Miles = 161 Kilometers	1 Gallon (US) = 3.785 Liters
1 Meter = 39.37 Inches	100 Kilometers = 62 Miles	1 Acre = 0.405 Hectare
1 Foot = 0.3048 Meter	1 Liter = 1.056 Quarts (US)	1 Hectare = 2.471 Acres
1 Kilometer = 0.621 Mile		

METERS TO FEET (Meters x 3.2808 = Feet)

100 m = 328 ft.	2500 m = 8202 ft.	5000 m = 16404 ft.	7500 m = 24606 ft.
500 m = 1640 ft.	3000 m = 9842 ft.	5500 m = 18044 ft.	8000 m = 26246 ft.
1000 m = 3281 ft.	3500 m = 11483 ft.	6000 m = 19686 ft.	8500 m = 27887 ft.
1500 m = 4921 ft.	4000 m = 13124 ft.	6500 m = 21325 ft.	9000 m = 29527 ft.
2000 m = 6562 ft.	4500 m = 14764 ft.	7000 m = 22966 ft.	

FEET TO METERS (Feet ÷ 3.2808 = Meters)

1000 ft. = 305 m	9000 ft. = 2743 m	16000 ft. = 4877 m	23000 ft. = 7010 m
2000 ft. = 610 m	10000 ft. = 3048 m	17000 ft. = 5182 m	24000 ft. = 7315 m
3000 ft. = 914 m	11000 ft. = 3353 m	18000 ft. = 5486 m	25000 ft. = 7620 m
4000 ft. = 1219 m	12000 ft. = 3658 m	19000 ft. = 5791 m	26000 ft. = 7925 m
5000 ft. = 1524 m	13000 ft. = 3962 m	20000 ft. = 6096 m	27000 ft. = 8230 m
6000 ft. = 1829 m	14000 ft. = 4268 m	21000 ft. = 6401 m	28000 ft. = 8535 m
7000 ft. = 2134 m	15000 ft. = 4572 m	22000 ft. = 6706 m	29000 ft. = 8839 m
8000 ft. = 2438 m			30000 ft. = 9144 m

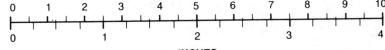

CENTIMETERS / INCHES

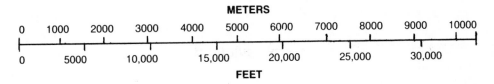

METERS / FEET

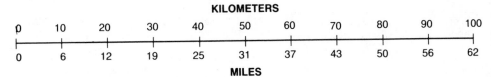

KILOMETERS / MILES

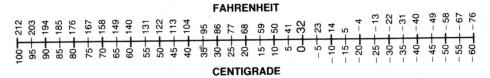

FAHRENHEIT / CENTIGRADE

Map Symbols

Town or Community..........	o☐☐	Peak and Prominent Ridge..........	✗
Buildings or Homes..........	o●	Stream or Creek, Desert..........	∼
Back Country Campsite..........	▲	Stream or Creek, Mountain..........	∼
Campsite..........	⬟	River, Large..........	∼
Campgrounds..........	⚓	Stream or Creek, Intermittent or Dry..	∼..∼
Church..........	⛪	Canyon Narrows..........	Ⓝ
Cemetery or Grave Site..........	†	Lake or Pond..........	⊕
Ranger Station..........	⚑⛪	Mine, Quarry, Adit, Prospect..........	↖↗
Airport or Landing Strip..........	✈ ✈	Water or Dry Falls..........	⟑
U. S. Highway..........	⬛⑧⑨	Spring or Seep..........	⚲
Utah State Highway..........	⬛㉔	Pass..........	⌣⌢
Road-Maintained..........	══ ══	Natural Arch..........	Ⓐ ∩
Road-4 Wheel Drive(4WD)..........	═══	Geology Cross Section..........	⊔
Track-Road, Unusable..........	▬ ▬ ▬	Pictograph..........	Ⓟⓘⓒ
Trail, Foot or Horse..........	▬▬▬▬	Petroglyph..........	Ⓟⓔⓣ
Route, No Trail..........	•••••	Cowboy Glyph..........	Ⓒⓖ
Peak or Summit..........	✗	Fremont Indian Ruins..........	Ⓡ

Abbreviations

Canyon..........	C. or Can.	Campground..........	C.G.
Lake..........	L.	Ranger Station..........	R.S.
River..........	R.	4 Wheel Drive Vehicle	4WD
Creek..........	Ck.	High Clearance Vehicle..........	HCV

REFERENCE MAP OF HIKES

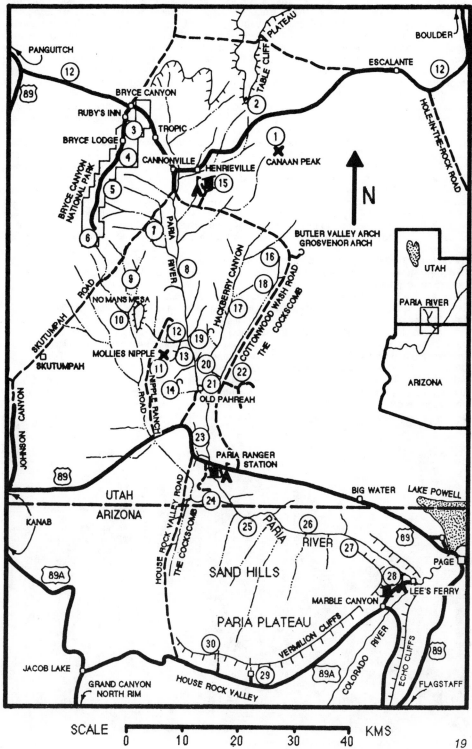

SCALE
0   10   20   30   40   KMS

Canaan Peak

Location and Access Canaan Peak, which rises to 2833 meters, is located about mid-way between the Bryce Valley towns of Tropic, Cannonville and Henrieville; and Escalante. It's also just to the southeast of Highway 12 as you pass through the area. The top part of Canaan Peak is made up of the same formation as is found at Bryce Canyon and Table Cliff Plateau, but its bright red limestone caprock is almost eroded away. All other surrounding hills or mountains have lost this Wasatch Formation cap, except Table Cliff Plateau, which isn't far away to the northwest. To get to the trail and trailhead on this mountain hike, drive along Highway 12, the link between Bryce Canyon and Escalante. Just northeast of mile post 45, turn south at the sign stating,*South Hollow and Canaan Peak*. Drive south about 8 kms on a rather good and well maintained dirt road. The starting point is just before you cross the upper part of Willow Creek. You can either park right on this main road--if you can see or find the trail markers on the trees; or drive the short dirt track to the metal stock tank, as shown on the map. Near this stock tank is a good place to camp.

Trail or Route Conditions It's probably easier to find the trail(which isn't used that often) if you'll use the little insert map to find and locate the metal stock tank just below Pole Spring. Best to park there, then head due south up the minor canyon towards the spring. After the dirt road peters out, watch closely for trail markers on the trees, which look like an "i". Once on the trail, it's fairly easy to follow, but the Forest Service doesn't remove dead-fall very often, so you'll have to jump over some downed trees occasionally. When you arrive on the west side of the main peak, the horse trail then intersects a very old logging road, which was unuseable for vehicles in 1987. At about that point, you can walk straight up the slope to the top-most ridge, then south to the summit; or continue around to the southwest or southeast side of the mountain and climb from there. The south face of the peak is very rugged.

Elevations Trailheads, about 2560 and 2600 meters; the summit, 2833 meters.

Hike Length and Time Needed Length to the top is about 3 to 4 kms, and will take only 3 to 4 hours to climb, round-trip.

Water At Pole Spring, but none on the mountain above that point.

Map USGS or BLM map Escalante(1:100,000), or Canaan Peak and Upper Valley(1:24,000).

Main Attraction A short day hike in a cool and little known mountain region, with many good camp sites. A nice place to visit in the heat of the summer.

Ideal Time to Hike From about mid-May until the end of October, but each year is a little different. Get there too early or too late, and you'll find muddy roads.

Hiking Boots Any dry weather boots or shoes.

Author's Experience The author had to hunt around for the trailhead, but after locating it, went quickly up the trail, and to the summit from the southeast side. He came down the west slope and returned to his car in less than 3 hours.

20   Canaan Peak, as seen from the southeast.

MAP 1, CANAAN PEAK

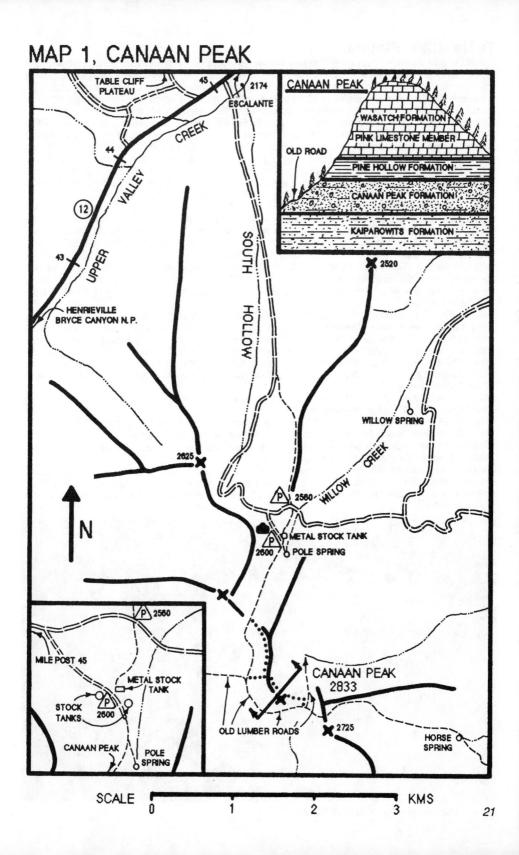

TABLE CLIFF PLATEAU

45

2174

ESCALANTE

CREEK

44

VALLEY

12

UPPER

43

HENRIEVILLE
BRYCE CANYON N.P.

SOUTH

HOLLOW

CANAAN PEAK

OLD ROAD

WASATCH FORMATION

PINK LIMESTONE MEMBER

PINE HOLLOW FORMATION

CANAAN PEAK FORMATION

KAIPAROWITS FORMATION

2520

WILLOW SPRING

2625

2560

WILLOW

CREEK

METAL STOCK TANK

2600

POLE SPRING

N

2560

MILE POST 45

METAL STOCK
TANK

STOCK
TANKS

2600

CANAAN PEAK

POLE
SPRING

OLD LUMBER ROADS

CANAAN PEAK
2833

2725

HORSE
SPRING

SCALE

0   1   2   3   KMS

21

Table Cliff Plateau

Location and Access Table Cliff Plateau is located about half way between Escalante and the Bryce Valley towns of Tropic, Cannonville and Henrieville. Table Cliff Plateau, or at least its very southern tip known as Powell Point, is one of the most prominent landmarks in southern Utah. To reach this hike, drive along Highway 12 between Henrieville and Escalante. The shortest route to Powell Point, can be found by leaving the highway very near mile post 44, and driving towards Pine Hollow; but this road is very rough and you'd need a HCV of some kind to make it to the trailhead at 2400 meters. To reach the normal route, drive further along the highway to near m. p. 45, and drive northwest from there to the Garden Spring area; or leave the highway halfway between m. p. 46 and 47. Again drive northwest toward Garden Spring. This loop road was in very good condition for all vehicles in early summer, 1987. Just southwest of Garden Spring is the sign pointing out the trail, but if you go just a bit south of the sign, you'll see a rough road heading toward Water Canyon. Most vehicles can probably make it up this old logging road to the trailhead at 2500 meters.

Trail or Route Conditions From the Trailhead at 2500 meters, there's a fairly well marked, but little used trail, to the top of Table Cliff Plateau. Once on this trail it should be easy to follow. It heads up the steep escarpment of the Plateau, then meets the rather good "home made" vehicle track running south to Powell Point. Once on this track, walk to where the road ends and a foot trail begins. Then it's a short walk through the bristlecone pines to Powell Point. A shorter second route comes up from Pine Hollow. There are a number of old logging roads in that area, so you follow which ever one seems to lead in the direction you're going. The track leading towards "running water" is an easy route, then the very steep(but not dangerous) slope up the escarpment to the top, and finally by road and trail to the Point.

Elevations The trailheads, 2390, 2400 and 2500 meters; the highest point is 3125 meters.

Hike Length and Time Needed The sign at the Garden Spring Trailhead reads "6 miles", or 10 kms, to Barney Top and to Table Cliffs. This surely means it's 10 kms to Powell Point from that trailhead, making it about 8 or 9 kms from the upper trailhead in Water Canyon. It's about 7 kms to Powell Point from the Pine Hollow area. If you park at Garden Spring, better plan on an all day outing, round-trip. But it's a shorter day-hike, and a half-day hike for some, if you go in from Pine Hollow, or Water Canyon Trailhead.

Water In early June, the author found running water in upper Pine Hollow and in Water Canyon(a year-round flow). There's no water on top.

Map USGS or BLM map Escalante(1:100,000), or Upper Valley and Pine Lake(1:24,000).

Main Attraction Splendid views, a cool summer hike, and quiet campsites

Ideal Time to Hike From late May to late October, but each year is a little different.

Hiking Boots Any dry weather boots or shoes.

Author's Experience The author walked the Pine Hollow route from his camp near the highway. He came down Water Canyon, but failed to locate the top part of the trail. He later found it at the bottom of the escarpment near the upper trailhead. Then it was road-walking back to his car in 5 hours, round-trip.

22   The east face of Table Cliff Plateau.

MAP 2, TABLE CLIFF PLATEAU

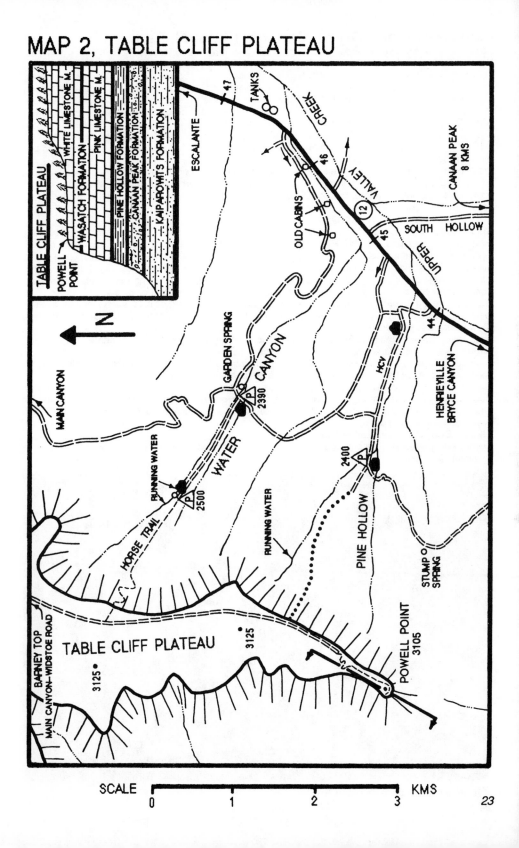

TABLE CLIFF PLATEAU

WHITE LIMESTONE M.

PINK LIMESTONE M.

WASATCH FORMATION

PINE HOLLOW FORMATION

CANAAN PEAK FORMATION

KAIPAROWITS FORMATION

POWELL POINT

N

ESCALANTE

TANKS

CREEK

CANAAN PEAK
8 KMS

12

OLD CABINS

VALLEY

SOUTH HOLLOW

UPPER

45

46

47

44

GARDEN SPRING

CANYON

P
2390

HCV

HENRIEVILLE
BRYCE CANYON

MAIN CANYON

WATER

RUNNING WATER

P
2500

HORSE TRAIL

RUNNING WATER

P
2400

PINE HOLLOW

STUMP
SPRING

BARNEY TOP

MAIN CANYON—WIDBTSOE ROAD

TABLE CLIFF PLATEAU

3125

3125

POWELL POINT
3105

SCALE

0   1   2   3   KMS

23

Fairyland Trail, Bryce Canyon National Park

Location and Access Included in this book are four maps covering the trails in Bryce Canyon National Park. This is the most northerly of the four, and is the most northerly of all trails in the park. The Fairyland Trail winds it's way down through canyons and *hoodoos*, and also follows the rim of Bryce Canyon for a good part of its length. This walking path is located about due east of the park visitor center and North Campground. One can begin the hike at Fairyland Point. To get there, take the first road running to the east just after you enter the park as you drive south from the Ruby's Inn area. This turnoff is *before* you arrive at the visitor center and park fee station. At Fairyland Point is a parking lot and view point only. Sunrise Point is another beginning point. Once inside the park just follow the signs. It's near the old historic Bryce Canyon Lodge. Another starting point is anywhere within the confines of the North Campground.

Trail or Route Conditions The Fairyland Trail, as is the case of all trails in this national park, is a constructed walking path and well maintained. There is no place where one might get lost, and all trail junctions and points of interest are well sign-posted. This trail makes for easy walking, for those accustomed to hiking. It's an up and down hike all the way.

Elevations From 2465 meters, down to about 2200 meters.

Hike Length and Time Needed This hike is divided into two parts; the Fairyland Trail, running down into the canyons; and the Rim Trail. If you start at Sunrise Point and walk down along the Fairyland Trail, then it's just over 8 kms to Fairyland Point. From Fairyland Point back along the rim to Sunrise Point, is just over 5 kms. So the length of the loop is about 13 kms. You can shorten it just a bit, if you begin at the campground or Fairyland Point, thus eliminating the short walk to Sunrise Point. Some people can do this loop-hike in as little as 3 hours, but for most it's 4 or 5 hours.

Water There are no springs or running water anywhere along this trail, so if it's warm weather, be sure to take some water with you. In cooler weather, and if you're a fast and fit hiker, you can likely make it OK without water or a lunch.

Map Bryce Canyon National Park(1:31,680), which can be bought at the visitor center. The newer 1:100,000 scale metric map doesn't show all the park trails.

Main Attraction Easy access, a good and well maintained trail, very little other foot traffic, and at least the second best area of the park for walking through and seeing the *hoodoos*.

Ideal Time to Hike May through October. Mid-summer can be a bit warm, as the altitude is only moderately high. Winter hiking could be fun too, for the properly equipped hiker, but it's not marked for winter use. Snow cover is generally light in this section of the park during winter, but in some years it can be a meter or more deep.

Hiking Boots Any dry weather boots or shoes.

Author's Experience The author started at Sunrise Point and made the hike in about 3 hours on a very cool May morning.

Typical scene along the Fairyland Trail.

MAP 3, FAIRYLAND TRAIL, BRYCE CANYON N. P

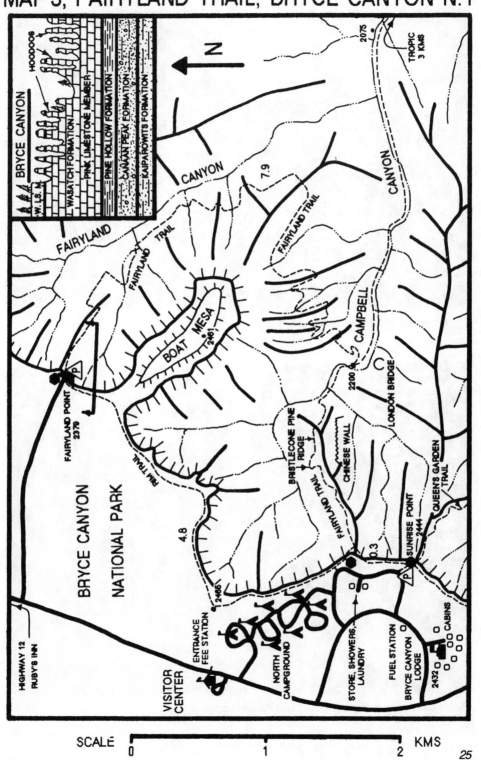

SCALE 0 1 2 KMS

The old and historic Bryce Canyon Lodge.

Rental Cabins, which are part of the Bryce Canyon Lodge.

The Tropic Canal, seen just south of Ruby's Inn. It was built in 1892, to take water from the East Fork of the Sevier River, into Bryce Valley and Tropic.

Wall Street, along the Navajo Trail.

Navajo, Peekaboo, Queens Garden Trails, Bryce Canyon

Location and Access The several trails on this map are near the center part of Bryce Canyon National Park, and are in the area which has the most visitation. These trails may be the most touristy of all, but the scenery is also the best in the park. It's here you can walk right through the narrow canyons of *hoodoos*, the erosional spires so prominent in this section of the park, and for which the park is famous. There are three stating points for trails heading off over the rim. They are: Sunrise, Sunset and Bryce Points. The first two are the most used, since they are very near the lodge, cabins and campgrounds. There are paved roads to each trailhead, and nowadays, the roads are kept open on a year-round basis.

Trail or Route Conditions All trails on this map are in good condition and well maintained. All junctions are signposted, and in some places there are benches to sit on for a rest. Walking is very easy and very enjoyable, especially for those visiting the park for the first time.

Elevations Sunset Point, 2431 meters; Sunrise Point, 2444; Bryce Point, 2529; and the bottom of the Navajo Trail, about 2280 meters.

Hike Length and Time Needed On the map are some large dots and numbers in between. These numbers represent the kilomage between dots. None of the distances are very great. To walk down the Navajo, then do the Peekaboo Loop Trail, and finish the hike by walking up the Queens Garden Trail to Sunrise Point, and finally back to the starting point at Sunset Point, is to walk about 10.5 kms. This can be done in as little as 2 hours by a fast hiker, but most would want about 4 hours, or about half a day for the trip. Some would want to take a lunch and drinks and spend more than half a day on this hike, especially if one were to take in some short side trips, such as the walk through Wall Street.

Water There is no running water anywhere in this area, so plan to take your own. When the wranglers are running dudes down the trails on horseback, and around the Peekaboo Loop, they usually turn on the water in a tap located near the toilets, as shown on the map. But it's best not to rely on this tap water, as it may not be on when you get there.

Map Bryce Canyon National Park(1:31,680). Buy this at the visitor center. The newer 1:100,000 scale metric maps aren't so good when it comes to showing trails inside the park.

Main Attraction The trails on this map give the hiker the best opportunity of any location in the park, to walk through and see at close quarters, the famous bright red spires of Bryce Canyon called *hoodoos*.

Ideal Time to Hike May through October, but mid-summer can be a little warm at lower altitudes. Because of relatively light snowfall, it's also possible to hike these trails in winter. However, in some winters the snow can pile up to more than a meter deep. Each year is different.

Hiking Boots Any dry weather boots or shoes.

Author's Experience The author worked one summer at the lodge, so has been on these trails often. Lately, he re-walked the suggested hike above, in a couple of hours.

Part of the Queens Garden Trail, located near the lodge.

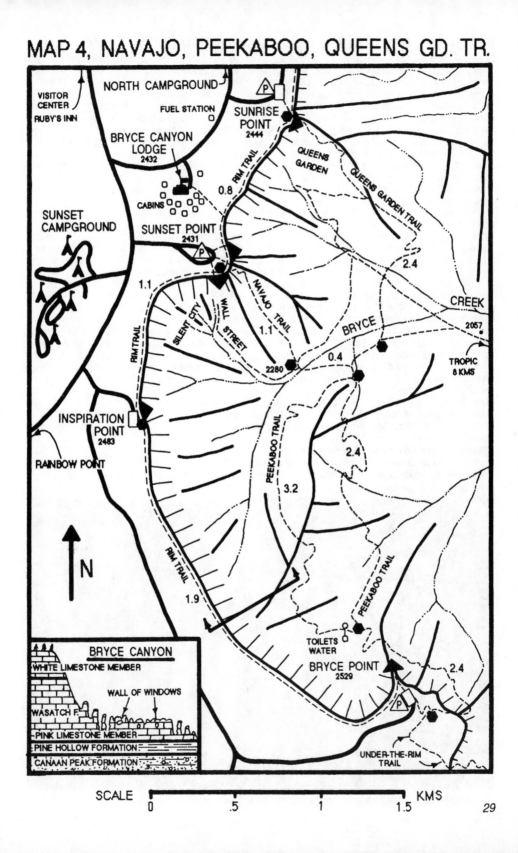

VISITOR CENTER
RUBY'S INN

NORTH CAMPGROUND

FUEL STATION

SUNRISE POINT
2444

QUEENS GARDEN

QUEENS GARDEN TRAIL

BRYCE CANYON LODGE
2432

RIM TRAIL

0.8

CABINS

SUNSET CAMPGROUND

SUNSET POINT
2431

P

2.4

CREEK

1.1

RIM TRAIL

SILENT CITY

WALL STREET

NAVAJO TRAIL

1.1

BRYCE

2280

0.4

2057

TROPIC 8 KMS

INSPIRATION POINT
2483

RAINBOW POINT

PEEKABOO TRAIL

2.4

3.2

N

RIM TRAIL

1.9

PEEKABOO TRAIL

TOILETS WATER

BRYCE POINT
2529

2.4

P

UNDER-THE-RIM TRAIL

BRYCE CANYON

WHITE LIMESTONE MEMBER

WALL OF WINDOWS

WASATCH F.

PINK LIMESTONE MEMBER

PINE HOLLOW FORMATION

CANAAN PEAK FORMATION

SCALE

0   .5   1   1.5   KMS

Under-the-Rim Trail, Bryce Canyon National Park

Location and Access This rather long trail runs from Bryce Point near the center of Bryce Canyon National Park, south to Rainbow Point, which is at the very southern end of the park. This trail runs north-south along the base of the Pink Cliffs, and offers both day and overnight hikes. In recent years, the entire park road system has been kept open on a year-round basis.

Trail or Route Conditions Being in a national park, one will expect this trail to be in good condition--and it is. It is well marked, so one can't get lost; it is well signposted, especially at trail junctions; and there are signs along the trail indicating campsite locations. Because this hike is long, it's necessary to camp one night, at least for most. There are seven campsites along the trail, all in the shade of giant ponderosa pines. See these listed on the map. These campsites are almost never crowded, as there aren't many hikers along this trail. This is a wilderness hike, even though it's near a busy highway. Be sure to get your free camping permit at the visitor center before staying overnight on this trail(in late summer of 1987, rangers told the author of the closing of two campsites. They apparently open and close periodically?).

Elevations Bryce Point, 2529 meters; low point on the trail, about 2050(but most is much higher), and Rainbow Point, 2776 meters.

Hike Length and Time Needed From Bryce Point to Rainbow Point is about 35 kms. This means that the average hiker will need two days. However, a fast hiker can do it in one long day with an early start and two cars. Water is scare along this trail, so day-hiking is worth considering. Also, consider doing the hike in stages, by using one of the connecting trails, thus shortening the hike, and eliminating the need to carry water for camping. The connecting trails are called: Sheep Creek, Swamp Canyon, Whiteman, and Agua Canyon Trails. If using the Whiteman Trail, remember to park at the picnic site about 400 meters south of the actual trail. The picnic site and car-park are marked, but where the road and trail meet, is not. You can't see the trail as you drive along in your car, but after you park, you can find it easy as you walk along the road. On the map, distance between dots is in kms.

Water One major problem along this hike is lack of water. In Spring just after the snow melts there's usually running water in most creek bottoms, but they dry up later on. Consult park rangers at the visitor center before hiking. Iron Spring has a good flow, but is undrinkable; Birch Spring has a small discharge, and may be dry late in summer. Lack of a good water supply, is the reason this is not a popular backpacking trail.

Map Bryce Canyon National Park(1:31,680). Buy it at the visitor center.

Main Attraction A forested trail hike along the base of the Pink Cliffs.

Ideal Time to Hike May would give you much more water on the trail, otherwise from about May through October.

Hiking Boots Any dry weather boots or shoes.

Author's Experience The author hiked the entire trail, but in four stages, using all connecting trails. This took two days to complete. The hike from Bryce Point to Sheep Creek Trailhead, then the walk along the highway back to his car, took about 4.5 hours.

The middle part of the park is the best place to see the famous Bryce Canyon Hoodoos.

MAP 5, UNDER-THE-RIM TRAIL, BRYCE C. N.P.

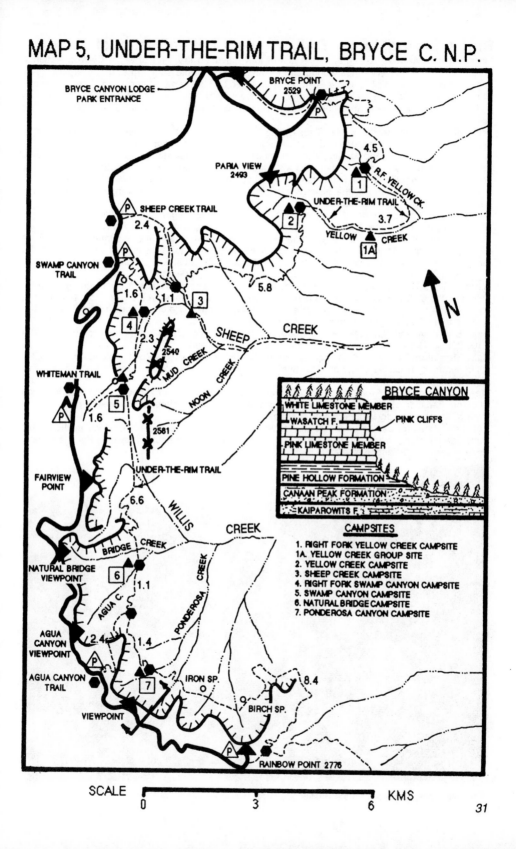

BRYCE CANYON LODGE
PARK ENTRANCE

BRYCE POINT
2529

4.5

PARIA VIEW
2493

R.F. YELLOW CK.

1

UNDER-THE-RIM TRAIL

SHEEP CREEK TRAIL

2.4

2

3.7

YELLOW   CREEK

1A

5.8

SWAMP CANYON
TRAIL

1.6   1.1

3

4

2.3

2540

MUD CREEK

SHEEP   CREEK

NOON CREEK

WHITEMAN TRAIL

5

1.6

2581

UNDER-THE-RIM TRAIL

FAIRVIEW
POINT

6.6

WILLIS   CREEK

BRYCE CANYON

WHITE LIMESTONE MEMBER
WASATCH F.   PINK CLIFFS
PINK LIMESTONE MEMBER
PINE HOLLOW FORMATION
CANAAN PEAK FORMATION
KAIPAROWITS F.

NATURAL BRIDGE
VIEWPOINT

BRIDGE   CREEK

6

1.1

AGUA C.

PONDEROSA   CREEK

AGUA
CANYON
VIEWPOINT

2.4   1.4

AGUA CANYON
TRAIL

7

IRON SP.

8.4

BIRCH SP.

VIEWPOINT

RAINBOW POINT 2776

CAMPSITES

1. RIGHT FORK YELLOW CREEK CAMPSITE
1A. YELLOW CREEK GROUP SITE
2. YELLOW CREEK CAMPSITE
3. SHEEP CREEK CAMPSITE
4. RIGHT FORK SWAMP CANYON CAMPSITE
5. SWAMP CANYON CAMPSITE
6. NATURAL BRIDGE CAMPSITE
7. PONDEROSA CANYON CAMPSITE

N

SCALE

0   3   6   KMS

Riggs Spring Loop Trail, Bryce Canyon National Park

Location and Access This map is the last of four, covering the trails of Bryce Canyon National Park. Shown here is the Riggs Spring Loop Trail, at the extreme southern end of the park. The beginning of this hike is at Rainbow Point, which is at the end of the paved park road. In recent years all roads in Bryce Canyon, including this one to Rainbow Point, have been open on a year-round basis. At Rainbow Point are toilets and drinking water. No food or other accommodations are provided at that point.

Trail or Route Conditions The Riggs Spring Loop Trail is a well maintained walking path, and is used moderately often. Because of the availability of water at two locations on the trail, it is one of the better hikes in the park, and certainly one of the better areas for backcountry camping. From Rainbow Point, you can do the loop-hike either clockwise or counter clockwise, it doesn't matter. Once you get down below the rim of the Pink Cliffs, then it's an up and down hike, until you once again walk back up to Rainbow Point. Some of the nicest views around can be had from Yovimpa Point along the Bristlecone Loop Trail, a walk worth taking.

Elevations Rainbow Point, 2776 meters; Yovimpa Pass, 2548; Riggs Spring, 2269 meters.

Hike Length and Time Needed The total length of this loop-trail which includes Riggs Spring, is about 14 kms. If you take the shortcut and exclude Riggs Spring, then it's less than 13 kms. Fast hikers can do this hike in half a day, but for many it's an all day trip. However, of all the trails in the park, this one has some of the nicest campsites, so you might consider spending a night on the trail. Riggs Spring is the best campsite, with good water and lots of shade and grass.

Water Riggs Spring has a good, year-round flow. Yovimpa Pass has a good spring as well. However, the Corral Hollow Campsite is normally without water, unless you arrive at the right time in spring, when some water is available for a short period of time in the creek bed. There's also water pumped from Yovimpa Pass up to the parking lot at Rainbow Point.

Map Bryce Canyon National Park(1:31,680), which can be bought at the park visitor center. The 1:100,000 scale metric maps don't show trails very well in the park.

Main Attraction The highest and coolest part of the park is at Rainbow Point, making it a nice hideout in summer. Because of the availability of water, this trail is one of the nicer hiking and camping areas in the park.

Ideal Time to Hike From about early to mid-May, until the end of October. Each year is a little different. Because of the higher altitudes, this can be enjoyed throughout the summer.

Hiking Boots Any dry weather boots or shoes.

Author's Experience As usual the author was in a hurry on this loop-hike, which included the short side trip along the Bristlecone Loop Trail, and he did it all in 3 hours. Yovimpa Point is a good place to see old bristlecone pine trees.

The Pink Cliffs, as seen from the Bristlecone Loop Trail.

MAP 6, RIGGS SP. LOOP TR., BRYCE C.N.P.

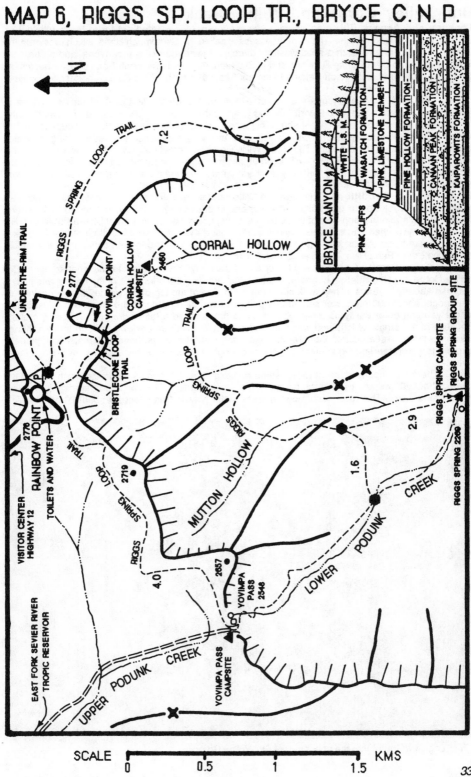

N

BRYCE CANYON

WHITE L.S.M.
WASATCH FORMATION
PINK LIMESTONE MEMBER
PINE HOLLOW FORMATION
CANAAN PEAK FORMATION
KAIPAROWITS FORMATION

PINK CLIFFS

RIGGS SPRING LOOP TRAIL

7.2

UNDER-THE-RIM TRAIL

CORRAL HOLLOW

• 2771

YOVIMPA POINT

CORRAL HOLLOW CAMPSITE
▲ 2460

LOOP TRAIL

BRISTLECONE LOOP TRAIL

P

RAINBOW POINT 2778

SPRING LOOP

RIGGS SPRING

TOILETS AND WATER

TRAIL

• 2719

MUTTON HOLLOW

2.9

RIGGS SPRING CAMPSITE

RIGGS SPRING GROUP SITE

RIGGS SPRING 2269

1.6

LOWER PODUNK CREEK

VISITOR CENTER
HIGHWAY 12

RIGGS SPRING LOOP

4.0

• 2657

YOVIMPA PASS 2546

EAST FORK SEVIER RIVER
TROPIC RESERVOIR

YOVIMPA PASS CAMPSITE

UPPER PODUNK CREEK

SCALE |—————|—————|—————| KMS
0   0.5   1   1.5

33

Bull Valley Gorge and Willis Creek

Location and Access This map includes two canyon gorges located not far to the southwest of the small town of Cannonville. The route of access is called the Skutumpah Road, which runs from the area south of Cannonville, in a southwesterly direction towards these two canyons, and on past the Swallow Park and Deer Spring Ranches and to Skutumpah. This Skutumpah Road ends(or begins) at the top or upper end of Johnson Canyon to the northeast of Kanab. Thus it's the shortest link between Kanab and Cannonville.

This road is generally open to all vehicles from around the first of April until sometime in November. But each year is different. During years with dry winters, it's possible to travel it all the time, except in the week or two right after a big storm. Parts of this road just to the south of the Bull Valley Gorge Bridge are made of clay, which becomes very slick when wet; while along the steep dugway just south of the old Clark Ranch on Willis Creek, is sometimes icy in the coldest part of the year. In the winter of 1986-87, two 4WD's slid off this part of the road, and had to be pulled out. In the warmer half of the year, the clay beds dry quickly after storms, and it's a good road for all vehicles with a fair amount of summer traffic.

Trail or Route Conditions There are no trails what-so-ever in these canyons; you simply walk down the dry creek bed in Bull Valley, or along and in the small creek flowing through Willis Creek Gorge. If you make the loop-hike of these two canyons, using the middle part of Sheep Creek as a link between the two, then you will walk along a seldom used 4WD track in the bottom of the dry Sheep Creek. About twice a year, cattle grazing permit holders, take in or bring out cattle, from the middle part of the Upper Paria River Gorge via Sheep Creek.

In Willis Creek, you simply walk in or out of the canyon with no obstacles what-so-ever. Bull Valley Gorge is a little different however. Park and/or camp on the north side of the bridge, and just up the road about 75 meters. Then walk along the north side of the top of the gorge, and to the west of the bridge, about 300 meters or so. At that point you can step right into the creek bed. Just below where you can enter easily, is a big log jam. This has created a fall or dropoff of about 5 meters. Because of the tangle of logs and limbs, it's rather easy to climb up or down through this overhang. It's easier than it first appears. Be sure and take along a short rope, perhaps a 10 meter-long piece of parachute cord(standard equipment in your pack, right!) to lower or raise packs, especially large ones.

There's a second route, a rather steep rock climb, which begins along the north side of the gorge, about 200 meters west of the bridge. This Crack Route, as it's called on the map, is marked with a stone cairn. This route up or down a crack in the Navajo Sandstone, is about 20 meters high

The "Log Jam Route" into the upper part of Bull Valley Gorge.

MAP 7, BULL VALLEY GORGE—WILLIS CREEK

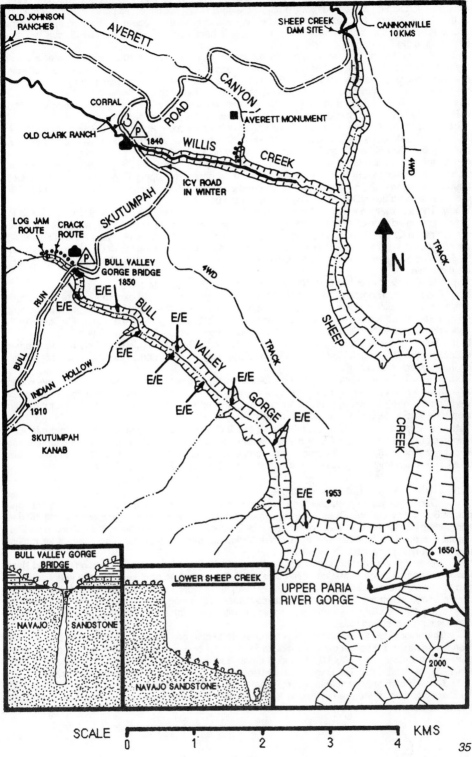

OLD JOHNSON RANCHES

AVERETT

CANYON

ROAD

SHEEP CREEK DAM SITE

CANNONVILLE 10 KMS

CORRAL

OLD CLARK RANCH

P

1840

WILLIS   CREEK

AVERETT MONUMENT

ICY ROAD IN WINTER

4WD

SKUTUMPAH

LOG JAM ROUTE

CRACK ROUTE

P

BULL VALLEY GORGE BRIDGE 1850

E/E

BULL

RUN

E/E

E/E

4WD

N

TRACK

BULL

E/E

VALLEY

E/E

E/E

INDIAN HOLLOW

E/E

GORGE

E/E

TRACK

SHEEP

1910

SKUTUMPAH KANAB

E/E

E/E

E/E

1953

CREEK

1650

BULL VALLEY GORGE BRIDGE

NAVAJO   SANDSTONE

LOWER SHEEP CREEK

NAVAJO SANDSTONE

UPPER PARIA RIVER GORGE

2000

SCALE   0   1   2   3   4   KMS

35

and nearly vertical, but it too is easier than it first appears. It has lots of hand and foot holds, but with some loose rock. The author has used this route three times, once with a large pack, which he had to pull up behind him on two pitches, with a parachute cord. Most people would prefer the Log Jam Route to the Crack Route, but between these two entry points in the bottom of the gorge, is another chokestone and minor fall of about two meters. Going back up this dropoff might be difficult for some, but it's not a life threatening obstacle.

There's also another route into or out of the gorge, located about 100 meters or so below, or to the east of the bridge. The author came up this route once, but those unaccustomed to rock climbing may feel uneasy using this entry/exit(E/E) point. On the map are other *possible* entry/exit routes to the gorge. One can also get into the gorge via Averett Canyon or Sheep Creek.

Elevations Bull Valley Gorge Bridge, 1850 meters; trailhead on Willis Creek, 1840; and the junction of Bull Valley Gorge and Sheep Creek, the low point on the hike, about 1650 meters.

Hike Length and Time Needed The distance of the hike down Bull Valley Gorge, then up Sheep and Willis Creek to the road, is about 20-22 kms. Combine that with the 2.5 km walk along the road between the two trailheads, and you have an all day hike; a *long* all day hike for some. Most hikers can do this in one day however. It's also possible to do the hike in two days, making an overnight camp in the lower part of Sheep Creek, near where it enters the Upper Paria River Gorge. There's running water(presumably year-round) and good campsites down there. If taking in big packs, it's likely easier to go down Bull Valley Gorge, rather than up.

Water There is running water in Willis Creek in the upper part of the gorge, probably on a year-round basis. You could probably drink this water as-is in *winter* time, as the land above the road is a *summer* grazing range for cattle. Bull Valley Gorge is dry, as is most of Sheep Creek. Water does begin to flow out of seeps in the lower part of Sheep Creek, as the red colored lower parts of the Navajo Sandstone begins to be exposed. This should be good water in summer, as the cattle at that time are up higher in the mountains.

Map USGS or BLM map Kanab(1:100,000), or Bull Valley Gorge(1:24,000).

Main Attraction The upper two or three kms of each gorge has some extremely narrow passages, similar to the Buckskin Gulch. Also, the scenery in the lower part of Bull Valley Gorge, with the huge Navajo Sandstone walls and dotted with pine trees, is worth seeing. Also the unusual bridge over the upper part of Bull Valley Gorge, and the 1954 accident scene where 3 men were killed.

Ideal Time to Hike From sometime in April on through October. This time period offers the best chance for the Skutumpah Road to be open and dry. May or June, and September or October, might be the ideal times to actually do the hiking.

Hiking Boots Willis Creek is small and you can usually hop right across, but it's best to have wading type shoes for that part of the hike. Bull Valley Gorge has no running water, but just up the gorge from the bridge, is one pool which holds water for a few days or a week after each storm. So for the entire loop-hike, wading type shoes are recommended.

Author's Experience The author first tried the Bull Valley Gorge hike on a very cold mid-April morning, but found the water and mud pool near the bridge, and turned back. A month later that pool was dry and he made two more trips into the gorge at that time. On another trip he went down Willis Creek on his way into Deer Creek, in the middle part of the Upper Paria River Gorge.

The Bull Valley Gorge Bridge

One of the more spectacular and unusual bridges you'll ever see is the one spanning the upper part of Bull Valley Gorge. The top part of this extremely narrow gorge is only about one meter wide, and perhaps 35 or more meters down. The rock involved is the famous Navajo Sandstone, perhaps the most prominent formation on the Colorado Plateau, and perhaps the most famous for making narrow slot-type canyons.

This bridge was first built sometime in the mid-1940's, by Marian Clark, Ammon Davis and Herm Pollock. The first stage of that operation involved using a winch to drag several large logs across the gap to serve as a foundation for the bridge. Then planks were laid across the logs, making a rather simple bridge which was first used by local cattlemen. This was the first time Bryce Valley and the Kanab and Johnson Canyon areas were linked. A later event forced the county to upgrade the bridge which is safe and sound today.

That event was the accident which occurred sometime on Thursday, October 14, 1954. Three men died as their pickup got out of control and slid off the bridge and wedged in the upper part of the gorge. The victims were Max Henderson, 33, and Hart Johnson, 37, both of Cannonville, and Clark Smith, 32, of Henrieville. The Garfield County News carried the story in the October 21 edition.

Quoting from the newspaper report, *"They started out Thursday to set up a deer hunting camp on rangeland one of the men owned in Kane County. When they had not returned by Saturday, a search was started for them.*

From above, this is what the bridge over Bull Valley Gorge looks like.

Bull Valley Gorge Bridge from below. Notice the pickup still in place.

The narrows of Willis Creek, just below the Skutumpah Road.

The Averett Monument, in the lower part of Averett Canyon.

A party led by Kendall Dutton of Cannonville, crossing the Bull Valley Gorge bridge, at 1 p.m. Sunday, sighted the pickup truck lodged in the narrow gorge about 50 feet[15 meters] below the bridge.

Bodies of two of the victims were still wedged into the truck, the third body had fallen clear and crashed to the Gorge floor almost 200 feet[60 meters] lower down"[the author believes 35 meters is a closer figure, but hasn't heard of anyone putting a tape to it].

The Highway Patrol and county Sheriff were called in and the rescue operation started. Garfield County Sheriff Deward Woodard was in charge of removing the bodies, "a hair-raising operation. His son, Paul Woodard, with a rope around his waist, worked for hours sawing away parts of the truck-- including the steering column--in order to free the bodies[Herm Pollock recalls they also used an acetylene torch for awhile]. He worked at the dizzy height above the canyon floor, with the swaying truck threatening to give[way] under him at any time. When one of the bodies was released from the truck, the weight almost pulled 22 men over the edge as the slack in the rope was suddenly snapped up.

According to the Sheriff, in reconstructing the accident, the light pickup truck the men were riding, stalled on the south side of the bridge and rolled backwards and into the gorge, dropping 50 feet[15 meters] before the narrowing sides crushed the cab and the men inside it."

Hart Johnson was buried in the Georgetown Cemetery, south of Cannonville; Max Henderson was buried in the Cannonville Cemetery, north of Cannonville; and Clark Smith was buried in the Henrieville Cemetery. Tombstones date from October 14, 1954.

Since the accident, the Bull Valley Gorge Bridge has been rebuilt. It appears workers simply pushed trees and large rocks down into the narrow chasm where they became lodged in the narrow top part. Then a bulldozer must have pushed more rock and debris on top of that, making a very solid and much wider bridge than was first built.

When you stop there today, walk along the north side of the gorge and to the west of the bridge, and from a view point you can still see the pickup lodged in the narrow defile. As you walk along the bottom of the gorge you also have a fine view of the truck from below. Because the pickup is sitting high and dry and protected somewhat by the bridge, it will be there in the same position for a long time to come.

Averett Monument

Another interest thing to see in the immediate area is the Averett Monument(some people spell it Everett). First the story behind the grave.

In August of 1866, a Mormon cavalry company from the St. George area was ordered by Erastus Snow, to go on an expedition to the Green River against Black Hawk and his marauders. This company, under the command of James Andrus, left the southern Utah settlements, and went past Pipe Springs, Kanab, up Johnson Canyon, and northeast to the upper Paria River Valley. This was before there were any settlements and traveling was rough.

By the time they reached the spot where Cannonville is today, many men were sick. It was decided to send these men back home. So six men and 14 head of disabled horses headed back. Along the way the small group was attacked by Indians. Elijah Averett Jr. was in the lead, and it was he who was shot and killed. The rest of the group escaped, and managed to circle around and return to the main unit in the upper Paria. The Indians, presumably Navajos, were pursued, but escaped. Later Averett was buried on August 27, 1866, where he died. This is in the bottom of what is now called Averett Canyon. The place is right on the old trail which was used by early stockmen and settlers before the present road was built.

Later, and in 1871, Frederick S. Dellenbaugh wrote about visiting the place in his diary. He stated he came across the grave marked by a sandstone slab with E. A. cut on it, which the wolves had dug out, leaving the human bones scattered around. Later, local cowboys reburied the bones and erected a cedar post with Averetts name on it. Many years later, the boy scouts of Tropic put that cedar post in their little museum in Tropic, and replaced it with a permanent stone marker that you see there today.

The best way to get there, is to drive from the old Clark Ranch on Willis Creek, in a northeast direction on the Skutumpah Road toward Cannonville. After about 2 or 2.5 kms, you'll drop down into the dry Averett Creek wash. Park on the road, and walk down canyon about 600-700 meters(8 minutes of fast walking). You know you're there when you see water begin to seep out of the creek bed, and when you can see an old trail running up the east side of the canyon. The monument is about 8 or 10 meters above, and about 30 meters back from the creek bed, on a low bench and on the right or west side. It's in a small clearing, surrounded by cedar trees. You can also come up from the bottom and from the narrows of Willis Creek. At the place is the original round stone with E. A. carved on it, and the larger, newer monument.

Just above the bridge in Bull Valley Gorge.

Another scene in Bull Valley Gorge, just above the famous bridge.

Bull Valley Gorge, two or three kms below the bridge.

Upper Paria River Gorge

Location and Access The Upper Paria River Gorge is that part of the river between Cannonville and the old Pahreah townsite. Some might extended this upper gorge on down to Highway 89. The Lower Paria River Gorge is from the Highway 89 bridge down to Lee's Ferry and the Colorado River. Like the Lower Gorge, this upper part has rather good and easy access.

You can start at either end and walk all the way through, but you'd need two cars. Or you can park at either end and head for the middle part of the gorge, then return the same way. To reach the upper part, drive south out of Cannonville on the paved road and in the direction of Kodachrome Basin and the Skutumpah Road. Cross over the Paria Creek bed(on the way toward Kodachrome B.), and drive two or three kms or a little more, to where you can park and enter the main canyon from one of the side drainages, such as Little Dry Valley. All routes in are easy walking. You can also enter or exit the gorge via Sheep or Willis Creek, or the slightly more difficult, and very exciting, Bull Valley Gorge.

To enter at the lower end of the gorge, drive along Highway 89, about half way between Page and Kanab. Between mile posts 30 and 31, and at the sign stating *"Old Pahreah and Pahreah movie set"*, turn northeast and drive about 10 kms to near Pahreah on a rather good dirt and clay road(which can be slick in wet weather).

Elevations About 1750 meters along the Upper Paria trailheads; about 1850 at Willis Creek and Bull Valley Gorge; and 1440 meters at old Pahreah.

Hike Length and Time Needed Old timers who talk about using the gorge as a road between Cannonville and Pahreah, say it was 30 miles, or 50 kms, between the two settlements. But you can shorten that by nearly 10 kms by beginning from one of the side canyon drainages such as Little Dry Valley. This can be walked in one very long day, but you'd need a car at both ends. However, it's recommended you take several days; because there are many side canyons to see, such as Deer Creek, and some old cattle trails to explore. In three or four days one could have a fun hike.

Water There is a year-round flow in the Paria, but during the irrigation season, which is from sometime late in April until about the first of October, there's little or no water flowing down canyon past Cannonville. Most or all of the water in the gorge at that time, seeps out from the bottom of the Navajo Sandstone or the top layers of the Kayenta Formation. This is in the area below the White Cliffs, which begins near the bend of the river known as the Devils Elbow.

There are many small seeps in the upper part of this map and in the gorge near Devils Elbow, which should be drinkable as-is. Also, most major side canyons have a small stream. If you will walk up any of these canyons to where the spring or seep begins, then that water is drinkable as-is. In winter months there are cattle in the canyons, so some precautions should be taken, such as taking water directly from a spring, using Iodine tablets, or filtration. However, in the summer months, from about mid-May until the end of October or the first part of November, there are no cattle in the canyon. They are taken out during this time period and put on the higher summer mountain ranges. With the rather steep gradient, the stream flows fast and will wash out the microbes which can give hikers stomach troubles.

It's during this time of year, and when there has been a long dry spell, that the water in this upper gorge is as clear as any mountain stream you'll ever see, and which the author has drank many times. About the only sediment entering the creek at this time is the small amount of sand being washed down by Kitchen Creek. However, when you get into mid or late summer, and with the presence of thunder shower activity, the water is often times very muddy.

For those who want to be on the safe side and drink only spring water, there are two fine springs on the west side of the canyon about straight across from the mouth of Hogeye Canyon. Another good source, perhaps the best in the gorge, is the historic Crack Spring. This spring is about 2-3 kms up stream from the mouth of Deer Creek Canyon and about half a km down canyon from Lone Rock. Walk close to the west wall and look and listen carefully for the water coming out of a cluster of small cottonwood trees.

Map USGS or BLM map Kanab and Smoky Mountain(and a small corner of Panguitch)(1:100,000), or Calico Peak, Deer Range Point, Bull Valley Gorge and Cannonville(1:24,000). Be sure and carry either of these sets of maps, as this hand-drawn sketch is not that accurate. The two metric maps are recommended(1:100,000).

Main Attraction The sites of the old Dugout, Carlo, Kirby, Hogeye and Seven Mile Flat Ranches. Petroglyphs at the mouths of Kitchen Canyon, Deer Creek, and Rocks Springs Creek. Pictographs inside Deer Creek; the only panels in the area. Cowboyglyphs at Crack Spring, Lone Rock and other sites. A number of old historic cattle trails, and many good campsites and solitude.

Ideal Time to Hike Spring or fall, with the very best times being from late March to mid or late May, and from mid or late September into early November. Summers are hot, and late spring and early summer(late May through June and into July) brings the small gnats and large horse and deer flies.

Hiking Boots Wading boots or shoes. If you're planning to do the entire gorge hike, which is rather

MAP 8, UPPER PARIA RIVER GORGE

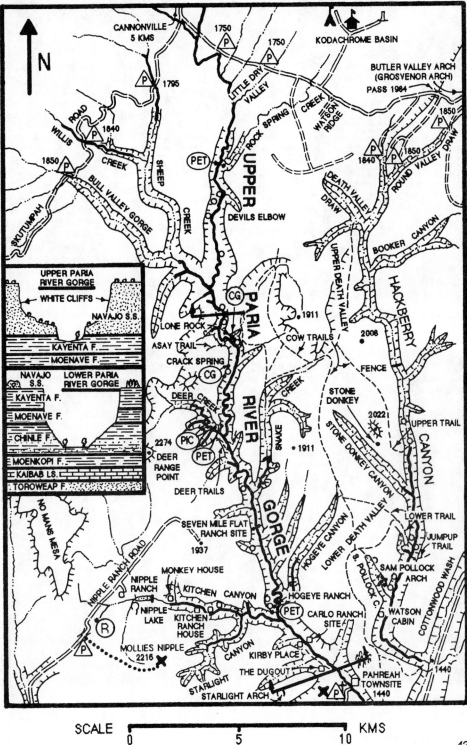

N

CANNONVILLE
5 KMS

1750
P

1750
P

1795
P

KODACHROME BASIN

BUTLER VALLEY ARCH
(GROSVENOR ARCH)
PASS 1984

WILLIS ROAD

1840
P

1850
P

SKUTUMPAH

BULL VALLEY GORGE

SHEEP CREEK

CREEK

PET

UPPER

LITTLE DRY VALLEY

ROCK SPRING CREEK

WATSON RIDGE

DEATH VALLEY DRAW

1840
P

1850
P

1850
P

ROUND VALLEY DRAW

DEVILS ELBOW

PARIA

UPPER DEATH VALLEY

BOOKER CANYON

HACKBERRY CANYON

UPPER PARIA RIVER GORGE
→ WHITE CLIFFS
NAVAJO S.S.

KAYENTA F.
MOENAVE F.

NAVAJO S.S. | LOWER PARIA RIVER GORGE
KAYENTA F.
MOENAVE F.
CHINLE F.
MOENKOPI F.
KAIBAB LS.
TOROWEAP F.

CG

LONE ROCK
ASAY TRAIL

CRACK SPRING

CG

DEER CREEK

2274
PIC
DEER RANGE POINT
PET

DEER TRAILS

RIVER

• 1911

COW TRAILS

• 2008

FENCE

STONE DONKEY

SNAKE CREEK

• 1911

STONE DONKEY CANYON

2022

UPPER TRAIL

LOWER DEATH VALLEY

LOWER TRAIL

NO MANS MESA

NIPPLE RANCH ROAD

SEVEN MILE FLAT RANCH SITE

• 1937

MONKEY HOUSE

NIPPLE RANCH

KITCHEN CANYON

R

NIPPLE LAKE

KITCHEN RANCH HOUSE

P

MOLLIES NIPPLE
2216

GORGE

HOGEYE CANYON

HOGEYE RANCH

PET

CARLO RANCH SITE

CANYON

KIRBY PLACE

THE DUGOUT

STARLIGHT

STARLIGHT ARCH

SAM POLLOCK ARCH

S. POLLOCK C.

JUMPUP TRAIL

WATSON CABIN

COTTONWOOD WASH

PAHREAH TOWNSITE
1440

P

X

1440

SCALE
0   5   10   KMS

Near the Devils Elbow, in the Upper Paria River Gorge.

The best water hole in the Upper Paria River Gorge is Crack Spring.

long, try and have a sturdy pair of shoes or boots. Many people take an old pair of shoes to "wear out" on a trip like this, but if they're too old or battered, they fail to give support to the foot and may not last to the end of the hike. So consider taking a pretty good pair of shoes, even though the wading will shorten their life.

Author's Experience The author has been up canyon from old Pahreah four times visiting the old ranches and trails, and Hogeye, Deer Creek and Kitchen Canyons. These were all day hikes, which took from 8 to 9.5 hours. Another day he walked from the side canyon west of Little Dry Valley down to Crack Spring, had lunch, and returned, in 7.5 hours. Another time he walked down Willis Creek to Deer Creek Canyon, on a two day trip, which should have been at least three days. On the authors last visit, he walked from old Pahreah to as far as Deer Creek and the cow trails in that area, in less than 8 hours, round-trip.

Trail or Route Conditions There are no trails as such in this canyon, but as you begin or end your hike, and in the bottom part just above old Pahreah, you'll be able to use some of the original old wagon roads which went from Pahreah to some of the ranches up the canyon and to Cannonville. The Smoky Mountain map shows the old road accurately to where it ends at the Kirby Place. Today there is an occasional vehicle using this track, mostly ORV's, which are ruining some parts of the canyon bottom.

It must be brought to the attention of everyone, that as of the Spring of 1987, the Utah State Legislature passed a package of four bills which have to do with ORV's. Quoting now from a letter from the Governor of Utah, Norm Bangerter, to the author; ....*the statute specifies that all public land shall be presumed closed to the use of off highway vehicles unless designated as open by the agency or entity controlling said land*. In the case of the Paria River, the agency is the BLM. These laws went into effect on July 1, 1987.

Unfortunately, the BLM has designated this area as open for these three and four wheeled ORV's to run the canyon, in what is considered an *existing road way*. The problem is, they don't always stay on the *existing road*. So these new laws haven't done a thing to curb the destruction caused mostly by these three and four wheeled ORV's.

There are also grazing permit holders who go into the middle part of the canyon occasionally in 4WD's to take in or bring out cattle. This is usually in about mid-May, and in the period at the end of October or the first part of November. These permit holders have a reason to be there, and are not just out there joy-riding, as are most recreation vehicle owners.

At about the Kirby Place and going north, these tracks fade away, as the canyon narrows; then you'll be walking in the flood-gutted canyon bottom. Grazing permit holders get into the upper part of this gorge via Sheep Creek, but the early day wagon route was right down the Paria and past Devils Elbow. Walking is easy all along this creek bed.

Beginning now in the upper end of the gorge. You'll first be walking in a shallow canyon, but soon it narrows and begins to deepen, as the river begins to cut down into the Navajo Sandstone. Remember that while the river is downcutting, the walls are rising; that is, the top of the Navajo is higher to the south than to the north. In other words the rock formations slope down to the north.

At the mouth of Rock Springs Creek, you'll see an isolated and lone standing butte, which must be a part of an old abandoned river channel. On the west side of this butte, and 6 or 8 meters off the ground, you'll see some pretty good petroglyphs. They must have been put there when the river bed was much higher.

Down river from Rock Springs Creek, is a big bend in the canyon, which old timers call the *Devils Elbow*. At that point the canyon is rather deep and moderately narrow. The white sandstone walls are the Navajo Sandstone, which form the White Cliffs all across the region.

In the area of the Devils Elbow, you'll begin to see many small seeps along the sides of the stream channel, and that the creek begins to grow in volume. In summer, the upper part is totally dry, or nearly so, and the water you often see in the Paria downstream, actually begins here.

As you near the place where Sheep Creek enters from the west, you begin to see red sandstone in the canyon bottom. This is the bottom part of the Navajo Sandstone. Then just a bit further down stream, and in the area of Lone Rock, you'll see the top part of the Kayenta Formation. The Kayenta tend to form little benches. As you walk south, the river continues to downcut, and the beds rise at the same time. From this area on down, most of the major side canyons have some kind of a water supply, either a flowing stream or good springs.

About 2.5 kms below the mouth of Sheep Creek, you'll see two fences come together part way across the canyon bottom. In between the fences, and on the west side of the canyon wall, is a cattle trail running up to the top of Asay Bench. The triangle shaped fence allows the cattle to come down to the river to drink, but doesn't allow them access to the rest of canyon. This is one route to the upper part of Deer Creek, where one can look for one very good panel of big horn sheep petroglyphs. One Cannonville cattleman mentioned this panel to the author, but the author didn't find it.

Just a bend or two below the Asay Bench Trail, is a big rock standing in the river channel. This is what old timers call *Lone Rock*. Look closely on its sides, and you'll see numerous old signatures or cowboyglyphs. Some of these date back to last century, but some of the older ones are now becoming indistinct.

About a half km below Lone Rock, and on the west side of the canyon, is *Crack Spring*. You'll have to walk close to the west wall and watch carefully to be able to see or hear the water coming out of the crack in the wall. It's on a narrow little bench, with many small cottonwood trees, and is hard to see unless you're close by. In the old days, when wagoneers were running from Cannonville to Pahreah, they always made this place their lunch stop, thus making the whole trip in one long day.

Kay Clark of Henrieville, remembered a trip he took with his father in April, 1920. They started in Cannonville and headed for Pahreah. They were carrying several sacks of grain, evidently to be sold to sheep herders in the lower valleys. When they made their lunch stop at Crack Spring, there were several other wagons already there. Since they were riding in comfort in a White Topped Buggy with fringes, some of the other drivers made comments as to how, *they were really traveling in style*. In those days, the White Topped Buggy was like a Mercedes, and the ordinary wagons used by most local people, were like Model T Fords.

Years ago someone placed a 5 cm pipe into the crack, making it easier to get a drink. The pipe is still there, and it always has a good flow. Since the space right at the spring is rather small, it would be best to camp on the opposite side of the river under some big cottonwood trees. Camping over there would also leave the spring site clean and pristine.

On either side of this spring on the lower canyon wall, are many very old cowboyglyphs or signatures of travelers. Those which are black in color, were made by placing axle grease on a finger, then writing a name. This grease prevented the sandstone from flaking away, so what you'll see there today, are many raised letters or signatures which literally stand out on the wall like Braille writing. Other people carved their names into the sandstone with a sharp metal instrument.

About half a km below Crack Spring, you come to some tight turns of the river, and high above are four or five alcoves on the east side of the canyon. One or two seem to have developed into arches. Just below these goose necks, is the mouth of Deer Creek Canyon. This is the best side trip you can take while hiking the Upper Paria River Gorge, so plan to camp and spend time in this one.

Deer Creek

Deer Creek Canyon is moderately narrow, with the canyon walls being vertical and made up of the red colored lower Navajo Sandstone and Kayenta Formation. This canyon is similar to places in the Lower Paria Gorge or even the lower end of the Buckskin Gulch, where the campsites are located.

Inside the canyon is a crystal clear, year-round flowing stream, which begins flowing at the base of the falls about 2 kms up from the Paria. Someone told the author there was some running water above the falls, but surely that would be seasonal. Along the stream are many fine campsites under large cottonwood trees. The walls of the canyon are red, but the benches you'll be camping on are white Navajo sands, which have blown off from the White Cliffs above.

As far as this water is concerned remember; cattle will be in this canyon from about late October or early November, on through about mid-May. At that time the cows are taken to their summer ranges. After the cattle are gone the water should soon be drinkable as-is, as it flows quickly out of the canyon.

If you're interested in petroglyphs and pictographs, this is one of the best little canyons around to see them. Right at the mouth of the canyon is one long panel of petroglyphs, including one glyph which is like a tit-tac-toe box. You'll have to climb a cedar tree to have a close look at this one.

Just inside Deer Creek about 100-150 meters, and on the north side, are several pictographs and petroglyphs. At one time, it looks as though someone tried to chop one of them out of the wall with an ax--but was unsuccessful. About a km up canyon from the Paria, is the best pictograph panel around. There are actually two panels. One you can crawl up to and see close-up; the other is out of reach. This second one faces west, and must have been made before part of the wall below it collapsed. These panels for the most part are untouched by vandals--so can't we keep them that way?

About two kms up the canyon you'll come to a blocking falls. This is as far as you go from inside the canyon. Below the falls is where the water begins to flow. It's in this upper part, that you'll find many white sand benches and large cottonwood trees, which combine to make some of the best campsites anywhere. If you wish to get upon top of the Cad or Asay Benches, you'll have to get there via the Asay Bench Trail or Deer Trails, just south of the mouth of Deer Creek.

Continuing down the Paria Canyon now. About 200 meters below the mouth of Deer Creek, is a fence across the canyon bottom. About 100 meters below the fence, and on the east side, is the beginning of the *Death Valley Trail*. This trail is well constructed, and was used to run cows from the Upper Death Valley and Snake Creek areas, down to water in the Paria Canyon. It's in good condition and easy to find and follow.

DEER CREEK CANYON

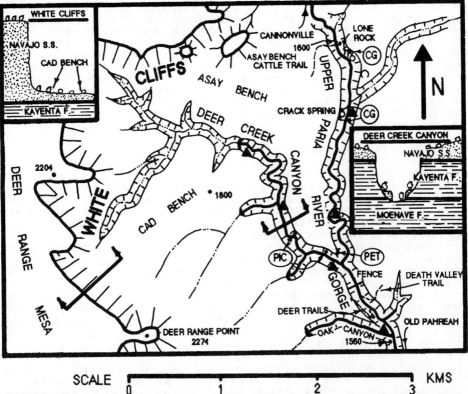

Map labels:
- WHITE CLIFFS
- NAVAJO S.S.
- CAD BENCH
- KAYENTA F.
- CLIFFS
- ASAY BENCH
- CANNONVILLE 1600
- ASAY BENCH CATTLE TRAIL
- LONE ROCK
- CG
- CG
- CRACK SPRING
- DEER CREEK
- CANYON
- UPPER PARIA
- N
- DEER CREEK CANYON
- NAVAJO S.S.
- KAYENTA F.
- MOENAVE F.
- DEER
- RANGE
- MESA
- WHITE
- 2204
- CAD BENCH
- 1800
- RIVER
- GORGE
- PIC
- PET
- FENCE
- DEATH VALLEY TRAIL
- DEER TRAILS
- OLD PAHREAH
- DEER RANGE POINT 2274
- OAK CANYON 1560

SCALE 0 1 2 3 KMS

Alcoves in the east wall, just above Deer Creek Canyon.

About 100 meters below the beginning of the Death Valley Trail, and on the west side of the canyon, is the beginning of the trail known by cattlemen as *Deer Trails*. This too is a constructed trail, and is easily seen from the other side of the canyon and from the canyon bottom. If you follow this one up, you'll find yourself upon the rim of the lower end of Deer Creek Canyon. From one of several perches on the rim, you'll have fine views of both the White Cliffs and the canyon bottom.

A half km below both of these trails is *Oak Canyon*, a tributary coming in from the west, and about 1.5 kms below it is the mouth of *Snake Creek*. Snake Creek has a good, year-round flowing stream along all of it's lower end. If you walk up this canyon, you'll find many campsites, and two side canyons. One rancher told the author you can climb out of one of these side canyons and up to Death Valley, but cattle or horses can't make it. Most of the water in Snake Creek comes out just below the falls in the main canyon, but some water begins to flow about 50 meters above this water fall. When cattle are in the region, they often come down to just above the falls to get at water in the top part of the Kayenta Formation.

Seven Mile Flat Ranch

About 2 kms below the mouth of Snake Creek is a place where the canyon opens up a bit and become wider. This is Seven Mile Flat. It got its name because it was about 7 miles, or 11 kms, above the town of Pahreah. Kay Clark, an old time cattleman from Henrieville, was too young to remember much, but was told this is where a man by the name of John W. Mangum had a small ranch, which people referred to as the Seven Mile Flat Ranch. As the story goes, it was a summer time place, with a cabin and some kind of corrals. At the ranch, they raised, among other things, sugar cane, from which they made molasses. In winter they lived in Pahreah town.

Kay Clark does remember that at the northern end of the flat area and on the west side of the river, he saw the remains of a small molases mill. There was somekind of a foundation and the old rollers, which were used to squeeze the juice out of the sugar cane. It's possible you might find something there today.

No one can say for certain what the exact dates were when this ranch was occupied, but Kay thinks it must have been at about the same time Pahreah was prospering, which was in the late 1870's and up until about 1883. That's when the first of the big floods hit the Paria and started the migration out of the valley. It must have been one of these first floods(later floods occurred in 1884 and 1896) which took out the buildings, and started washing out the entire bottom of the canyon. Today, there is nothing more than a broad washed out river flood plan.

From the Seven Mile Flat area down to the mouth of Hogeye Canyon, there isn't much to see, except a couple of side canyons on the east. At the very mouth of Hogeye, is an abandoned meander or river channel. Right out in the middle of the rather flat area is a rounded butte, which apparently resembled a hogs eye, thus the name, *Hogeye Canyon*. Hogeye is another of the major side canyons of the Paria River, which is discussed in another hike. It does have a good year-round running water supply and many good campsites.

Hogeye Ranch

Right at the mouth Hogeye Canyon and on the flats surrounding the Hogeye Butte, is the location of another old ranch, the Hogeye Ranch. Herm Pollock of Tropic thought it was first settled and used by an Ernest Mangum. But Marian Clark, who is a little older(in his 90's in 1987) and who still lives in Cannonville, thought is was a John W. Mangum.

Both sources believed this summer ranch was occupied in the years after people started leaving Pahreah town, but no on knows for certain when it was first used. Herm remembers a small wooden shack on the north side of Hogeye Butte, and Marian remembers a small two meter square stone storage building of some kind. Goats were raised, and some farming was done in summer. The big floods of 1883-84 or 1896 must have lowered the creek bed to the point they could no longer get water up to the farmland. Nothing remains today, except a lot of Cheat or June Grass, indicating the place was heavily used by someone at some period in time.

Just northwest of the Hogege Butte is a good spring coming out of the west side of the canyon; and just to the southwest of the butte is another spring, which made the site a good one, as far as water is concerned.

About a km below Hogeye is *Kitchen Canyon*, which is discussed in another hike. But right at the mouth of this canyon, is a good panel of petroglyphs and cowboyglyphs. Be careful of Kitchen Creek water; it drains the Nipple Ranch area, which has cattle year-round.

On the east side of the Paria Canyon, opposite the mouth of Kitchen Canyon, is where the Marian Mangum family(or perhaps one of his sons) had a dugout, and what must have been a garden and summer ranch area. The author was made aware of this place after all his hikes were finished, so there may or may not be any ruins of that site today.

Pictographs inside Deer Creek Canyon.

From the canyon rim, looking northeast into Deer Creek Canyon.

Kirby Ranch

About a km below the mouth of Kitchen Canyon, on a bench just west of the creek, and under a large cottonwood tree, are the Kirby Place ruins. The only thing left to see is the rock chimney. The old cabin was either burned down or the logs were hauled away to build another house or barn someplace else.

As with the other ranches in the area north of old Pahreah, not much is known for sure about this ranch site. But everyone agrees that it is the Kirby Place, and that it was first occupied from the years of about the mid-1870's on through about the time of the first flood to hit the valley. Kay Clark says it was the typical summer ranch site. Apparently the Kirby family lived in Pahreah during the winters, then had cows and a small garden at the ranch in summer. Herm Pollock believes the Kirby family left for Arizona after the 1884 flood, which left their irrigated land high and dry.

Carlo Ranch

About 200 meters due east of the Kirby house chimney, on the opposite side of the canyon, and sitting out in the middle of a sagebrush flat, is the foundation and chimney of the Carlo Ranch house. Herm Pollock remembers this family when he was just a boy of 12 years.

The year was 1922 and it was Christmas time. For most of that fall Herm and his father Sam Pollock, had stayed in the town of Pahreah. The Pollocks lived in Tropic, but they were in the Pahreah area with a sheep camp, and were also in the business of supplying food and supplies to other sheep camps in the region.

On Christmas morning with nearly half a meter of snow on the ground, Sam loaded up two boxes of food and other supplies, and put them on two mules. He instructed 12 year old Herm to go up the canyon about 5 kms to the Carlo home, and present the family with the gifts of food. Herm vividly remembers the time, because it was the first time he ever played Santa Claus.

He also remembers the time well, because of how poor the Carlo family was. Their home was a one roomed cabin, made of logs and rocks. At that time it had no door, only a piece of canvas covering the opening. The only heat they had was from an open fireplace. When Herm first went in, he placed his hand on the inside of the doorway frame, which was covered with thick soot. When he pulled his hand back, it was covered black.

The several small children were dressed in rags, and were filthy dirty. Their normally red hair was black, because they had gone so long without bathing. Mrs. Carlo was dressed in flour sacks. Herm also remembered a story of one of the young boys. He had found an old blasting cap somewhere and was playing with it when it exploded. He had lost three fingers on one hand.

Herm Pollock went back home a week after this experience, but his father helped the Carlo family get through the winter. When spring finally came, Sam took a wagon to the ranch, and helped them get out. Later in the spring of 1923, the family left the country, and no one remembers if their old cabin was ever occupied again.

The only thing remaining of the Carlo Ranch home is this chimney.

If you're out looking for the old Carlo Ranch site, first find the Kirby Place, which is easier to locate. Then walk 200 meters due east--across the creek, a low flood plain flat, then upon a sagebrush flat. It must be about 30 meters or so from where the steeper canyon wall comes down to the tall sagebrush.

Going down canyon from the Kirby Place, and on the west side of the river, you can get onto one of two of the old original roads and walk most of the way to Pahreah. At the mouth of Dugout Canyon(called Deer Range Canyon on the USGS maps), the two tracks meet. If you continue on this single track, about half a km south or below the mouth of Dugout, you'll see on the right, just as you go down a little decline, several old logs, posts and a depression in the ground. This is believed to be what is called The Dugout.

The Dugout

The Dugout is just one of several old ranch or homestead sites along the Paria River, just above the old Pahreah townsite The site was situated up against a low embankment; actually along the edge of an old river channel. First earth was removed, then logs were built up on the sides and on the top. Dirt may or may not have been put on the roof, but it must have been a rather cool place in summer and warm in winter, because it was at least partly underground.

No one alive today seems to know who built The Dugout, or who lived in it first, but several old timers from Tropic and Henrieville, remember the time John (Long John) Mangum and family lived there. This was in the late 1920's and early 1930's, and may have extended to about 1934, according to Wallace Ott and Kay Clark. The wife of John Mangum was named Oma, and whose maiden name was Carlo. The Mr. Carlo of the Carlo Ranch was her brother.

In about 1934 the Mangums, either John or brother Marian, had a cabin at the mouth of Kitchen Canyon. At that place, they once had a fine corn field on the flat at the mouth of the canyon. Herm Pollock remembers this time period well, because the Mangums lived there for two years, then were washed out by a big flood which rolled down Kitchen Canyon and the Paria on July 10, 1936. During this same flood, Pollock was stranded for two and a half days on the Carlo Bench(around the old cabin) with a herd of sheep. He had nothing to drink but muddy flood water.

Some time in the middle 1930's the Mangums began working on a ranch in Five Mile Valley south of Pahreah, which they homesteaded. Herman Mangum got title to it in June, 1937. This was at Cottonwood Spring and was called Five Mile Ranch by most people, but some called it Cottonwood Ranch. They lived there until 1942, then headed for Idaho.

Continuing south from The Dugout. Perhaps the last thing to see in the Lower Paria River Gorge, besides Pahreah ghost town, is the line of cottonwood trees marking the original ditch or canal which provided water for Pahreah homes and gardens. This canal began about a km below The Dugout, and about two kms above Pahreah on the east side of the river. It's where the stream is pushed to the west by a rocky bend from the east. You can see the very slightly visible remains of the canal, by following the broken line of cottonwood trees down to the townsite.

The Kirby Place. All is gone but the fireplace chimney.

Bullrush Gorge and Deer Range Canyon

Location and Access The location of Bullrush Gorge and Deer Range Canyon is about half way between Johnson Valley and Cannonville. Johnson Valley is about 16 kms east of Kanab. If driving east from Kanab on Highway 89, turn north into Johnson Canyon from between mile posts 54 and 55. At the north end of the Johnson Canyon is the Skutumpah Road, which links the valley with Cannonville. Be sure and carry the metric map *Kanab,* to be sure and find the right valleys and roads. It's probably best to park right on the road where Bullrush Hollow Creek crosses it. You could also park at the corral in Swallow Park, or if you have a HCV or 4WD, you could get closer to the head of Deer Range or Tank Canyon.

Trail or Route Conditions There are no trails here, except for the occasional cow trail. So for the most part you'll be right in the dry creek bed of either canyon. The walking is easy. Between Bullrush and Deer Range Canyon, you'll be walking along a very sandy 4WD track which runs down to the LeFevre Cabin and on toward the Nipple Ranch and Nipple Lake. This road is so sandy in its lower parts, only a fool would attempt to drive it, even with a 4WD(it is possible to drive it in wet, or wet and cold weather--which makes sand-trap driving possible). There are no obstructions anywhere except for one minor fall in Tank Canyon, which you can skirt easily by climbing the west side slope.

Elevations From 2025 or 2075 meters, down to 1850 near the metal water tank.

Hike Length and Time Needed If you park on the road in Bullrush Hollow, walk down canyon, and up Deer Range and Tank Canyons, then due west cross-country to your car, it will be 25-26 kms. This is an all-day hike for anyone, and a very long all-day hike for some. You could also take in No Mans Mesa on the same hike, and spend a couple, or three days in the area.

Water Both canyons are dry, except for running water in upper Bullrush G. in spring only. Cattlemen have piped water from Adams Spring, southeast of Adair Lake, down to the metal water tank and to a tap just beyond the LeFevre Cabin. The author isn't sure if the water is allowed to run year-round or not, but it was running in late April, 1987. If there are cattle in the area, then water will be in the pipe. Always have plenty of water in your car.

Map USGS or BLM map Kanab(1:100,000), or Rainbow Point and Deer Spring Point(1:24,000).

Main Attraction The gorges are only moderately narrow, but the best part is in the lower end of Deer Range Canyon. The walls are broken down and not sheer, allowing ponderosa pines to grow in the cracks and crevasses, making a unique scene. It's similar to the Huang Shan(Mountains) of China, where pines grow out of seemingly solid granite.

Ideal Time to Hike Spring or fall, but it's possible in summer too.

Hiking Boots Any dry weather boots or shoes.

Author's Experience The author parked on the road in Bullrush Hollow, walked down the gorge, then up Deer Range and Tank Canyons, and finally cross-country back to his car, all in 6.5 hours. But you'll want more time than that.

Typical scenery in the lower Park Wash and Deer Range Canyon.

MAP 9, BULLRUSH GORGE—DEER RANGE C.

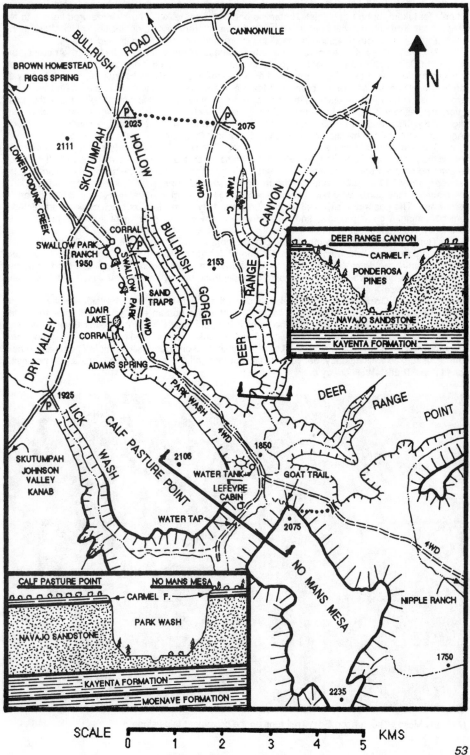

N

BULLRUSH ROAD

CANNONVILLE

BROWN HOMESTEAD
RIGGS SPRING

SKUTUMPAH HOLLOW

2111

LOWER PODUNK CREEK

P 2025

P 2075

4WD

TANK C.

DEER RANGE CANYON

CORRAL

P

SWALLOW PARK RANCH
1950

SWALLOW PARK

SAND TRAPS

BULLRUSH GORGE

2153

DEER RANGE CANYON

ADAIR LAKE

4WD

CORRAL

ADAMS SPRING

PARK WASH

DEER RANGE CANYON
CARMEL F.
PONDEROSA PINES
NAVAJO SANDSTONE
KAYENTA FORMATION

DRY VALLEY

P 1925

LICK WASH

CALF PASTURE POINT

SKUTUMPAH
JOHNSON
VALLEY
KANAB

2106

WATER TANK

4WD

1850

DEER RANGE POINT

LEFEVRE CABIN

GOAT TRAIL

WATER TAP

2075

4WD

NO MANS MESA

NIPPLE RANCH

CALF PASTURE POINT
NO MANS MESA
CARMEL F.
PARK WASH
NAVAJO SANDSTONE
KAYENTA FORMATION
MOENAVE FORMATION

1750

2235

SCALE   0   1   2   3   4   5   KMS

53

Lick Wash and No Mans Mesa

Location and Access All the canyons, cliffs and mesas on this map make for an interesting area, not only for hikers, but for geologists, botanists and historians alike. The hike featured here is to No Mans Mesa. You can reach it from about half a dozen different routes, but including Lick Wash in the access route, rounds out a description of all the interesting canyons in the immediate area.

No Mans Mesa is a remnant of the former plateau which extends to the north. At one time it was part of Calf Pasture and Deer Range Points, but erosion has left it high and dry, and surrounded by unclimbable cliffs. It's 6-7 kms long and about 2 kms wide. The walls you see are white Navajo Sandstone, which are part of the prominent feature of southern Utah known as the White Cliffs. The capstone is the Carmel Formation, a more erosion resistant rock than the Navajo. The top of the mesa is very flat, except it tilts to the north and northwest, as shown on the geology cross-section. The height of the cliffs range from 200 meters in the north, to about 400 meters at the south. The altitude ranges from about 2075 meters on the north end, to about 2235 meters on the higher south tip.

The author has found two routes to the top. One is up the east side of the north point; the other is the old *Jepson Goat Trail*. In 1927, a local rancher by the name of Lewis Jepson built a trail up the extreme northern end of the mesa. He had 800 Wether goats there in the spring and summer of the first year, and 1300 to 1500 goats on the mesa the second spring, 1928(one source states 3000). One story says the goats were taken to the mesa top to hide them from the bankers who had a lean on their owner. The goats did fairly well for the short time they were there, but lack of water prevented it from becoming a good pasture, and has prevented any further grazing of livestock there since. Essentially, No Mans Mesa is untouched by the hand of man and is very pristine.

The soaring White Cliffs make it one of the more scenic areas in this book. To get there, use the Skutumpah Road, which links the upper end of Johnson Canyon with Cannonville. Also, have along the *Kanab* metric map(1:100,000), which shows almost the entire Skutumpah Road. You can park where Lick Wash crosses the road; or in Swallow Park, perhaps at the corral east of the old Sears Riggs Ranch house.

Trail or Route Conditions You'll walk right down the dry creek bed in Lick Wash, which has some short but interesting narrows, then use cattle trails near the bottom end, which will take you to the LeFevre Cabin(which was brought into the canyon from the East Fork of the Sevire River in the mid-1960's). If you walk down Park Wash below Swallow Park and Adair Lake, you can use an old and very sandy 4WD track which runs to the LeFevre Cabin, and on south to the Nipple Ranch and Nipple Lake. This makes walking easy, but you'd better not try to take a vehicle down there, as it's one hell of a sand trap. That's 4WD country only!

No Mans Mesa. The Jepson Goat Trail runs up the prominent talus slope.

MAP 10, LICK WASH–NO MANS MESA

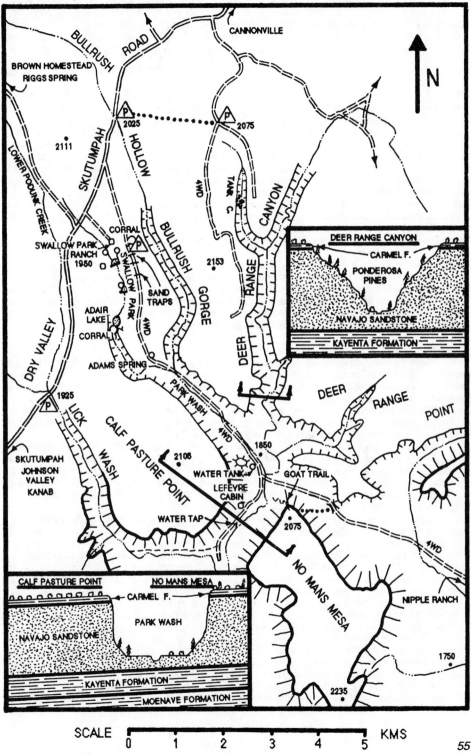

CANNONVILLE

BULLRUSH ROAD

N

BROWN HOMESTEAD
RIGGS SPRING

LOWER PODUNK CREEK

SKUTUMPAH HOLLOW

2111

P 2025

P 2075

4WD

TANK C.

DEER RANGE CANYON

BULLRUSH GORGE

CORRAL
SWALLOW PARK
RANCH
1950

SWALLOW PARK

SAND
TRAPS

2153

DEER RANGE CANYON
CARMEL F.
PONDEROSA
PINES
NAVAJO SANDSTONE
KAYENTA FORMATION

DRY VALLEY

ADAIR
LAKE

CORRAL

4WD

ADAMS SPRING

PARK WASH

DEER RANGE

POINT

P 1925

LICK WASH

CALF PASTURE POINT

4WD

2106

WATER TANK
LEFEVRE
CABIN

1850

GOAT TRAIL

SKUTUMPAH
JOHNSON
VALLEY
KANAB

WATER TAP

2075

4WD

NO MANS MESA

NIPPLE RANCH

CALF PASTURE POINT
NO MANS MESA
CARMEL F.
PARK WASH
NAVAJO SANDSTONE
KAYENTA FORMATION
MOENAVE FORMATION

1750

2235

SCALE   0   1   2   3   4   5   KMS

As you approach the north end of No Mans Mesa, which is in full view as you walk down Park Wash, notice the talus slope on the northwest corner. This is where the goat trail is. You'll actually have to go up this talus slope a third or nearly half way, before you can see the trail. Once on the route, it's easy to follow. The top part of the trail which zig zags around some minor cliffs is very obvious and is still in good condition. At the very top is a wire gate and short fence which kept the goats on top. Just a 100 meters away from the top of the trail on the east side, is another way of getting up or down, but there's no trail up that slope.

Elevations From 1925 meters at Lick Wash car-park, to 1950 at the Swallow Park Ranch; the LeFevre Cabin, about 1850; top of the goat trail, 2075 meters.

Hike Length and Time Needed If you make the loop-hike of Park and Lick Wash, and include the side trip to the top of the goat trail, it'll take you all day, and a very long day for some. The distance, if you include the walk back to your car on the road is about 25-26 kms.

Water There are several springs in Swallow Park, plus Adair Lake, but all the canyons are dry. Don't plan to use the water in Swallow Park, as there are livestock there all the time. However, ranchers and the BLM have constructed a water pipeline from Adams Spring southeast of Adair Lake, down Park Wash to a metal water tank, and to a water tap just below the LeFevre Cabin. When there's cattle in the area, there's water in the pipe. Because of its moderate elevation, cattle may be there year-round.

Map USGS or BLM map Kanab(1:100,000), or Rainbow Point and Deer Spring Point(1:24,000).

Main Attraction An old historic trail and grand views of the nearby park lands and White Cliffs from the top of the mesa. Lick Wash has some short, but interesting narrows, and some pine-clad cliffs near the bottom end. Adair Lake is interesting.

Ideal Time to Hike Spring or fall, but the moderate altitude makes it possible to hike in summer too.

Hiking Boots Any dry weather boots or shoes.

Author's Experience He parked where Lick Wash crosses the Skutumpah Road, walked down Lick Wash to the LeFevre Cabin, then around to the east side of No Mans Mesa, and climbed it along the route shown. He later came down the goat trail, and returned via Park Wash and the Swallow Park Ranch. This took a little over 7 hours, round-trip. You should plan on more time than this, or plan on camping one night, and taking two, maybe three days, for the trip.

Swallow Park Ranch

From the *Biography of John G. Kitchen*, it appears the first settler at Swallow Park was Frank Hamblin. This had to have been in the late 1870's, or more likely in the 1880's, extending into the 1890's, and perhaps past the turn of the century. For several years, he was the only neighbor John G. Kitchen had at the Nipple Ranch.

Swallow Park is a high valley, at just under 2000 meters elevation. It's located along the Skutumpah Road, and about half way between the upper end of Johnson Valley and Cannonville. It's also just south of the southern end of Bryce Canyon National Park.

If the memories of some of the old timers are good, the second owner of the ranch was a man named George Adams. George married Minda, one of the daughters of Frank Hamblin, thus giving him a toehold on the ranch. His name is on the spring, southeast of Adair Lake. Wallace Ott believes he got there sometime after the turn of the century. Actually, it was November 23, 1917, when George first got official ownership from the government, under the homestead act. There are no other records of land ownership prior to that time.

Adams owned the ranch only a couple of years, then sold the lower part of the valley around what they called Swallow Park Lake to Jackson Riggs, in December, 1919. Just prior to this sale, William Sears Riggs in November, 1919, settled and filed ownership on the northern part of the valley. In 1926, W.S. Riggs then bought more land from the Federal Government, which was an enlargement of his original 160 acres. Sears Riggs is the one who built the first house at the ranch, which is still there today. His name is also on the rather good spring near the head of Lower Podunk Creek, just south of the south tip of Bryce Canyon, and along the Riggs Spring Loop Trail.

Wallace Ott, who is now semi-retired and who lives in Tropic, bought the entire spread on December 11, 1940. He lived there part time, using it as a summer range or ranch, until 1955. During his stay at the Park, part of the property was sold to John H. Johnson, in March, 1945.

Wallace Ott sold out entirely to one of his relatives, Layton Ott, in December, 1955. Less than a month later, John H. Johnson sold his part of the Park to Calvin C. Johnson of Kanab, who still holds title to that land. So presently, it's Johnson and James D. Ott who own two different parts of the old Swallow Park Ranch and most of the land which is considered Swallow Park.

At the Park today, you'll see the old house built by Sears Riggs, and a couple of other old buildings just southwest of the house. There are in the valley a couple of small dams and duck ponds

This is the very top of the Jepson Goat Trail on No Mans Mesa.

Looking south along the east side of No Mans Mesa.

which are full all the time, and which are fed by several springs. Near the largest pond is an old yellow camp wagon with the name, *Camp Burge*, painted on it. Perhaps the most interesting thing to see, is Adair Lake. This was always known to old timers as Swallow Park Lake. It's at the southern end of the park, and right at the beginning of a little narrows section of upper Park Wash.

The lake is actually on a fault line, or just to the east of the fault. The earthquake line is the cliffs you can see from up valley. The west side has been raised, thus creating the lake just to the east. The lake and a swamp have always been there, but one of the early owners, and someone before Wallace Otts time, put up a very low dam, maybe a meter or less in height, to create a slightly larger lake.

The lake is there year-round; throughout wet and dry years. On two occasions Wallace Ott attempted to plant bass in the lake, but apparently it was too shallow to sustain them throughout the winter. Presently in the lake, and for as long as anyone can remember, are *salamanders*, or what the locals call *water dogs*. The lake also has an abundant waterfowl population.

At the bottom end of the lake, and right on top of the low and almost invisible dam, is a corral. Wallace Ott used this corral to hold cattle for spraying, but other owners used it as a kind of trap. They would herd cattle or horses up Park Wash from the area of No Mans Mesa. When they reached the corral, they were as good as got, and in one easy operation.

Adair Lake is easy to get to, and although it's on private land, it seems the owner shouldn't worry about visitors walking to it, because there's nothing there to disturb.

From half-way up the goat trail, looking at the tip of Calf Pasture Point and Park Wash.

The huge white cliffs of Calf Pasture Point, with the LeFevre Cabin in the lower right.

The old Riggs Home, in the middle of Swallow Park. Pink Cliffs are in the background.

Mollies Nipple

Location and Access Mollies Nipple is located just a few kms north of Highway 89, about half way between Page and Kanab. On some older maps of the area, it's called the White Cone. This name comes from the white Navajo Sandstone which the cone, or nipple, is made of. At the very summit of the peak is the brown and more erosion-resistent capstone. The author believes it could be the Carmel Formation, but it could also be a harder iron layer within the Navajo. The name Mollies Nipple, comes from the wife of John G. Kitchen, whose name was Molly. Read more about John G. Kitchen and his ranch under *Map 12, Kitchen Canyon*.

Probably the easiest access and hiking route to the mountain, begins west of the peak. From Highway 89, turn north right at mile post 37. This rather good, and now maintained road, was built by an oil company which made a test hole near point 1937 meters. It's now maintained by the county, for access to the Nipple Ranch. This road is good, except right near the pass at 1825 meters, where there's a big sand trap. Going down the other side toward the ranch, there are more sandy places too. Get to or near the pass and park.

You can also come in from Starlight Canyon, and old Pahreah. Leave Highway 89 from between mile posts 30 and 31, to reach old Pahreah and the nearby movie set.

Trail or Route Conditions From the pass at 1825, walk southeast up the slope to the top of the ridge. From there you'll see your objective. Walk down a prominent ridge, across the valley, and up another prominent ridge west of the Nipple. Head up the peak itself from the southwest. There's a minor hikers trail as you near the summit. After a couple of minor pitches, you're on top. You could also come in from the road labeled, *Sand Trap Alley,* or route-find in from Starlight, or possibly Kitchen Canyon.

By using the Nipple Ranch Road and by parking at the pass of 1825 meters, you can also include in your hiking day, a quick look at the only cliff dwellings in the immediate area. From the pass, walk down the road about 700-800 meters to the northeast, and to the valley bottom. This is actually the West Swag. At the bottom, make a 180 degree turn to the right, and walk southwest in the bottom of the valley to the head of what could be called the south arm of the West Swag. Right at the southern end, and under the overhang are two cliff dwellings. These rock and mud structures have been partially destroyed by time, cattle and white men.

The strange thing about these ruins is that they are under an overhang and facing north--the first this author has seen. The Indians who inhabited this site were likely a part of what archeologists called the Virgin Anasazi. But the site is very near to the transision zone of the Sevier, Great Basin, or Fremont Culture area, and the Anasazi Cultures to the south. Just north of the ruins, and along the east facing wall, are some minor petroglyphs.

Mollies Nipple from the west, and from along the normal route.

MAP 11, MOLLIES NIPPLE

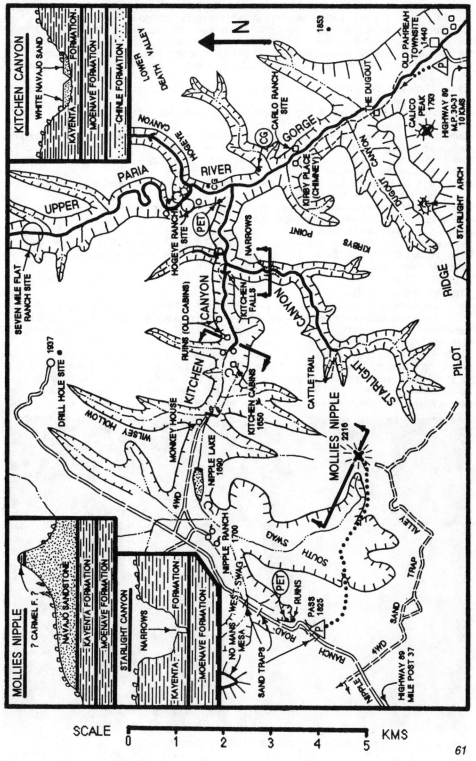

SCALE

0   1   2   3   4   5   KMS

Elevations Mollies Nipple summit, 2216 meters; the pass, 1825; old Pahreah, 1440 meters.

Hike Length and Time Needed From the pass on the Nipple Ranch Road, it's about 5 kms to the peak. A fit hiker can do this round-trip in about half a day; but others may want to take a lunch, water, and spend a day. It's much further from old Pahreah, but some could do it from there in one very long day. But a two day trip, camping in Starlight Canyon, would be fun. You could also go up Kitchen Canyon to the old Kitchen Cabins and climb from there, but you're supposed to get permission from the land owner, Calvin C. Johnson first(tele. 801-644-2384-Kanab). No problem; he just wants to know who is on his land, which is from about the old cabin ruins to the Nipple Ranch Road, in the bottom of Kitchen Canyon.

Water Carry your own on the normal route, but there's good water in Starlight Canyon, and from springs in Kitchen Canyon.

Map USGS or BLM maps Kanab and Smoky Mountain(1:100,000), or Deer Range Point and Calico Peak(1:24,000).

Main Attraction A beautiful peak, a fun half day hike(normal route), and excellent views. Along the Paria are petroglyphs at the mouth of Kitchen Canyon and old ranch sites. And just northeast of the pass 1825 meters, are the Kitchen Canyon cliff dwellings. On the way in you can visit the abandoned Burch Ranch and the old King Mine.

Ideal Time to Hike Spring or fall, but it can be climbed year-round. In winter, the sand traps don't usually trap, especially if they're wet or frozen.

Hiking Boots Any dry weather boots or shoes(except, if you come up the Paria River, you'll need waders for that part, and in lower Kitchen Canyon).

Author's Experience From the pass, the author made it to the summit in one hour, 15 min. He then went north to the Monkey House, Nipple Lake and Ranch, and walked the road back to his car. Round-trip was 4 hours and 15 min. Don't attempt to drive to the Nipple Ranch unless you have a 4WD vehicle and permission.

The Burch Ranch

On your way to climb Mollies Nipple via the standard route, you may want to stop and visit one of the abandoned ranch sites along the way. One of the last ranches to be built and used in the Paria River drainage, was the Burch Ranch. This old homestead is located in the northwestern corner of section 33, R3W, T41S. To get there, drive north from Highway 89 right at mile post 37, which is the Nipple Ranch Road. Drive about 10 kms, to where you see the Kitchen Point Corral and old stone building on your right. This is an old CCC camp, dating back to the mid-1930's. From the corral, look for an old track running due west. Follow this track west 100 meters, and park at the locked gate just before the wash. Then you can walk through the wash bottom, along an old track to the west, then north a ways, and finally to the west again to the ranch site. It's about 1.5 kms WNW of the Kitchen

Anasazi Indian cliff dwellings in the upper part of Kitchen Canyon.

Point Corral.

Part of the land you'll be walking over is private, belonging to Calvin C. Johnson of Kanab. To rightfully explore the site, you should first telefone him and get permission. There's really nothing out there to disturb, but as a matter of respect, call him first at 801-644-2384. It was Calvin Johnson who the author interviewed for this Burch Ranch story.

In the early 1930's, Dood Burch, his wife, and two young sons, Robert and Omer, migrated from Texas to the House Rock Valley area, which is just south of the Vermilion Cliffs and Paria Plateau. They lived there a couple of years, then homesteaded this ranch in about 1934 just below where Deer Spring Wash and Park Wash meet.

The first thing they did was to build a small house out of lumber and a storage cellar behind. The cellar was dug out of the hill side, and lined with rocks. It was likely a place for food storage, but they may have also lived in it. They built several corrals, a small dam to create a pond, and a blacksmith shop. Their water came from a small spring on a hillside just south of the home and cellar. At one time they had water piped to the house, where they raised a small garden.

One interesting feature of their home was that Mrs. Burch built a special floor, like nothing the author has ever heard of. When she had collected enough old fruit jars, she turned them upside down and placed them in the floor of the cabin. They must have been packed very close together so they wouldn't break. On top of the bottles, she laid goat hides. This according the Calvin Johnson, who later bought the place. When the author visited the place, there were a number of old bottles around, but apparently at a later date they installed another floor made of wood.

The Burches were horse and rodeo people. They brought with them a number of quarter horses, and also ran goats in the hills around the ranch. They apparently supplied part of the stock animals during the rodeo season in southern Utah and northern Arizona.

Evidently the Burches had marital problems. They never officially got a divorce, but he took off for Texas not too long after they had settled in at this ranch. Sometime later he was killed when his horse threw him as it stepped in a gopher hole and stumbled. Mrs. Burch ended up raising the boys by herself.

County records show the patented land was obtained officially from the government in January, 1945. It was listed in the name of Omer Burch, the youngest of the two boys. Robert got married to a local girl and drove the mail truck for several years in the Kanab area, before moving to Provo, where he lived for the rest of his life.

Omer and his mother moved to Oregon in late 1947, when they sold the land to Johnson. Omer ended up as a brand inspector and continued in the rodeo stock business. After their departure, Johnson used the place as a kind of line cabin for several years afterwards, until the house and facilities literally fell apart and decayed. Parts of the house, cellar, and corrals are still there today.

Corn cobs and potsherds are all that remain of the Kitchen Canyon ruins.

Well preserved matate. Used with a mano, this is where they ground-up seeds and corn..

Very little remains of the old Burch Ranch, near Kitchen Point Corral.

The caved in roof of the cellar, at the old abandoned Burch Ranch.

Two kms north of Kitchen Point Corral and along the Nipple Ranch Road, is this old stockade type corral, originally built by John G. Kitchen, sometime in the 1880's or 1890's.

Kitchen Canyon

Location and Access Kitchen Canyon is located in the area north of Highway 89 about half way between Kanab and Page. Exit the highway between mile posts 30 and 31, at the sign stating *Old Pahreah and the Pahreah Movie Set*. Pahreah is about 10 kms off the highway on a good and well traveled dirt road(but which is slick in wet weather because of the Chinle and Moenkopi clay beds). The movie set is about 8 kms from the pavement.

Another possibility is to leave Highway 89 right at mile post 37, and drive about 25 kms up the Nipple Ranch Road to the Nipple Ranch. But the land down canyon from the Nipple Ranch to just beyond John G. Kitchens old cabins is private, and you'll need to call Calvin Johnson of Kanab to get permission to cross his land(801-644-2384). A simple fone call will insure permission.

The Nipple Ranch Road is very good, except it has sand traps beginning about 4 kms short of the ranch. For a nice hike, the route from old Pahreah is best. Even if you come up from old Pahreah, Calvin Johnson would prefer you call or let him know, if you're planning to see the old homestead and the Monkey House, which are both on the lower part of his land.

Trail or Route Conditions After parking your car near the end of the road not far from the Paria River, simply walk up canyon in the washed-out river bed. You'll be crossing the small Paria stream several times in the 8 kms or so to the mouth of Kitchen Canyon. Inside Kitchen Canyon, you'll also be walking in and beside the small Kitchen Creek. When you arrive at Kitchen Falls(just where Starlight Canyon enters), head up the steep slope on the north side of the falls and pass through an old gate, which at one time was a wagon road down to the Pahreah. About a km above the falls(which is about where the private land begins), you can get out of the creek bed, and walk on cattle trails on the north side of the "V" shaped erosional gully so prominent in Kitchen Valley. It's easy walking all the way.

Elevations Old Pahreah, 1440 meters; the old Kitchen Cabins, about 1650; and Nipple Lake, 1690 meters.

Hike Length and Time Needed It's about 8 kms from old Pahreah to the mouth of Kitchen Canyon, and another 5 kms to Nipple Lake. Plan on taking a lunch and spending the entire day seeing the Kitchen Valley historic sites. You could also camp in Starlight Canyon, where there's a good water supply, and no private land.

Water Lower Kitchen Canyon has running water year-round, and some springs at several locations in the valley. This water is good as-is, if you take it from the springs.

Map USGS or BLM maps Kanab and Smoky Mountain(1:100,000), or Deer Range Point and Calico Peak(1:24,000).

Kitchen Falls, located in the bottom end of Kitchen Canyon.

MAP 12, KITCHEN CANYON

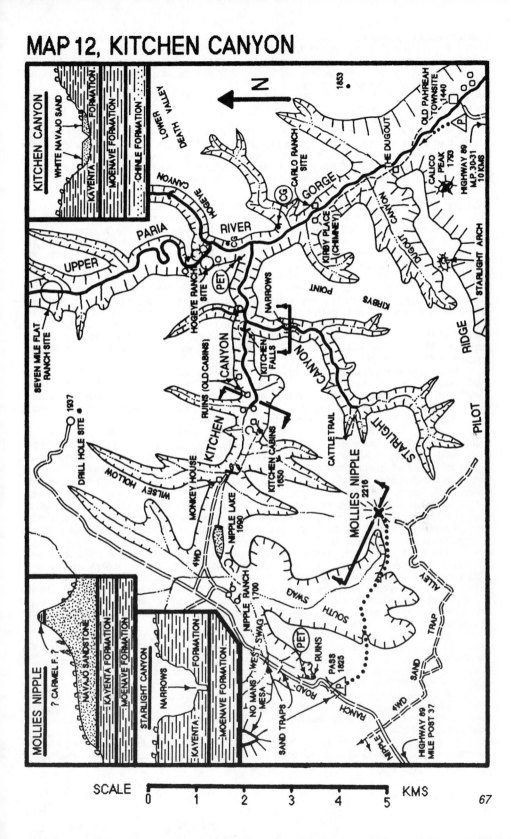

KITCHEN CANYON

WHITE NAVAJO SAND

KAYENTA FORMATION

MOENAVE FORMATION

CHINLE FORMATION

MOLLIES NIPPLE

? CARMEL F. ?

NAVAJO SANDSTONE

KAYENTA FORMATION

MOENAVE FORMATION

STARLIGHT CANYON

NARROWS

KAYENTA FORMATION

MOENAVE FORMATION

N

1853

OLD PAHREAH TOWNSITE 1440

CALICO PEAK 1793

HIGHWAY 89 M.P. 30-31 10 KMS

STARLIGHT ARCH

THE DUGOUT

CARLO RANCH SITE

DUGOUT CANYON

GORGE

PARIA RIVER

KIRBY PLACE (CHIMNEY)

POINT

KIRBYS

PILOT RIDGE

HOGEYE CANYON

CG

CG

PET

NARROWS

HOGEYE RANCH SITE

UPPER

SEVEN MILE FLAT RANCH SITE

KITCHEN FALLS

KITCHEN CANYON

STARLIGHT CANYON

CATTLE TRAIL

DRILL HOLE SITE 1937

WILSEY HOLLOW

RUINS (OLD CABINS)

KITCHEN CANYON

MONKEY HOUSE

KITCHEN CABINS 1650

MOLLIES NIPPLE 2216

4WD

NIPPLE LAKE 1690

NIPPLE RANCH 1700

SOUTH SWAG

VALLEY

TRAP

SAND TRAP

PET RUINS

PASS 1825

NO MANS WEST SWAG MESA

SAND TRAPS

RANCH ROAD

NIPPLE RANCH ROAD 4WD

HIGHWAY 89 MILE POST 37

SCALE

0 1 2 3 4 5 KMS

67

Main Attraction Kitchen Falls, Nipple Lake, the stone Monkey House, and the ruins of the oldest ranch in the entire region, the John G. Kitchen cabins and the Nipple Ranch. Along the Paria are petroglyphs and the chimneys of the old Kirby Place and the Carlo Ranch, as well as the ruins of the Dugout, once occupied by John Mangum and family. At or near the car-park is the old movie set, old Pahreah townsite and Pahreah cemetery.

Ideal Time to Hike Spring or fall, but perhaps also in winter warm spells. Summers are a little too warm for most people to enjoy.

Hiking Boots Wading boots or shoes.

Author's Experience He first saw the canyon from Mollies Nipple and from the pass at 1825 meters, then made two more foto trips into the canyon from Pahreah. One trip to Starlight, lower Kitchen and lower Hogeye Canyon, took about 9.5 hours, round-trip. Another trip to Seven Mile Flat and to the Monkey House, took 8.5 hours round-trip. It might pay to camp and spend a couple of days in the area, while visiting Starlight Canyon and Mollies Nipple on the same trip.

History of the Nipple or Mollies Nipple Ranch

One of the very first ranches to be built in the entire area is what most people call the Nipple Ranch. In researching the history of the ranch, the author obtained a copy of the *"Biography of John G. Kitchen"*, from Adrian Kitchen(a great grandson) of Wahweap on Lake Powell. This short history of the original founder of the Nipple Ranch, was compiled by a Nephi Johnson of Mesquite, Nevada, and Ramona Kitchen Johnson of Kanab. They got the information from John G. Kitchen, Jr. Here then is the history of John G. Kitchen and the Nipple Ranch, which has been edited slightly by the author.

John G. Kitchen was born in Canada in 1830. Very little is known of his childhood or his early youth. The first anyone knows of him was during the gold rush days of California. There at the age of nineteen his willingness to work, and his determination to get along in the world, began to assert itself. Money was plentiful at that time in California. A gold mine was to be had almost for the taking, but young Kitchen was not interested in a gold mine. His heart was set on a cattle ranch in the Rocky Mountains. So he worked at the job that paid the best, and saved his $11.00 per day, to make that cattle ranch dream come true.

In 1873 he arrived in Johnson, Utah[in Johnson Valley east of Kanab], with a herd of heifer calves, which he had purchased in and around St. George. Sixtus Johnson was then running the Dairy Ranch, two miles[3 kms] north of Johnson, and he took the calves to manage while Kitchen went back to his job in California for the winter. This arrangement lasted for several years, with Kitchen returning each fall with more calves, or money to buy more.

In 1878 he took a herd of steers to Nephi, Utah, to sell. While there and waiting for the train to load his steers, he became acquainted with Martha or Mollie Grice. She was waiting tables at the Seely Hotel, and keeping house for her uncle, William Grice. John married Martha and brought her back to the Dairy Ranch, which he had leased. There the couple lived until their first baby, Rose, was born. The following spring[1879] with the assistance of Nephi Johnson, they moved their cattle into Mollies Nipple Ranch.

The ranch received its name because of the peculiar shape and coloring of a large knoll or peak located to the south of the ranch and Kitchen Valley. Marthas nickname was Mollie, because it's common knowledge around the country this peak was named after Kitchens wife. This peak of course, is named Mollies Nipple. When you see it, you'll understand how it got the name.

Their life at the Nipple Ranch, though filled with hardships and disappointments, was successful. They started with meager beginnings, and built slowly as time and means would permit, while faced with drouth years, crop failures, menaces of gophers, squirrels, and chipmunks. For several years, Kitchen did all of his own riding on an old mare, "Dolly", upon which he carried food and a quilt for a bed when he was forced to camp away from home for a night or two. In later years he brought back a few blooded horses each fall or spring when he shipped his steers and thus built up a fine band of horses, along with his cattle.

Those first few years at Mollies Nipple Ranch were never to be forgotten by the Kitchens. They had a new country to conquer, land to clear, buildings and fences to be built, and cattle to tend. The cattle were so well taken care of, that other cattle men said jokingly, that "Kitchen knew where every cow laid down each night." He knew his cattle so intimately that many of them were given names, such as Betsy, Posey, Kill Deer, Brin, Blue Neck, Red Rony, and Jennette.

Most of his cows were red Durham, branded with the box brand on the left ribs, and marked with a Kitchen Slit in each ear. The Kitchen Slit was a circular cut just above and following the vein in the lower part of the ear, and is so called because Kitchen was the first man in Southern Utah to use that mark.

To build up a better grade of cattle, he used to bring in blooded bulls each fall or spring when he returned from taking his steers to the railroad. One of these was a roan Durham named Paddy, that cost him $500. The original cattle were Hereford stock.

This is the original Kitchen home. It has two fireplaces, both still standing.

Mollies Nipple to the south, and Nipple Lake.

A John Mangum helped the Kitchens with the buildings at Mollies Nipple. The corrals and fences were made of cedar logs and posts secured there in the valley and constructed in the stake and rider[or rip gut] style, which consisted of two posts set in the ground so as to form an X every 8 or 10 feet[2 or 3 meters] with a cedar pole rider placed in the saddle of the X to connect the pairs of posts[Only those who have tried to chop down a cedar tree with an ax, can appreciated the amount of work which went into this type of fence].

The buildings were of pine logs or native rocks laid up with mud. The roofs were of split pine logs. The split side was laid down, then covered with bark and about a foot[30 cms] of sand. It was on these roofs, warmed from the heat within, that the wild flowers first bloomed in the springtime.

The dwelling house, which consisted of two long rooms[actually two cabins and a store room placed next to each other], was constructed of hewed logs, in the shape of a "T". One room served as a kitchen, living and dining room, and was heated by the cook stove and fireplace. The other room had a large fireplace and it served as a bedroom and a school room. The floors of both rooms were unplaned lumber, but Mrs. Kitchen kept them scrubbed clean and white; "So clean you could eat off them", was a familiar family expression.

After their children became old enough, the Kitchens had a school teacher who boarded with the family every winter. These private tutors, boarded with the family and assisted with the ranch labor when not teaching. Among these teachers were Robert Laws, Lydia Johnson, Jim Burrows, and a Mr. Ramsdale.

A little distance from and at the back of the home, was the cellar and smoke house. These buildings were of much the same construction as the ranch house, except that the cellar was excavated about six feet[2 meters] in the ground. Here many bushels of fruit and vegetables were stored in winter, and milk and butter were kept cool in summer. The smoke house was constructed of rock, and here Kitchen cured beef, pork, and venison.

While their home was still being built, another child was born to them. For this occasion, Martha went to Pahreah, where she could have the assistance of other women during childbirth. The child was a boy and they named him John G. Kitchen, Jr. Their next two children were Rosena and Mattie, born at Nipple Ranch. Their fifth child, Una, was born in Kanab.

In addition to stock raising, Kitchen farmed and always had a garden to keep his family alive. There were several large springs that boiled up at the foot of the mountains, creating meadow land for several miles up and down the valley. These springs he dammed up, and used for irrigation purposes. He would store the water for several days, and until the ponds were full, then run the water off onto his crops. It was on the hillside just above the ditches that he used to build his hot beds. Early in the spring he would level off a small space on the mountain side, where the sun shone early and late, and was protected from the cold. Here he would plant some of his seeds.

Before he began irrigating each spring he would carry water for the young plants. After he began irrigating, the hot beds were so located that he could scoop water from the ditches onto the plants with a shovel. He raised cabbage, cauliflower, squash, turnips, carrots, potatoes, corn, watermelon, rye, and hay. One year he raised over 800 bushels of corn. He had a span of oxen, Ben and Brady, to assist him with the farming, and other heavy work such as hauling wood and securing rocks for building.

Because of the lack of roads and long distances to any settlement, there was practically no demand for his produce, except what his own family, hired help, and stock consumed. He delighted in taking a packload of vegetables to his Hamblin friends at Swallow Park some 7 or 8 miles[11 or 12 kms] to the northwest. And each fall he enjoyed taking part of a beef to Pahreah, and distributing it among his less fortunate friends.

As his cattle increased and financial conditions improved, Kitchen purchased the Meadows Ranch from Chet Patrick[In Dunk Findlays history of his familys Findlays Ranch, he states that Alexander Duncan Findlay sold his squatters rights of the Meadows to Kitchen for 50 head of steers]. This ranch was northwest of the Nipple, not far below the Pink Cliffs on Meadow Creek. It's just to the northwest of the present day Deer Spring Ranch. It was used primarily as a summer ranch. There he added dairying to his ranching activities. Some summers he milked as many as 50 cows. From the milk, they made butter and cheese, which were packed and stored for winters use at the Nipple[Dunk Findlay states that a man by the name of Joe Honey lived in a dugout Kitchen had built as a shelter at the Meadows for one winter, to preserve Kitchens claim to the land].

At the Meadows Ranch, with the assistance of Edwin and John Ford and Thomas Greenhalgh, he built a dugout shelter[it's still at the upper end of the Meadows today] and large corrals and fences. One night the cowboys had five hundred head of three and four year old steers ready to drive to the railroad the next morning. About two o'clock in the morning something frightened them, and they stampeded. The cowboys were camped only a short distance from the corral and when they heard the cattle running and bellowing, they rushed to the scene. The corral was built on a sidehill, and on the down hill side, the cattle were piling up and being trampled. Fear seized the cowboys, lest so many

In about the middle of Kitchen Canyon, stands the Monkey House.

There are numerous old cowboyglyphs on the door frames of the Monkey House.

would die, so they spent the rest of the night fighting the steers back from the downhill side of the corral. The next morning revealed one steer dead, and several lame and bruised.

Another interesting event happened just south of Kitchens Ranch. One winter Ira Hatch of Panguitch, Utah, had his sheep camp in the high country close to Mollies Nipple. One afternoon it began to storm, and it snowed all night. The next morning the sheep bunched up beneath cedar trees, unwilling to brave the deep, newly fallen snow. Still the storm continued. For three days it snowed and when the storm finally broke, Hatch and his sheep were virtually prisoners in four or five feet[about a meter and a half] of snow.

Hatch left his freezing, starving sheep and made his way to the Nipple Ranch for help. Kitchen took one team, Ned and Colonel, cut down a tree, and dragged it around to make trails for the sheep to follow into lower country where the snow wasn't so deep.

During the summer of 1895, Kitchen let Ebbin Brown dairy at the Meadows Ranch and paid him $1.00 per head for all the three and four year old steers he could gather. He gathered 500 head. Then Kitchen and other cowboys gathered another 500 head and drove them to the railhead at Milford. Here they were loaded on cattle cars and shipped to Kansas City, Missouri, and to Omaha, Nebraska. Young John Jr. accompanied his father on this trip, traveling with and tending the cattle until they reached their destination. It was on this trip, and while in Salt Lake City on their return journey, that his father gave him the gold watch which he still carries(1947) and treasures so much, and a bicycle, which was the first one ever owned in Kanab.

At the lower end of the canyon there were clumps of squawberry bushes. Every fall Piute Indians would came to the Nipple country to hunt deer and to gather squawberry brush to make baskets. Kitchen made it a practice to buy two baskets, two tanned deer hides, and several deer hams from them each fall. The baskets were used to haul laundry and for storing dried fruits and vegetables. The deer hides were used to make belts, saddle strings, harness parts and shoe laces. The deer hams were cured in the smoke house and eaten during the winter.

One interesting story is told about the "tally stick" method of keeping track of calves branded. Whenever Kitchen went out to brand calves, he would carry a short stick in his back pocket. When he branded a calf, he would whittle a notch in the stick. In the evenings after he had returned to the house, the notches were transferred to a much larger tally stick, which was 8 or 10 feet[2.5 or 3 meters] long and kept overhead on the rafters in the kitchen. Whenever he desired a count of the seasons branding, he would take down the tally stick and count the notches. One side represented the heifers, the other side the steers. It was when his branding count reached enormous figures that he became known as "The Cattle King of Southern Utah." It was estimated at one time that he owned about 5000 head of cattle, ranging from St. George on the west, Panguitch on the north, and to the Colorado River on the east and south[When Dunk Findlay of Kanab heard about the 5000 head of cattle, he doubted very much that the country could have sustained that many. Maybe 2000 could have been a closer figure].

Kitchen was a great lover of knowledge, and so that the children might have an advantage of better schooling, and his family enjoy some of the finer things of life, he appointed George Adams foreman of his ranch, and moved the family to Kanab in the early 1890's. This move seemed to climax his career, and his star of success began waning. Liquor had always been his weakness, so while in Kanab and with plenty of leisure time and money, drinking got the upper hand. Trouble began brewing, which ended in the divorce courts.

The loss of his family was a great blow to Kitchen. Mollie ended up marrying Joe Honey, a man who once worked for Kitchen. Sorrowing, Kitchen made a liberal settlement both of alimony and for the education of his children, which Thomas Chamberlain faithfully administered. He sold his stock cattle to Scott Cutler and Hack Jolly, who moved them out of the country. The remnant of the box brand was sold to Johnny Findlay.

In 1898, Kitchen went to Lee's Ferry, where he lived only a short time. He died very suddenly, and under mysterious circumstances. A rider was dispatched to Kanab with the news. Young John rode in haste all night, but the body was already buried when he reached the Ferry.

Thus ended the career of a man with clouds of uncertainty hovering about the cause of his death as well as about the disposal of his property. In his will he bequeathed to each of his daughters $20,000, and to his sons $25,000, but through faulty administration, the fortune was dissipated. Although his family spent years in the inheritance courts, not a dollar was ever recovered.

In 1904, his children erected a monument to his memory at Lee's Ferry Cemetery. It reads, "John G. Kitchen, Born 1830, Died July 13, 1898."

After the death of Kitchen, there seems to be a gap in history of the Nipple Ranch. Evidently, it was in the courts for some time. Some of the old timers in the area thought it may have gotten into the hands of two men named Hunter and Clark, then after a time it may have been taken over by a Jim Henderson. However, the first recorded transfer of the property(Kane County Courthouse) was on July 2, 1908. The land, part of a grant of 100,000 acres, was given to the state of Utah by the Federal government, for the use of *"Institution for the Blind"*.

The next transfer of ownership was on March 11, 1912, when the Cross Bar Land & Cattle Co. purchased the ranch land from the state of Utah. Later, on May 7, 1927, a John H. Johnson bought the land from Kane County, apparently for back taxes owed by the cattle company. The last time the land changed hands, was on January 16, 1956, when present owner Calvin C. Johnson, bought it from John H. Johnson.

At the ranch today, Calvin has a small headquarters located to the west of Nipple Lake, along with several corrals. Hikers are asked to stay away from this part of the ranch. Down canyon and a couple of kms to the west or above the Kitchen Falls, are the ruins of the old Nipple Ranch. The author has seen the ruins of an old chimney in one location, and a rock wall just to the west of the chimney, as shown on the map. Just to the west of these ruined cabins, is the Kitchen house. It's in rather good condition, considering its age. The roof has collapsed, but the log walls and the two chimneys are still standing. When the author first saw the twin chimneys and rooms, he thought it was the home of an old Mormon polygamist. Instead, the second room was for the school teacher. Nearby is an old corral, made in the "stake and rider" fashion. The holes you'll see in the corral gate posts, are said to have been made by Kitchen who used a hot iron poker, to run through the posts. Nearby, are the ruins of the smoke house and other structures.

From Kitchens house, you can walk along an old seldom used road to the northwest. After about a km, you'll see some of Calvin Johnsons work in erosion control. Crossing the valley is an earthen dam, and just to the north of it is a rock cabin, called the Monkey House.

The Monkey House

The Monkey House was built in 1896 by a Dick Woolsey, and at the mouth of what the USGS maps call Wilsey Hollow. It's made of stones, and it sits up against a large boulder. When Woolsey and his wife first settled in at this location, they had with them a monkey. The monkey was kept in a box or cage on top of a pole near the cabin. When someone approached the homestead, the monkey would chatter loudly. This is how the rock dwelling got its rather famous name.

Inside the cabin and on the wooden doorway structure, are many names of early cowboys. A new roof has been added, and the ramada has been taken off from the original structure, evidently in the years John H. Johnson owned the land. But it's in good condition today. Behind the cabin is a small pen or corral in a small opening of the cliff.

About another km or two to the west of the Monkey House, is Nipple Lake. Evidently there has always been a small and shallow pond there in a swampy area, but today, you'll see a low dam, maybe a meter high, which backs up the clear blue water to form the lake. This is an unusual site in the dry land. All the time you walk the canyon bottom, you'll see to the south, the ever present Mollies Nipple, towering above the landscape, for which the ranch is named.

If you're coming into the area to climb Mollies Nipple from the pass marked 1825, you can see an old corral built and used by Kitchen. As you leave the Highway 89 right at mile post 37, you'll drive north on the Nipple Ranch Road. After about 6 kms you pass the old King Mine on the right. After about another 4 kms or so, you'll see on the right or east, a corral and stone house which is the old CCC camp at Kitchen Point. It's now used by Calvin C. Johnson of Kanab. To the west of this corral is the old Burch Ranch.

Drive north from the CCC corral about 2.5 kms and at the mouth of the first canyon coming in from the east, is an old stockade type corral(with the poles standing upright and stuck in the ground). This is the old Kitchen Corral of lower Park Wash.

For those who like to explore, drive about another km north of the Kitchen Corral and to the mouth of Box Elder Canyon coming down from the east. You can walk up this canyon to reach Mollies Nipple. Somewhere at the head of this canyon and before you reach the Nipple, is an old "stake and rider" fence, which runs from northeast to southwest from the Nipple area toward the head of Box Elder Canyon. The author looked for it, but found nothing. Calvin C. Johnson can perhaps give you a more accurate idea of just where it's located. This fence is of historic value because of the way it was constructed and when it was built.

Starlight Canyon

Location and Access Starlight Canyon is located not far north of Highway 89, about half way between Kanab and Page. It's also just to the east of Mollies Nipple, a prominent landmark in southern Utah. To get there, leave Highway 89 between mile posts 30 and 31, at the sign stating *old Pahreah ghost town and Pahreah movie set*. This dirt road is very good and maintained, but it can be slick in wet weather because of the presence of the Chinle and Moenkopi clay beds. It's about 8 kms to the old movie set, and another 2 kms to old Pahreah. Park somewhere along the river.

Trail or Route Conditions From where you'll be parking, you simply walk north in the flood plain of the canyon bottom. You'll cross the creek several times on your way to the mouth of Kitchen Canyon. Once inside Kitchen Canyon, you'll also be walking either right in the small creek or beside it. When you see Kitchen Falls just ahead, you'll also see Starlight Canyon coming in from the south. Walk straight up this narrow canyon, which also has a small stream. But it's very small, and at various times, may be dry in some places, . This canyon is lined with cottonwood trees up to where the water first begins to flow, then it's just a dry, sandy wash in the upper parts. Easy walking all the way.

Elevations Old Pahreah townsite, 1440 meters; bottom of Starlight Canyon, about 1550; base of Mollies Nipple and head of the canyon, about 1900 meters.

Hike Length and Time Needed It's about 8 kms from Pahreah to the mouth of Kitchen Canyon; another 1.5 or 2 kms to the bottom of Starlight Canyon; and about 10 more kms to the top of Mollies Nipple if you stay in Starlights' main channel. Consider it an all day hike from the trailhead to the upper end of the canyon and back. Strong hikers could climb Mollies Nipple on the same hike, but it would be a long all day hike.

Water There's running water, apparently the year-round, in the bottom half of Starlight. There's also a year-round flow in Kitchen Canyon, and there are some springs on the north side of the canyon in lower Kitchen. If there aren't any fresh signs of cattle, and since it's a fast flowing stream, you should be able to drink Starlight water as-is,

Map USGS or BLM maps Kanab and Smoky Mountain(1:100,000), or Deer Range Point and Calico Peak(1:24,000).

Main Attraction A short but very interesting narrows sections, a chance to climb the conspicuous Mollies Nipple, and total solitude in an unknown canyon. Along the Paria River, look for the chimneys of the old Carlo and Kirby Ranches, and the petroglyphs at the mouth of Kitchen Canyon.

Ideal Time to Hike Spring or fall, but it's also possible in winter. Summers are very warm.

Hiking Boots Wading boots or shoes.

Author's Experience On one trip the author walked from Pahreah, up to the Kitchen Cabins, up Starlight to where the water first begins to flow, then about half way up Hogeye Canyon and back to the car, in about 9.5 hours. Much too long to enjoy. If you're taking in Kitchen Canyon on the same hike, set up a camp in Starlight, and make it a two day outing.

The narrows of Starlight Canyon are short, but very interesting.

MAP 13, STARLIGHT CANYON

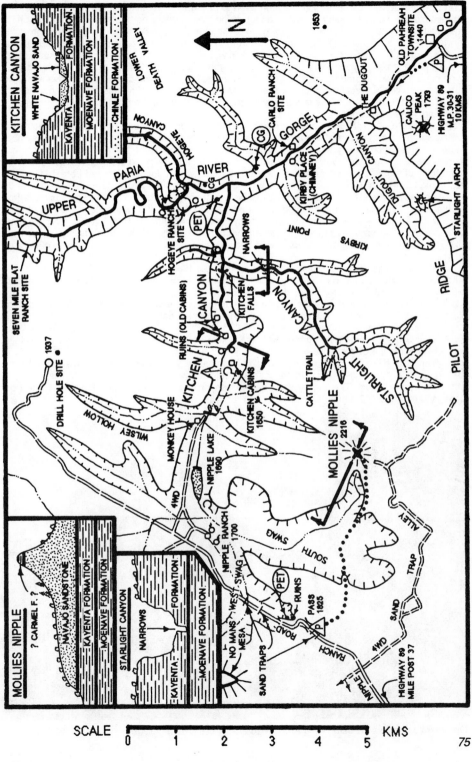

SCALE

0   1   2   3   4   5   KMS

75

Starlight Arch Hike

Location and Access Starlight Arch is located about half way between Kanab and Page, and just north of Highway 89. Old timers in the area used to called this Wedding Ring Arch. It's a part of a remnant piece of white Navajo Sandstone on top of the mesa directly north of the Pahreah Turnoff. At times you can see the arch from the highway, near the turnoff. To make this hike, turn off Highway 89 between mile posts 30 and 31(the Pahreah Turnoff) and drive in the direction of old Pahreah and the movie set. This is a good road, but it can be slick in wet weather. It's 8 kms to the movie set, which is the best place to park if you have a low slung car. If your car is higher off the ground than average, or if you have a shovel to smooth over some of the small gullies, then you can probably drive about two kms up the shallow Long Canyon to the west and to the car-park at 1475 meters. Some may want to park at point 1460 meters. This is the original old road to Pahreah from Kanab, and it's rough and rutted and never maintained.

Trail or Route Conditions One can reach Starlight Arch from any one of several little drainages flowing south from the area of the arch. The way the author took is shown with the route symbol. There is no trail, you simply follow the drainage, as it meanders down the minor canyon. You can shorten the hike considerably, if you shortcut across the meanders of the drainage. When you arrive at the base of the steep slope and begin walking across the vari-colored Petrified Forest Member of the Chinle Formation, swing around to the west and make the final ascent to the mesa top via the southwest face, which is only moderately steep and very easy to climb. You can see this route from the highway. Once on the mesa top, simply head north to the mass of white Navajo sitting atop the Kayenta Formation, where the arch is prominently seen. The author did not try, but is certain that a route can be found up through the terraces northeast of the arch. Walk from Pahreah up the Paria River, then turn west up Dugout Canyon(called Deer Range Canyon on USGS maps), north of the small No Mans Mesa.

Elevations Trailhead, 1475 meters; Starlight Arch, about 1900 meters.

Hike Length and Time Needed If you can drive to the 1475 meter car-park, then it's only about 5 to 6 kms to the arch. From the movie set, it's 7 or 8 kms. This is about a half day hike for most, maybe 4 to 6 hours, round-trip. If you try the Dugout Canyon route, it's about 8 kms to the arch from Pahreah.

Water Take you own water. The campground at the movie set has no water.

Map USGS or BLM map Smoky Mountain(1:100,000), or Paria(1:62,500) and Calico Peak(1:24,000).

Main Attraction A fun mesa-top hike, with fine views. Lots of petrified wood enroute in the Petrified Forest Member of the Chinle.

Ideal Time to Hike Spring or fall, but it could be climbed in winter warm spells, or in summer heat.

Hiking Boots Any rugged pair of boots or shoes, but waders if you try the Dugout Canyon route.

Author's Experience The author went up the canyon shown, had a good look down the north slope, and returned in 3 hours.

Old timers called this Wedding Ring Arch. Maps today call it Starlight Arch.

MAP 14, STARLIGHT ARCH HIKE

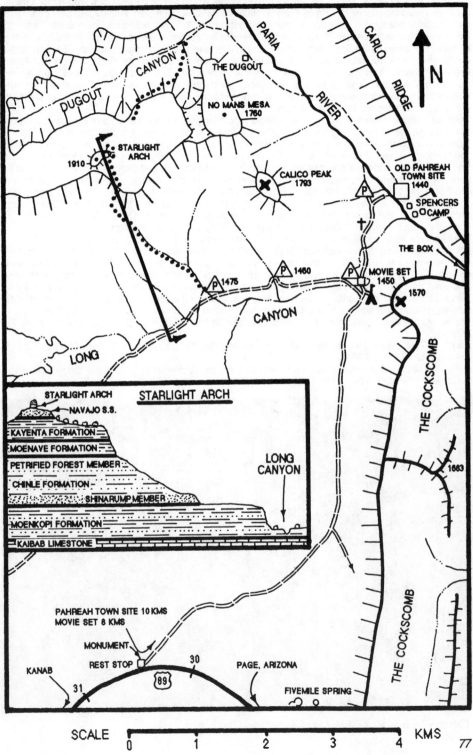

DUGOUT CANYON

PARIA RIVER

CARLO RIDGE

N

THE DUGOUT

NO MANS MESA
1760

STARLIGHT ARCH

1910

CALICO PEAK
1793

OLD PAHREAH TOWN SITE
1440

P

SPENCERS CAMP

THE BOX

P 1475

P 1460

P

MOVIE SET
1450

1570

LONG

CANYON

THE COCKSCOMB

STARLIGHT ARCH

STARLIGHT ARCH
NAVAJO S.S.
KAYENTA FORMATION
MOENAVE FORMATION
PETRIFIED FOREST MEMBER
CHINLE FORMATION
SHINARUMP MEMBER
MOENKOPI FORMATION
KAIBAB LIMESTONE

LONG CANYON

1683

THE COCKSCOMB

PAHREAH TOWN SITE 10 KMS
MOVIE SET 8 KMS

MONUMENT

REST STOP

KANAB

31

30

89

PAGE, ARIZONA

FIVEMILE SPRING

SCALE
0   1   2   3   4   KMS

Kodachrome Basin Trails

Location and Access This book covers mostly areas which are wilderness and with no foot trails, but it also includes places like Bryce Canyon National Park, which is very touristy and crowded. This map includes something in between those two extremes. It is Kodachrome Basin State Park. It's located only about 3 or 4 kms directly south of Henrieville, but you can't approach it from there, except by trail. Get there by driving south out of Cannonville, and follow the signs. It's about 5 kms to the first junction, then after about another 7 or 8 kms, you'll turn left off from the Cottonwood Wash Road to enter the park. You must pay a small fee at the entry point. The road is graveled all the way(well maintained), and has promise to be paved soon. Inside the park are two resident rangers, a newly built campers store(with camping supplies and horseback rides), a campground and picnic site(both with water), and several constructed trails.

Trail or Route Conditions For the most part the hiking trails are in the area of the park northwest of the rangers residence. Right next to the campground, is the beginning of the Eagles Nest Trail. It takes you up a steep trail to a pass, now known as Eagles Nest Pass, at 1935 meters. From this pass you have a fine view of the basin below, that is worth the walk. To the south of the campground is the Panarama Trail. It too is a constructed trail, which takes hikers into and through another section of the park. At its far end is Panarama Point, an overlook situated on a rock outcrop, which allows one another good view of the rock monoliths in the park. This walk is along a sandy trail and is well signposted. On the other side of the park is a short trail through some cliffs to the minor Shakespear Arch. Another site to see, but which you can drive to, is Chimney Rock. Get there by driving northeast from the ranger station on a road which could be slick in wet weather.

Elevations Rangers residence, 1765 meters; the campground about 1800 meters.

Hike Length and Time Needed The walk to Eagles Nest Pass is only about one km or less, and will take you only 10 or 15 minutes, one way. The Panarama Trail, which makes a loop-hike, is something like 3 or 4 kms, round-trip. You could do this one is about an hour, but you may want more time than that. The distance to Shakespear Arch is less than a km, and will take you less than 10 minutes for the one-way walk. While there are no trails around some sand pipe towers just west of the rangers residence, it can make an interesting walking area for someone looking for good fotos.

Water At Ott's campers store, the picnic site, and at the campground(but not enough water for bathing).

Map USGS maps Henrieville and Cannonville(1:24,000), and Utah Travel Council Map 5, Southwestern Utah(1:250,000).

Main Attraction Red rock spires and cliffs, and a constructed campground, for those who enjoy that type of camping. Also, a rare geologic feature known as *Sand Pipes*.

Chimney Rock, in the eastern part of Kodachrome Basin State Park.

MAP 15, KODACHROME BASIN TRAILS

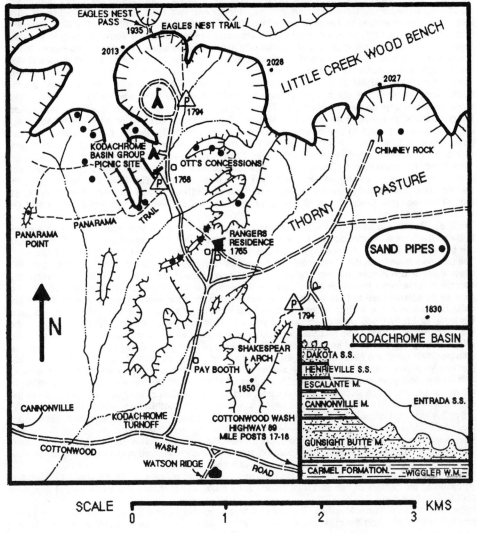

Ideal Time to Hike Spring or fall, but the park is open and can be visited year-round.
Hiking Boots Any dry weather boots or shoes.
Author's Experience The author walked all the trails in about half a day.
Sand Pipes of Kodachrome Basin Within the park are some unusual geologic features called Sand Pipes. They occur almost no where else. In the park, they are found mostly in the red colored Gunsight Butte Member of the Entrada Formation. They seem to be concentrated in the areas to the west of the rangers residences. These pipes are lighter colored than the surrounding rock, and average about 20 meters high, and about 8 meters in diameter. The sand making up the pipes is normally much courser than the surrounding rock. It's been thought they came about by the injection of liquefied sand, perhaps triggered by an earthquake and possibly initiated by cold water springs.

Round Valley Draw

Location and Access Round Valley Draw is one of the main tributaries of the upper part of the much larger Hackberry Canyon. Use this map for access into the upper end of Hackberry. The location is about half way between Kodachrome Basin State Park and the Butler Valley Arch(the name first applied to the arch), more commonly known as Grosvenor Arch. If you're coming in from the Bryce Canyon area, drive south out of Cannonville and follow the signs to Kodachrome Basin. When you arrive at the Kodachrome Turnoff, continue straight east. Drive another 10 kms to the small sign on the right(it was gone the last time the author was there), which points the way into *Hackberry Canyon*. This could be one of your entry or exit points. Or better still, continue east on this Cottonwood Wash Road, climb a steep dugway, and go over the pass marked 1984 meters. Near there you'll see a fence and cattle guard. Turn right, or south, and drive down this never maintained, but good track, to either of the car-parks shown. The Slickrock Bench Car-park is the best one; it allows you easy access to the lower part of the narrows. Probably the best entry route is the one going down the Draw itself. From the pass of 1984 meters, continue down the hill and second dugway to the dry creek bed signposted *Round Valley Draw*. Just beyond is a turnoff to the south, again signposted, *Rushbed Road*. Drive south on this road about 3 kms, to where you cross the dry creek bed for the second time and park where you can. This is the Round Valley Draw Car-park, and it's the second of the two normal ways of entry to the narrows of the Draw. If you're coming from Highway 89, turn off between mile posts 17 and 18, and drive north on the Cottonwood Wash Road for about 54 kms to the Rushbed Road.

Trail or Route Conditions From the Round Valley Draw Car-park, you walk right down the creek bed about 1.5 kms. At that point you see exposed, the top layer of Navajo Sandstone. This is where the slot canyon begins. You can get in where it first cuts into the Navajo, but it's a little difficult. Or you can bench-walk on the north side of the narrows for about 200-300 meters until you come to a stone cairn which marks another steep, but fairly easy route down into the depths. To some this second route in looks fearsome at first, but it's easier than it first may appear. Take a short piece of rope or parachute cord to help those not accustomed to rock climbing. Take it slow and easy and most hikers can make it OK. In the bottom of the narrows, it's much like the Bull Valley Gorge or Buckskin Gulch. As you walk down canyon you will come to a large boulder which you pass on the left. Fifty meters beyond this first boulder, you'll come to another large chokestone. This has created a falls or dropoff. You could jump off, or lower members of your group down with a rope, but you can also go down the crack between it and the wall. If you're about 180 cms(about 6 ft.) tall or taller, you can easily *chimney* down this crack, by placing your feet on the wall and your back against the rock, and by wiggling your way downward. This is just difficult enough to make it fun. After another 50 meters or so, you come to perhaps the deepest and darkest section of the hike. In the middle of this narrow part, there's another chokestone which has formed still another falls. You could jump off this 2.5 or 3 meter high dropoff, but if you're of average height, you can spread your legs, one foot on each side of the canyon wall, and work your way over the falls. If you're there soon after a storm, you may have a small pool below both of these falls, but it's never very deep. Down canyon there are still more narrows, but no more obstacles. After passing through the narrows, you could return the same way, or exit to the Slickrock Bench Car-park, then rim-walk back to your car.

Elevations The two main car-parks are both at 1850 meters altitude, while it's about 1775 meters elevation at the bottom of the Slickrock Bench entry route. That makes the lower part of the gorge about 75 meters deep.

Hike Length and Time Needed It's about 5 kms from the Round Valley Draw Car-park to the junction of the Draw and the main Hackberry Canyon. If you were to hike down the narrows, then exit at the Slickrock Bench route(a walk-up), and rim-walk back to your car, it would take about half a day, depending on how long you want to enjoy the narrows.

Water Take your own water, and have a good supply of it in your car. There are no good springs or wells anywhere near.

Map USGS or BLM map Smoky Mountain(1:100,000), or Slickrock Bench(1:24,000).

Main Attraction Another deep, dark and narrow Navajo Sandstone slickrock canyon, two kms of which are equal to the Buckskin Gulch.

Ideal Time to Hike Spring or fall are best, but it can be done year-round. There doesn't seem to be any water seeping into the bottom to make icy walking conditions during winter, and it's very cool in the narrows during summer. June is the very best time, because it's the driest month in this region.

Hiking Boots If you're there right after rains, take wading shoes. Otherwise, you can get by with dry weather footwear.

Author's Experience On one trip the author went down in late March, and found half a meter of snow on the narrows floor, which had slid off the walls. There was no water in any of the potholes then. He went down again in June, a week after heavy rains, and found some mud in the low places, but no pools of water. He has entered or exited all four routes into the Draw.

MAP 16, ROUND VALLEY DRAW

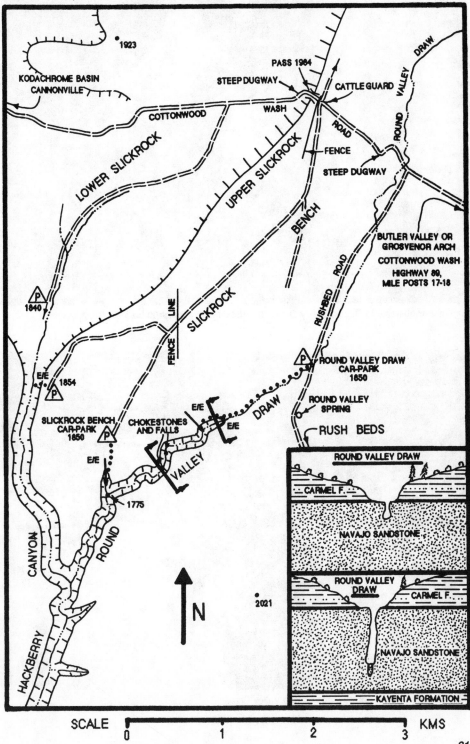

1923

KODACHROME BASIN
CANNONVILLE

PASS 1964
STEEP DUGWAY
CATTLE GUARD

COTTONWOOD
WASH

ROAD

FENCE

ROUND VALLEY DRAW

LOWER SLICKROCK

UPPER SLICKROCK

BENCH

STEEP DUGWAY

BUTLER VALLEY OR
GROSVENOR ARCH
COTTONWOOD WASH
HIGHWAY 89,
MILE POSTS 17-18

RUSHBED ROAD

P
1840

FENCE LINE

SLICKROCK

E/E
1854
P

P
ROUND VALLEY DRAW
CAR-PARK
1850

ROUND VALLEY
SPRING

SLICKROCK BENCH
CAR-PARK
1850
P

CHOKESTONES
AND FALLS

E/E
E/E

DRAW

RUSH BEDS

E/E

VALLEY

1775

ROUND

ROUND VALLEY DRAW

CARMEL F.

NAVAJO SANDSTONE

CANYON

HACKBERRY

N

2021

ROUND VALLEY
DRAW

CARMEL F.

NAVAJO SANDSTONE

KAYENTA FORMATION

SCALE
0   1   2   3   KMS

81

One minor obstacle in Round Valley Draw. It's just difficult enough to be interesting.

The beginning of the narrows into Round Valley Draw.

Winter snows stay long, as the sun doesn't reach the bottom of Round Valley Draw.

One way to get past the second obstacle, is to chimney up and around the chokestone.

Hackberry Canyon

Location and Access Hackberry Canyon is one of three long canyon hikes in this book, and it's one of the best around when considering availability of water, good scenery, pleasant campsites and interesting things to see. This canyon lies just east of the Upper Paria River Gorge. The road you'll be using, whether you go in at the head of the canyon or enter from the bottom, is the Cottonwood Wash Road.

From the Bryce Canyon area, drive east, then south through Tropic and Cannonville, and first follow the signs to Kodachrome Basin State Park. At the Kodachrome Turnoff, continue driving east on the Cottonwood Wash Road about 10 kms until you see a small sign on the right(south) indicating the road to Hackberry Canyon(that sign was gone the last time the author was there!). Most cars can be driven down this never-maintained road for about 3 kms. A shovel might help you get a little further along.

Another possibility is to drive further along the Cottonwood Wash Road, up a steep dugway, and over a pass marked 1984 meters. Just beyond this is a fence and cattle guard. Turn right or south, and drive this never-maintained and seldom-used, but rather good track to its end on the Slickrock Bench. See *Map 16, Round Valley Draw*, for a better look at the entry routes.

Still another alternative, is to drive along the Cottonwood Wash Road 'till it crosses the Round Valley Draw, then turn south on the *Rushbed Road*. Drive about 3 kms to where you cross the creek bed for the second time; then park and walk in via Round Valley Draw. This will be the most difficult of the three entry points, but also the most fun. Read the route description on *Map 16*.

You can reach this same area from Highway 89. Between mile posts 17 and 18, turn north onto the bottom part of the Cottonwood Wash Road. From the highway, it's about 20 kms to the bottom of Hackberry, or about 55 to 60 kms to the side roads mentioned above.

Trail or Route Conditions All the way you'll be walking right down the creek bed of the canyon. The upper half is dry; while the lower end has a small stream. The easiest entry point is to come right down the main Hackberry Canyon, but it's also the least interesting. For the adventurous sort, it's recommended you come right down the narrows of the Round Valley Draw. Take a rope or parachute cord to lower your pack into, and past two minor falls in the upper part.

The author didn't see, but has heard good things about Booker Canyon. It has some minor dry falls, and Ponderosa pines grow out of slickrock in its upper reaches.

About 8 kms below Booker Canyon, you may see the first spring or seep. A little further along, and as you see the huge Navajo wall in front of you on the left, and as water is starting to flow, look to your right(west), and you'll see a fence on a bench. At that point is a constructed cow trail out of the canyon.

This is called the Upper Trail. Herm Pollock of Tropic, believes this trail was first made by a group of Panguitch cattlemen in the last century. It was on this very narrow trail, as it runs along the rim of the canyon, that a cow once laid down right on the trail and died. Because it was very narrow, the other cows wouldn't step over her body. The end result was the choking death of many cows in the area which is now called Death Valley. Since this first disaster, the trail has been improved many times and by different cattlemen who ran stock in the Upper Death Valley. One of these men was Sampson Chynoweth. Members of the Ott family may have also improved it some, as it's a rather good trail today.

A bit further along is Stone Donkey Canyon, which has an excellent spring less than half a km from the mouth. Stone Donkey Canyon divides Upper from Lower Death Valley. The upper part of this canyon has some fine narrows and is a box canyon.

About a km down canyon from where the red beds of the Kayenta Formation(perhaps it's the red bottom of the Navajo?) first begin to show, is another cow trail out of the canyon to the west. At that point high on the east wall are several Navajo alcoves, and right at a place where the creek turns abruptly west, is a cowboyglyph, *W. M. Chynoweth, 1892,* about 5 meters above the creek. To the right of this is the constructed trail. This is mostly a natural break in the cliffs, but minor work has been done in the very lowest part. Just above the cliffs is a long sand slide which the cows walk going to or from the creek. This is called the Lower Trail, and is used today by cattle in the Lower Death Valley area.

Not far below the Lower Trail, and just above the little one meter high falls or jumpup, is another trail heading up and to the east towards the Rush Beds side of the canyon(to between Hackberry and Cottonwood Wash). For lack of a better name, let's call this one the Jumpup Trail. This is one the author hasn't seen.

Further along is Sam Pollock Canyon. Three kms up this canyon is an arch, with Sams name on it. At one point in this side canyon, you'll have to route-find to the right or north side of the canyon, to get around the falls, which otherwise block the way. It's an easy hike up.

Half a km down stream from the mouth of Sam Pollock Canyon, and on a bench on the west side of the creek, is the old Watson Cabin. Read the full story about this old cabin below. As the

MAP 17, HACKBERRY CANYON

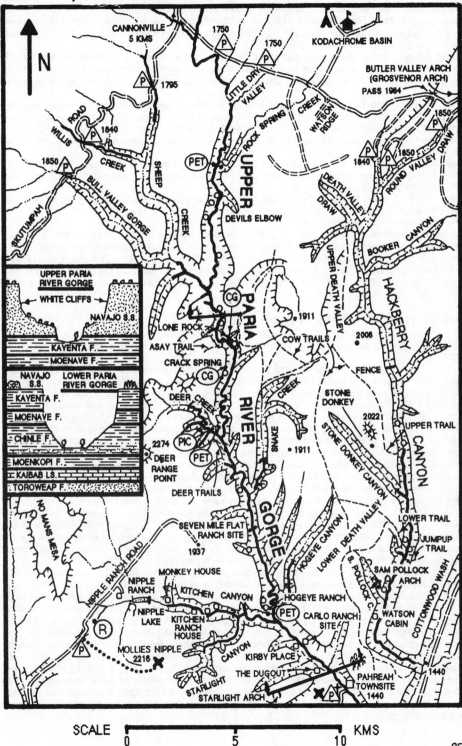

N

CANNONVILLE
5 KMS

1750

1750

KODACHROME BASIN

BUTLER VALLEY ARCH
(GROSVENOR ARCH)
PASS 1984

P 1795

P 1840

WILLIS ROAD

P 1850

SKUTUMPAH

BULL VALLEY GORGE

CREEK

SHEEP CREEK

LITTLE DRY VALLEY

ROCK SPRING CREEK

WATSON RIDGE

1850

P 1840 P 1850

ROUND VALLEY DRAW

PET

UPPER PARIA

DEVILS ELBOW

DEATH VALLEY DRAW

UPPER DEATH VALLEY

BOOKER CANYON

HACKBERRY

UPPER PARIA RIVER GORGE
WHITE CLIFFS
NAVAJO S.S.
KAYENTA F.
MOENAVE F.

LOWER PARIA RIVER GORGE
NAVAJO S.S.
KAYENTA F.
MOENAVE F.
CHINLE F.
MOENKOPI F.
KAIBAB LS.
TOROWEAP F.

CG

1911

2008

LONE ROCK

ASAY TRAIL

CRACK SPRING

CG

DEER CREEK

COW TRAILS

FENCE

STONE DONKEY

2022

UPPER TRAIL

CANYON

SNAKE CREEK

STONE DONKEY CANYON

2274

PIC

PET

DEER RANGE POINT

DEER TRAILS

1911

NO MANS MESA

SEVEN MILE FLAT RANCH SITE

1937

LOWER TRAIL

JUMPUP TRAIL

HOGEYE CANYON

LOWER DEATH VALLEY

S. POLLOCK C.

SAM POLLOCK ARCH

COTTONWOOD WASH

NIPPLE RANCH ROAD

MONKEY HOUSE

NIPPLE RANCH

KITCHEN CANYON

NIPPLE LAKE

KITCHEN RANCH HOUSE

HOGEYE RANCH

PET

CARLO RANCH SITE

WATSON CABIN

R

P

MOLLIES NIPPLE
2216

CANYON

KIRBY PLACE

THE DUGOUT

STARLIGHT

STARLIGHT ARCH

P

PAHREAH TOWNSITE
1440

1440

SCALE 0   5   10 KMS

85

canyon turns to the east, it cuts dramatically through the Navajo Sandstone part of The Cockscomb, before reaching Cottonwood Wash.

Elevations Trailheads, about 1850 meters; bottom of canyon, 1440 meters.

Hike Length and Time Needed This hike is around 28 to 30 kms long. It could be done in one long day, but who wants that? Normally, it takes 2 or 3 days for the walk, depending on how many side canyons or trails you visit along the way.

Water It begins to flow in the creek bed about 12-13 kms below where Round Valley Draw enters. It then flows all the way, or very near to, Cottonwood Wash. There's a good spring up Stone Donkey Canyon a ways, and there are several seeps or springs just below the minor falls, including a side canyon.

At times, usually the end of October or first part of November through about mid-May, there are cattle in the canyon, so try and take water directly from a spring, or consider purifying it first, at that time of year. In summer, and when there are no cattle around, it should be good as-is, as the Giardia are carried down with the free flowing water. The author has drank it often, without Iodine, and never died once.

Map USGS or BLM map Smoky Mountain(1:100,000), or Slickrock Bench and Calico Peak(1:24,000).

Main Attraction Good water, shady campsites, narrow side canyons, old historic cattle trails, an old homesteaders cabin, and solitude.

Ideal Time to Hike Spring or fall. In late spring and early summer, you'll be plagued by deer and horse flies(late May to early July). To avoid these pests, just wear long pants.

Hiking Boots Wading boots or shoes.

Author's Experience He has made 7 or 8 trips into the canyon, but only once did he walk all the way through. On that occasion, he left late in the evening and rim-walked above Round Valley Draw to about its confluence of Hackberry, and camped. Next day he hurried all the way through, and hitched a ride back to his car in the afternoon along the Cottonwood Wash Road. In the spring, summer and fall, you might see 20 to 30 cars on this road per day. Other trips were to see Round Valley Draw, Sam Pollock Arch and the cattle trails.

Frank Watson and the Watson Cabin

There's a rather well build and well preserved cabin in the lower end of Hackberry Canyon, and an interesting story behind it. It's called the Watson Cabin, after a man known locally as Frank Watson.

The mans real name was Richard Welburn Thomas, who came from Wisconsin. As the story goes, Thomas apparently had a quarrel with his wife one night, but early the next morning, he got up, left the house. He walked to the railway station where he boarded a train for the wild west. This is the story that's told, but he could have been a fugitive from the law. No one will ever know for sure.

After some wandering, it seems he ended up at Lee's Ferry, and under the employment of Charles H. Spencer. Spencer was the big time promoter who got lots of money from investors and tried to find a way to separate gold from the Chinle clay beds at Lee's Ferry. Spencer was at work at the Ferry between 1910 and 1912. It was at this time, Thomas changed his name to Frank Watson. Evidently Watson was a good all-around handy man and mechanic. It's been said by several men in Bryce Valley, that Watson was involved in the running of the paddlewheeler *Charles H. Spencer,* up the Colorado River and to Warm Creek, where they were to load coal and carry it down to the gold diggings at the Ferry. This whole operation failed in the end, and the miners left in 1912.

From Lee's Ferry, Spencer and his men went up the Paria River to the old town of Pahreah, and were involved in the same work there from 1912 to about the end of World War I. Watson was also there at that time, and it appears it was sometime during the war, that he went over Carlo Ridge and into lower Hackberry Canyon and built this cabin. It's been said that he had a rough trail from the cabin, over the ridge, and down to Pahreah, but no one knows of it's whereabouts today.

Herm Pollock, the rock hound out of Tropic, remembered the Watson Cabin as being well built. Watson made the wooden hinges on the door with only a pocket knife. About 150 to 200 meters south of the cabin, Watson had made a flume and a sluice or riffle box, both of which were painted bright yellow when Herm saw the place in 1922. Apparently, Watson had tried to do the same thing in lower Hackberry, as Spencer was trying to do over the ridge at Pahreah, and evidently without success.

George Thompson of Cannonville, and Herm Pollock, both remembered a little about the cabin and the time when Georges father, Jodi Thompson, tried to homestead the bench land where the cabin was located. Jodi and some of his brothers, went to the area sometime in about the mid-1920's, and tried for two seasons to grow crops and plant peach trees. They had dug a ditch by hand and with shovels only, and had successfully brought water from the creek above the cabin down to the bench where they grew vegetables. But in the second year they had a flash flood, which lowered the creek bed to the point where water couldn't be diverted to the bench, and that ended the garden scheme at the Watson Cabin.

There's an interesting story about one dark night in the cabin, as told by several old timers in Bryce Valley. Jodi and one of his brothers either got to the cabin late at night, or were sleeping there, when they heard rattlesnakes in the darkened room. With only candle light and a pitch fork with five prongs, they managed to spear one rattler with each prong. In the morning they stood the pitch fork up against the cabin wall with the five rattlers on it, and they nearly reached down to the ground.

According to Ken Goulding of Henrieville, Watson was employed by the Goulding family off and

The upper part of Hackberry, just below the Upper Trail.

The sandslide, which is part of the Lower Trail, into middle Hackberry Canyon.

on for several years herding sheep, apparently during the mid to late 1910's. At one time Watson lived in a tent, which was pitched behind the Goulding house in Henrieville. Ken recalled that one winter, Watson tore down an old Model A Ford, and put it back together again the next spring.

At about the end of World War I, and after the time when Watson had built his Hackberry Cabin and had worked for the Gouldings, he built a small store on what is now known locally as Watson Ridge. Watson Ridge is south of Henrieville, and due south of Chimney Rock, which is in Kodachrome Basin State Park. The store was small, and catered to the sheepmen who were numerous in the area at that time. He sold all kinds of supplies, but Ken Goulding remembers him selling candy, Bull Durham tobacco, and a boot leg whisky everyone called *Jamaica Ginger.*

This was in the early days of prohibition, and selling this rot-gut whisky was forbidden. The lady who owned and operated the only store in Henrieville, bought it from someone, then it was transported out to Watsons store, where they used to have some wild parties. It was sold and drank out at Watsons place, because it was so far away from the law.

To get to Watsons old store site, drive east on the Cottonwood Wash Road about one or two kms east from the Kodachrome Turnoff. Turn right or south, at the first road running south, and drive about 100-200 meters. It's near the crest of the hill, but on the west side. Today there's only some scattered tin cans, etc., marking the spot.

The last time Goulding saw Watson was in about 1921. Herm Pollock and the Otts pick up the story from there. After leaving the store on Watson Ridge, he likely went to the bottom of Heward Canyon, a tributary of Sheep Creek, which is just east of Bryce Canyon, and to the south west of Cannonville and Tropic. About 2 kms to the west of the old Johnson Ranch on Sheep Creek, is a very well built stone house along the road running up Heward Creek. This may have been built by Watson, since it was well built and is still in very good condition, except for the wooden roof, which has collapsed under it's own weight. Watson lived there, or perhaps just down canyon at the Johnson Ranch. While there, he apparently tried to developed a coal mine just west of the cabin for one or two winters(See the map "Bryce Valley & Skutumpah Road Ranches", on page 205).

To get to the Heward Canyon rock house, drive south out of Cannonville for about 4 or 5 kms, and turn west toward the old town site of Georgetown. From the Yellow Creek Road, turn south from just across the creek and head for Sheep Creek, and the sites of the old Henderson and Johnson Ranches and Heward Creek. About 2 kms west of the old Johnson Ranch, which is now owned by Colorado City people named Binion and Stubbs, is the rock house on the right side of the road.

Later he landed at the old W. J. Henderson Ranch, which is about 1.5 or 2 kms southwest of the Georgetown site, and just up the hill from where the James R. Ott Ranch was located. At this ranch, Watson lived with an old man named Hyrum "Hite" Elmer. Wallace Ott remembers when old Hite died, because Watson came down to their ranch to get a wagon to haul him off.

Sam Pollock Arch, in a side canyon of the lower Hackberry.

From the Henderson Ranch, Watson went back to Wisconsin to see his aging mother sometime in the mid-1920's. She was apparently very happy and surprised to see him, according to Ken Goulding. Since he had been gone for so long, and had lost touch with the family, his mother thought he surely must have been killed by Indians.

The well preserved Frank Watson Cabin, in the lower end of Hackberry Canyon.

Inside the Frank Watson Cabin.

Cottonwood Wash Narrows

Location and Access Featured here is a short narrows section in the upper end of Cottonwood Wash. These narrows aren't very long, but they are nearly as deep, dark and narrow as parts of the Buckskin Gulch, against which all narrows are judged. The location is very near the top of Cottonwood Wash, and about 7 kms south of the Butler Valley Arch(this was the name of the arch before the National Geographic Society came into the area in about 1948, and changed the name it Grosvenor Arch after their NGS President?). To get there, drive from Bryce Canyon on Highway 12, and through the towns of Tropic and Cannonville. From Cannonville head south and first follow the signs to Kodachrome Basin, but continue straight east on the Cottonwood Wash Road instead. Where you see the sign pointing out the direction to Grosvenor Arch, continue to drive south(rather than turn east), for about 7 kms. The only land mark to look for is a bridge on one of the two largest tributaries of the upper Cottonwood Wash. In the entire upper part of the Wash, this is the only place the road is bridged. At all other locations, the road just crosses dry washes. If you're coming up canyon from Highway 89, turn off the pavement between mile posts 17 and 18(the Paria River Ranger Station is between m.p. 20 and 21). From the highway to the above mentioned bridge is about 42 kms. When this access road is wet, stay away, it's impassable. But it tends to dry quickly in summer after rains, which are very infrequent.

Trail or Route Conditions Park near the bridge, and scramble down into the drainage. After just a few meters, you'll have a choice of going up the short section of Butler Valley Draw, or down the Cottonwood Wash Creek bed. Go up first, as that part is perhaps the best, then head down canyon. There are several very short side canyons and some high falls to see as well. After about 2 kms, you'll come out the bottom end and back to the road. These narrows are formed by a strange twist of the dry stream channel, which has cut into the ever present Navajo Sandstone.

Elevations Entry point, 1735 meters; bottom of narrows, 1675; the campsite at arch, l900 meters.

Hike Length and Time Needed You have only about 200 meters or so of interesting narrows up Butler Valley Draw, then about 2 kms of narrows where the main wash is back away from the road and where it cuts the Navajo. You can do the whole hike in one or two hours. Short, easy, interesting, fun and safe for the whole family.

Water Carry water in your car, as the well shown on the map doesn't always produce. The campsite at the arch is a dry one.

Map USGS or BLM map Smoky Mountain(1:100,000), or Butler Valley(1:24,000).

Main Attraction A very short, but interesting and easily accessible Navajo narrows, and the Butler Valley Arch. A great little walk, even for non-hikers.

Ideal Time to Hike About anytime, but summers are a little warm, and cold winter weather prevents the road from drying quickly after storms. Access can be a problem in winter, but otherwise the road is good and heavily used in the warmer months.

Hiking Boots Dry weather boots or shoes.

Author's Experience Once in early April, the author did this entire hike in about an hour.

90 Inside the Navajo narrows of the upper part of Cottonwood Wash.

MAP 18, COTTONWOOD WASH NARROWS

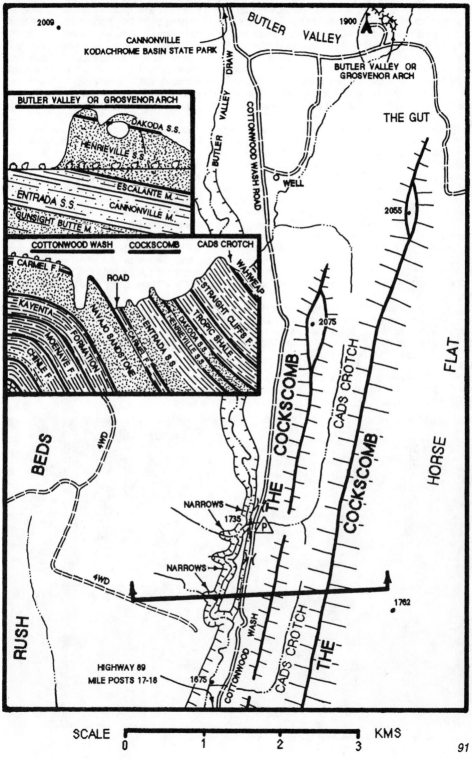

BUTLER VALLEY

2009 .

CANNONVILLE
KODACHROME BASIN STATE PARK

1900

BUTLER VALLEY OR
GROSVENOR ARCH

THE GUT

BUTLER VALLEY OR GROSVENOR ARCH

DAKODA S.S.

HENRIEVILLE S.S.

ESCALANTE M.

ENTRADA S.S.   CANNONVILLE M.

GUNSIGHT BUTTE M.

COTTONWOOD WASH   COCKSCOMB   CADS CROTCH

CARMEL F.

ROAD

WAHWEAP

STRAIGHT CLIFFS F.

TROPIC SHALE

KAYENTA
FORMATION

MOENAVE F.

CHINLE F.

NAVAJO SANDSTONE

ENTRADA S.S.

CARMEL F.

DAKODA S.S.

HENRIEVILLE S.S.

WELL

2055

BUTLER VALLEY DRAW

COTTONWOOD WASH ROAD

BEDS

4WD

2075

THE COCKSCOMB

CADS CROTCH

THE COCKSCOMB

HORSE   FLAT

NARROWS

1735

P

NARROWS

4WD

1762

RUSH

HIGHWAY 89
MILE POSTS 17-18

1675

COTTONWOOD   WASH

CADS CROTCH

THE

SCALE

0   1   2   3   KMS

Sam Pollock and Hogeye Canyons

Location and Access This loop-hike involves a couple of side drainages in the lower parts of the Upper Paria River Gorge and lower Hackberry Canyon. It takes in some historic sites and a traverse of some high mesa country between two major canyons. You have two starting points to choose from. One is at the mouth of Hackberry Canyon, where it drains into the lower Cottonwood Wash. Reach this car-park by leaving Highway 89 between mile posts 17 and 18, which is about 5 kms east of the Paria Ranger Station. This is the Cottonwood Wash Road. Drive about 20 kms to the mouth of Hackberry Canyon. The other starting point is at old Pahreah. Get there by exiting Highway 89 between mile posts 30 and 31, where the sign points to *old Pahreah and the movie set*. Drive about 10 kms to the car-park. Both of these access roads are maintained and heavily used in the warmer months, but both can be slick in spots during wet weather. However, during the warmer months, these clay roads dry quickly after rains.

Trail or Route Conditions Here's the recommended route. Park at the mouth of Hackberry and walk up canyon where it cuts through the Navajo narrows. Further up you pass the Watson Cabin on a bench above the creek; then less than a km away, enter the lower end of Sam Pollock Canyon. About a km up this canyon is a falls, which can be skirted on the north side. Further up on the right, is Sam Pollock Arch, named after a Tropic cattleman. From the arch, you head in a northwest direction over a divide and toward a Navajo rock which looks like a beehive. Walk around this rock on the right or east, and enter the upper part of Hogeye Canyon. Walk down Hogeye to the lower part where there's year-round water and many good campsites. Then finish the hike by walking down the Paria, past the ghost town site, and through what is called The Box. This is the part of the Paria which cuts through The Cockscomb. Just beyond The Box, turn north and walk the lower Cottonwood Wash back to your car. If starting at old Pahreah, then plan to make camp somewhere near the Watson Cabin. Also, consider some kind of alternate route involving some of the old cattle trails, which are described on *Map 20*.

Elevations Both car-parks 1440 meters; the high point along the divide, about 1775 meters.

Hike Length and Time Needed This loop-hike is about 36 to 38 kms, and should be considered a two day walk.

Water There's year-round running water in Hackberry, Hogeye(very good) and the Paria. There are also some good springs coming out of the west wall just north and south of the old Hogeye Ranch site.

Map USGS or BLM map Smoky Mountain(1:100,0000), or Paria(1:62,500) and Calico Peak(1:24,000).

Main Attraction Deep canyons, several historic ranch sites, good water and campsites.

Ideal Time to Hike Spring or fall.

Hiking Boots Wading boots or shoes.

Author's Experience The author made it into upper Hogeye from the mouth of Hackberry, but returned the same way to get fotos of the arch. Round-trip, about 7 hours. He has also been into Hogeye from old Pahreah, as well as hiking all the cow trails shown.

One of several minor waterfalls in the lower end of Hogeye Canyon.

MAP 19, SAM POLLOCK—HOGEYE CANYONS

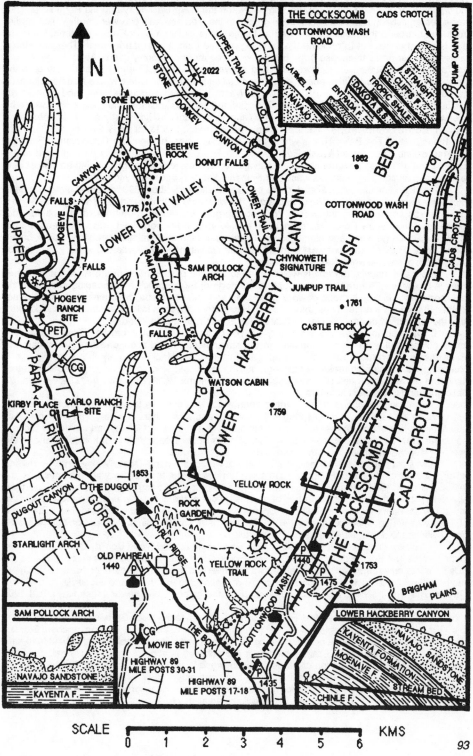

THE COCKSCOMB

CADS CROTCH

COTTONWOOD WASH ROAD

CARMEL F.

NAVAJO

ENTRADA F.

DAKOTA S.S.

TROPIC SHALE

STRAIGHT CLIFFS F.

PUMP CANYON

N

UPPER TRAIL

STONE DONKEY CANYON

2022

STONE DONKEY

BEEHIVE ROCK

DONUT FALLS

FALLS

CANYON

HOGEYE

1775

UPPER

FALLS

LOWER DEATH VALLEY

LOWER TRAIL

1862

BEDS

COTTONWOOD WASH ROAD

RUSH

SAM POLLOCK C.

SAM POLLOCK ARCH

HOGEYE RANCH SITE

PET

FALLS

CG

CHYNOWETH SIGNATURE

JUMPUP TRAIL

1761

CASTLE ROCK

LOWER HACKBERRY CANYON

WATSON CABIN

1759

KIRBY PLACE

PARIA

RIVER

CARLO RANCH SITE

1853

DUGOUT CANYON

THE DUGOUT

GORGE

CARLO RIDGE

ROCK GARDEN

YELLOW ROCK

CADS CROTCH

THE COCKSCOMB

STARLIGHT ARCH

OLD PAHREAH 1440

P

YELLOW ROCK TRAIL

COTTONWOOD WASH

1440

P

1475

S 1753

BRIGHAM PLAINS

THE BOX

CG

MOVIE SET

HIGHWAY 89 MILE POSTS 30-31

HIGHWAY 89 MILE POSTS 17-18

P

1435

SAM POLLOCK ARCH

NAVAJO SANDSTONE

KAYENTA F.

LOWER HACKBERRY CANYON

KAYENTA FORMATION

MOENAVE F.

NAVAJO SANDSTONE

STREAM BED

CHINLE F.

SCALE

0 1 2 3 4 5 6

KMS

Lower Death Valley Cow Trails

Location and Access Featured here are some of the trails and routes used by early day sheep and cattlemen in the high mesa country lying between the lower Hackberry and the Paria River. For over a century, sheep and cattle have been grazed in the area now called Lower Death Valley, and in areas south around the Rock Garden and a Navajo dome, called Yellow Rock. In recent years the BLM has sent crews out to relocate these fading historic trails and to mark them. There are three trailheads or car-parks to choose from, but two would be more commonly used. About 5 kms east of the Paria Ranger Station on Highway 89, and between mile posts 17 and 18, turn north onto the Cottonwood Wash Road. Drive about 16 kms and pull off the road to the left, where it comes closest to the confluence of the Paria and Cottonwood Wash. Or drive another 4 kms, and park at the confluence of Hackberry and Cottonwood. The third and perhaps least feasible access point would be to leave Highway 89 from between mile posts 30 and 31, and drive 10 kms northeast to old Pahreah.

Trail or Route Conditions The best marked and easiest trail to follow is the one running north from the middle of The Box. This is where the Paria River cuts through The Cockscomb. From the trailhead on the Cottonwood Wash Road, walk into The Box. About half way through, and at the contact point of the red Kayenta and white Navajo Formations, look for a trail running northwest, and up at a steep angle. This Box Trail was recently marked(1987?) and is easy to follow.

From the Hackberry Trailhead, cross the creek, and walk about 300 meters south from where Hackberry meets Cottonwood Wash, and along the west side of the drainage. There you will find a small canyon coming from the west. Walk up the gully less than 75 meters, and look for the beginning of the Yellow Rock Trail running up a slide area to the northwest. It's very steep at first. Follow it up, then go west, and along the south side of a huge bald Navajo Sandstone dome, called Yellow Rock. Finally head northwest to meet The Box Trail at the Rock Garden Junction. This junction is just south of several white Navajo pinnacles.

From this junction the trail is well marked to where it passes north of the Rock Garden, then fades in the sand. The trail circles around to the north of Sam Pollock Arch heading east, then zig zags northeast. Finally it drops down a sand slide and crosses a shallow drainage, before turning southeast following a ridge. Near the bottom of Hackberry Canyon, it follows another sand slide to the lip of the canyon, where the constructed part of the Lower Trail can be found.

If you're planning to *leave* Hackberry Canyon by the Lower Trail, it may be difficult to locate. If you're looking for this trail from inside the canyon, remember it's found about one km down stream from where the red Kayenta Formation first appears(in the upper Hackberry only the white Navajo is exposed). As the canyon makes a hard right turn to the west(going down canyon), about 5 meters above the present creek bed is a cowboyglyph, with the name *W. M. Chynoweth--1892*, written. At that corner and to the west is the trail.

There's still another cow trail further north which you can use to get out of Hackberry. Just down stream from the upper-most spring in the canyon, and where there is a very high Navajo wall on the east side, is a bench on the west side of the creek. On it is a short fence, and above the fence is the Upper Trail, so called because it allows passage to Upper Death Valley. It heads up and to the west in a shallow drainage to join the main north-south cattle route.

It was because of an incident on this trail that we get the name Death Valley, both Upper and Lower. About a century ago, Panguitch cattlemen ran cows in the area. They were the ones who first built a trail down to Hackberry Creek. But in those days it wasn't as good a trail as you see there today(since that time a better route has been blasted out of the cliff). It was very narrow, and cows had to step from one foothold to the next. Once a cow laid down right on the trail and died. The rest of the herd was too spooked to pass by her on the very narrow path. Since they couldn't get to water, they all choked to death, thus the name Death Valley.

You could use this Upper Death Valley Trail to skirt around Stone Donkey Canyon, and head south towards The Box, or down Hogeye or Sam Pollock Canyons. In the northern part of the area, the trails fade into *cow routes* only. Those who want to hike into the northern parts of this area, in Upper Death Valley, should have some good topo maps and expect to use their route find skills.

Elevations The trailheads are about 1440 meters; the highest point on the mesa top, about 1900 meters.

Hike Length and Time Needed From The Box Trailhead to the Rock Garden Junction is about 5 kms. From the Hackberry Trailhead up the Yellow Rock Trail to the same junction, is about 3 or 3.5 kms. From the Rock Garden Junction to the bottom of the Lower Trail in Hackberry, is about 9-10 kms. From the bottom of the Lower Trail to the mouth of Hackberry is about 6 kms. A nice half-day hike, would be to begin at either of the trailheads(on Cottonwood Wash), walk to the Rock Garden Junction, and return by the other trail, thus making a loop-hike, and maybe 4 or 5 hours walking. Fast hikers could begin at the Hackberry Trailhead, walk up the trail, enter Hackberry via the Lower Trail, then return down Hackberry to the trailhead. This would be an all day hike.

MAP 20, LOWER DEATH VALLEY COW TRAILS

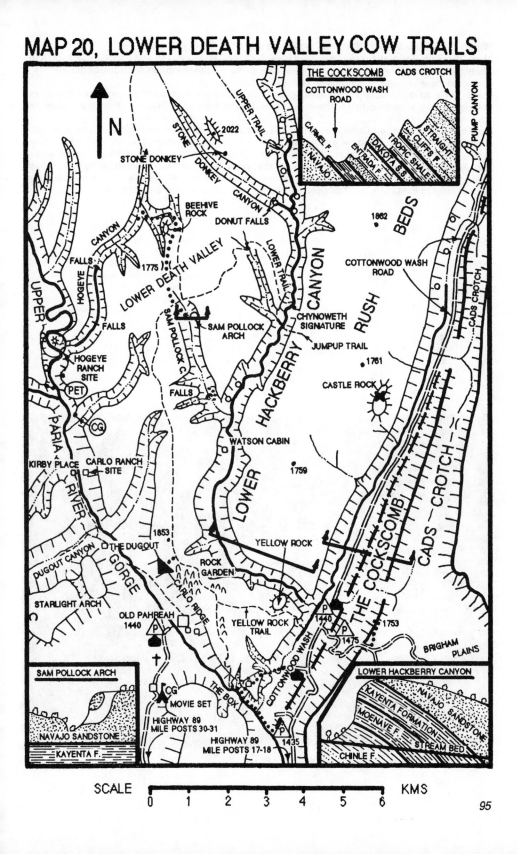

THE COCKSCOMB
CADS CROTCH
COTTONWOOD WASH ROAD
PUMP CANYON
CARMEL F.
NAVAJO
ENTRADA F.
DAKOTA S.S.
TROPIC SHALE
CLIFFS F.
STRAIGHT

N

STONE DONKEY CANYON
2022
UPPER TRAIL
STONE DONKEY
BEEHIVE ROCK
DONUT FALLS
HOGEYE CANYON
FALLS
1775
LOWER DEATH VALLEY
LOWER TRAIL
1862
BEDS
COTTONWOOD WASH ROAD
HACKBERRY CANYON
CADS CROTCH
UPPER
FALLS
SAM POLLOCK C.
SAM POLLOCK ARCH
CHYNOWETH SIGNATURE
JUMPUP TRAIL
1761
RUSH
HOGEYE RANCH SITE
PET
FALLS
CASTLE ROCK
CG
WATSON CABIN
PARIA RIVER
KIRBY PLACE
CARLO RANCH SITE
1759
LOWER
1853
THE DUGOUT
DUGOUT CANYON
GORGE
ROCK GARDEN
YELLOW ROCK
THE COCKSCOMB
CADS CROTCH
STARLIGHT ARCH
CARLO RIDGE
OLD PAHREAH 1440
P
YELLOW ROCK TRAIL
P 1440
P
1475
C 1753
BRIGHAM PLAINS
†
COTTONWOOD WASH

SAM POLLOCK ARCH
NAVAJO SANDSTONE
KAYENTA F.

CG
MOVIE SET
HIGHWAY 89 MILE POSTS 30-31
THE BOX
HIGHWAY 89 MILE POSTS 17-18
P 1435

LOWER HACKBERRY CANYON
NAVAJO SANDSTONE
KAYENTA FORMATION
MOENAVE F.
STREAM BED
CHINLE F.

SCALE
0 1 2 3 4 5 6
KMS

Water There is no water on the mesa, only in the canyons. Carry your own.

Map USGS or BLM map Smoky Mountain(1:100,000), or Paria(1:62,500) and Calico Peak(1:24,000).

Main Attraction A higher and cooler hike, strange rock formations, an overlook of old Pahreah, and some route-finding in a little known country.

Ideal Time to Hike Spring or fall are best, but it could be hiked in summer or in mild winter weather.

Hiking Boots Waders to reach The Box Trail and to use Hackberry Canyon; otherwise dry weather boots or shoes.

Author's Experience Once the author left late in the afternoon and entered The Box from Cottonwood Wash. He found the trail and went as far as the Rock Garden Junction, then returned, in 3 hours. The next morning, he found the Yellow Rock Trail at Hackberry Canyon, hiked it all the way to Sam Pollock Arch, and arrived in Hackberry via the Lower Trail. He then hurried up canyon and found the Upper Trail, before returning to his car via the canyon bottom. All in 9.5 hours. A very long day, but if the hike to the Upper Trail had been eliminated, it would have been a pleasant walk.

The Box, of the Paria River, and the beginning of The Box Trail.

Just above old Pahreah, is what the author calls The Rock Garden.

The Upper Trail, from Hackberry Canyon, up to Upper Death Valley.

The Hidden Cache Trail

The last hike to be added to this book happened quite by accident. While interviewing one of the old timers in Tropic, this story about an old hermit or possibly a German spy?, and a cache of food and equipment was told. Later the author tracked down the people who originally found the cache, and got the full story.

It begins on February 8, 1953. Harvey Chynoweth, his four sons, Jack, Gene, Wade and Ralph, and Harveys brother Will Chynoweth, were running cows in the lower Cottonwood Wash and out to the east of The Cockscomb on the flats called Brigham Plains. They had worked all day, and had arrived back at camp late. Camp was on the lower Cottonwood Wash, not far above where it flows into the Paria River, at the bottom end of The Box.

Since the valley bottom had been grazed out by cows, and there wasn't much feed for the horses, it was common practice for cowmen working in the area, to run their riding horses up on top of The Cockscomb to the west, where they could pasture at night. Up there they couldn't go far because of rough terrain and there was plenty of grass. Since Ralph was the youngest of the boys, he was chosen to take the riding stock up above the cliffs.

It was after dark, but there was a full moon and the sky was clear. Ralph recalls having trouble with one little sorrel pony which was trying to run away or something. At any rate, when the horses were left in the upper pasture, they were always hobbled, so they could be found and caught easy in the mornings. When Ralph finally got hold of the little sorrel, he began putting the hobbles on it. But then something caught his eye. The moonlight was so bright, it reflected off something metal. He went over to check it out and found a couple of small metal buildings, or sheds, or boxes. He could see inside one of them and saw that somebody had lived there. He returned to camp a little spooky and told the story. No one believed him. They thought he was dreaming or just telling stories.

The next morning they all went back to get the horses and saw in full light what was there. It was some kind of camp but hadn't been lived in for some time. There were two galvanized metal boxes or shelters, measuring only about 1.25 x 2 x 2.5 meters each, and a cave which had the entrance cemented up with a little rock wall.

Inside one of the boxes was a bed with blankets on it, all tucked in neatly; a small metal wood burning stove which was new and apparently hadn't been used; and an old .22 rifle which hung above the door. The .22 was a single shot, which broke in the middle to load, like some single shot shotguns you see. There were also several new denim shirts, underwear, socks, pajamas, two pair of boots, tooth brush, tooth paste, and neatly folded napkins. The clothing items were neatly put together and folded, like what you'd find in the military. Besides these things, was some kind of a military uniform. One man swears it was from WWI.

In the other metal shelter, and all very neatly packed away, was a food cache of sizable proportions. The food cache included jars or buckets of peanut butter, canned milk, chocolate, sugar, rice, flour, raisins, canned fish, sardines, corned beef, and other canned goods. Most of the cans had rusted badly, from the inside out apparently, and had leaked, spoiling the contents. Indications were that it had all been there for some time. One witness said they found one can of corned beef dated 1942.

Just behind the two metal shelters, was a small cave. The front of this cave, measuring about one by two meters, had been sealed up with a rock and mortar wall. The job was so well done, that in 1987 when the author saw it, it appeared as if it could have been made only a month or two before. The entrance passage was a small metal-framed window, like the kind you see in some homes or buildings of the WWII vintage. The inside of the cave had been dug out a bit, and it measured about 1.5 x 2 meters at the front end, and it tapered back to the rear of the cave for a distance of about 4 meters. Not much headroom, but cozy.

Inside the cave was found an electric hot plate and several five gallon(19 liter) water storage jars full of water. The fact that they had not frozen and broken the jars, indicates how well insulated the cave was in winter. There were also a dozen batteries of various kind, and some witnesses said there were radios too, but not everyone agreed on that point.

Right in the corner next to the window-entrance, are three wires which were built into the rock and mortar wall. These wires led outside to a wind mill contraption and a generator mounted on a rock behind the cave. The single blade propellor was 4 or 5 meters long, and mounted horizontally(instead of vertically as is usually the case). The cave had built-in wiring so that electricity generated by the wind mill generator outside, could be used for lights, cooking, and by the radio? inside.

According to the newspaper report in the March 19, 1953, *Garfield County News* in Panguitch(a week later in the Kanab paper), all identifiable marks on the generator and other equipment found, had been scratched off. Even the numbers on a thermometer had been removed!

According to the Chynoweths, as soon as they got back home, they immediately called the Sheriff of Kane County, Mason Meeks, and told him of the situation. Shortly thereafter, the Sheriff

MAP 21, THE HIDDEN CACHE TRAIL

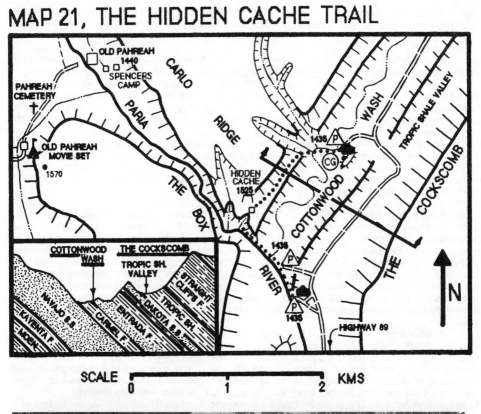

SCALE
0   1   2   KMS

The Hidden Cache, showing one metal storage box and behind, the cave.

and Highway Patrolman Merrill Johnson, Merle(Peaches) Beard, and others, went to the cache and removed what items were left. There are two conflicting stories--the Chynoweths and the Sheriffs--as to what items were originally discovered, and what the Sheriff took out. Merrill Johnson said nothing was removed?

Sheriff Meeks sent a report to the FBI. Later they contacted Meeks and it was their speculation that whoever set up the place had likely been a spy of some kind from the WWII era.

There were several different theories advanced as to who built the cache: he was a deserter from the army and on the run; that he was a draft dodger; he was just an old hermit, who happened to have been in WWI; he had worked for Charles H. Spencer in the gold diggings at old Pahreah, and had returned to hideout; and because some of the clothing items had foreign labels(French), some thought he may have been a spy of some kind. The radio and generator equipment prompted this idea.

There's also endless speculation as to how this person may have gotten all the equipment and food there without detection. At that time, which must have been in the mid-1940's, there were no roads in the area except the one to old Pahreah. When this story finally came to light, there was all kinds of talk about it, and then people started remembering events that had happened in the previous years, which may have had a connection with the cache.

The one which seems to hold the most credibility is the story told by Calvin C. Johnson of Kanab(the man who now owns the Nipple Ranch). He remembered the time as being in 1944 and/or 1945. On several occasions he and other cattlemen in the area of old Pahreah, had seen a Willis Jeep parked inside The Box, and at the bottom of the cliffs where the cache was later found. Calvin also remembers that he and others had talked to the owner of the Jeep on several occasions as they met on the deserted road between The Box, just below Pahreah, and Kanab. The man was in his 30's, had a trimmed beard, was always dressed up in an old army uniform, and spoke with somekind of a foreign accent. He never did say much, and the conversations were always short; like howdy and goodby. Calvin recalls that the boys he rode with on the range, called this fellow, *our little German spy!* Apparently this had more meaning in 1953 when the cache was discovered, than it did at the end of WWII.

Another event happened in 1963, which may have had a connection with this place. At that time, the Sheriff of Kane County was Lenard Johnson. His people lived in Short Creek(now called Colorado City, Arizona). He had a pilots licence and once while flying in the area between Hurricane Mesa and Short Creek, spotted another cabin from the air. Later, they went to it on the ground, and found another small cabin full of food, similar to the cache at Pahreah. Nothing else was found in that cache, but everyone familiar with the two sites, seemed to think there was a connection.

Location and Access The location of the camp and cache, called The Hidden Cache, for lack of a better name, is just above the confluence of the Paria River and Cottonwood Wash. To get there, leave Highway 89, from between mile posts 17 and 18, and turn north onto the Cottonwood Wash Road(this location is just east of the Paria Ranger Station). Drive about 16 or 17 kms to the confluence of the Paria and Cottonwood. You can enter The Box at that point, which is likely the easiest entry point. Or you can drive up the road a ways to where there are some good campsites. From where you come near to the confluence, the road then runs north a ways along the Tropic Shale Valley, but to the east of the Dakota Sandstone part of The Cockscomb. After less than a km, the road turns west, and heads down to the main Cottonwood Wash creek bed. Just as the main road turns north inside the Cottonwood Wash, you turn west and drive along a seldom used road down into the cottonwood trees to a place with several old foundations. These old foundations were built by Alex Joseph and his polygamist family before they were run out and had to settle down the road a ways at Big Water. Park there under one of the big trees.

Trail or Route Conditions From the car-park at the confluence of the Paria and Cottonwood, walk up into The Box less than a km from the car-park. As you enter the box, you'll immediately pass two minor gullies on your right or north, then a fence across the canyon bottom. Just beyond the fence, and on your right, or north, is a small canyon. Head up and into this canyon. After just a short distance and on the left side, you'll begin to see a trail heading straight up the canyon bottom. Around 500 meters from the river, and just after you begin to level out, you'll see the first gray metal shelter, and just behind it the second box and cave. This route is the shortest and easiest of the two.

From the old camp of Alex Joseph, walk down the usually dry creek bed 200 meters or so, then head up a kind of slide and slope to the southwest, on the south side of a canyon which has two drainages coming together. You'll see a faded trail up this steep slope. Once on top, you'll see a wall of Navajo rock running from just west of you, to the southwest. You walk southwest and parallel to this wall, but not up close. Stay to the southeast of the wall a ways. Eventually you'll see the hideout.

Elevations The trailheads, about 1435 meters; The Hidden Cache, about 1525 meters.

Hike Length and Time Needed From either trailhead or car-park, it's no more than 1.5 kms to the hideout. If you know the route exactly, it's only a 20-25 minute walk. But if it's your first trip, it may take awhile to find the place. Using The Box route makes finding the cache a little easier.

Water Have drinking water in your car. The Paria River water at that point isn't too bad if you have to use it, but you should filter or purify it first.

Map USGS or BLM map Smoky Mountain(1:100,000), or Paria(1:62,500).

Main Attraction A short hike to what has become a legendary Hidden Cache.

Ideal Time to Hike Spring or fall are best, but can be done year-round.

Hiking Boots Dry weather boots or shoes, but if you're going up through The Box, you'll have to cross the creek two times; but it's not deep ordinarily.

Author's Experience The author went up from the Cottonwood Wash side, and had to hunt for the place, but it still only took 40 minutes to find. After taking fotos, it only took about 20 minutes to return to the car.

This is the box which had a bed, clothes and a .22 rifle.

Inside the cave is Mason Meeks, looking over a battery, and Merle Beard(at window).
Foto by Merrill Johnson(1953 foto).

The Cockscomb

Location and Access One of the most striking land forms of southern Utah is the feature known as The Cockscomb. The Cockscomb is a fold in the earths crust, more properly called a monocline, which has created a rather sharp erosional ridge. This ridge-line runs north-south, from just south of Canaan Peak in the north, down to about Highway 89. This is the part that stands out most, and has the sharpest ridges. This same feature runs south into Arizona. It goes by the *geologic* name of the East Kaibab Monocline. The *geographic* name is The Cockscomb. From Highway 89, you can follow it south on what is called the House Rock Valley Road. In the area of Highway 89A, in the House Rock Valley, you can see it running further south to Saddle Mountain and on into the Grand Canyon. However, this northern section is the most rugged and the most interesting part to see. Cottonwood Wash, and the road by the same name, run right down the middle of The Cockscomb Valley, from the Butler Valley Arch(Grosvenor Arch), down to the Paria River. While one can hike up to the crest of the ridge from anywhere along Cottonwood Wash, the route described here is perhaps the easiest and has some of the best views. To get there, exit Highway 89 between mile post 17 and 18, and drive about 20 kms to a point 200-300 meters below where Hackberry Canyon reaches Cottonwood Wash. You can park there, or drive half a km east and up a rather good road to where it steepens, then park. Very low geared or powerful vehicles can make it to the pass, where the road runs on east to Brigham Plains. Parking at the bottom of the hill is best for most cars.

Trail or Route Conditions If you have parked at the base of the steep part of the road, then you have only to walk about one km to the pass overlooking both Brigham Plains and The Cockscomb Valley. At the pass, or low break in the highest cockscomb-shaped ridge, walk about due north and angle up to the left as you climb to the highest part of the ridge crest. One could walk along the crest, or walk along the bottom of Cads Crotch, an eastern valley to The Cockscomb. Most people would be happy just to reach the point marked 1753 meters.

Elevations From about 1475 meters, up to 1753, or perhaps a little higher to the north.

Hike Length and Time Needed From the Cottonwood Wash Road to the pass in The Cockscomb, is less than 2 kms. From the pass to the high point is another half km. The round-trip hike can be done easily in a couple of hours.

Water Take your own water, and always have extra water in your car.

Map USGS or BLM map Smoky Mountain(1:100,000), or Calico Peak(1:24,000).

Main Attraction An interesting look at an unusual geologic feature fully exposed. Geology students shouldn't miss this one, as it is one of the shortest and most interesting hikes in this book. The view from the top is spectacular.

Ideal Time to Hike Spring or fall, but it can be climbed anytime.

Hiking Boots Any boots or shoes, but a rugged pair if you intend to do much hiking along the ridge.

Author's Experience The author parked at the bottom of the steep part of the road, and walked from there. Round-trip was about an hour and a half.

A grand view from the top of The Cockscomb, looking north. Castle Rock left.

MAP 22, THE COCKSCOMB

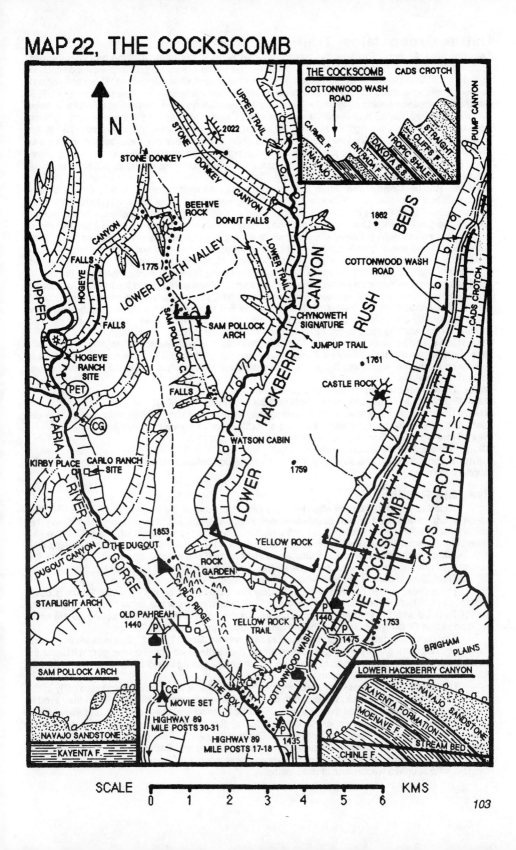

THE COCKSCOMB

CADS CROTCH

COTTONWOOD WASH ROAD

PUMP CANYON

CARMEL F.

NAVAJO

ENTRADA F.

DAKOTA S.S.

TROPIC SHALE

STRAIGHT CLIFFS F.

N

UPPER TRAIL

2022

STONE DONKEY CANYON

STONE DONKEY

BEEHIVE ROCK

DONUT FALLS

CANYON

HOGEYE

FALLS

1775

LOWER DEATH VALLEY

LOWER TRAIL

1862

BEDS

COTTONWOOD WASH ROAD

CADS CROTCH

UPPER

FALLS

FALLS

HOGEYE RANCH SITE

PET

CG

SAM POLLOCK C.

SAM POLLOCK ARCH

FALLS

CHYNOWETH SIGNATURE

JUMPUP TRAIL

1761

CASTLE ROCK

LOWER HACKBERRY CANYON

RUSH

WATSON CABIN

1759

KIRBY PLACE

CARLO RANCH SITE

PARIA RIVER

1853

THE DUGOUT

DUGOUT CANYON

GORGE

STARLIGHT ARCH

CARLO RIDGE

ROCK GARDEN

YELLOW ROCK

LOWER

HACKBERRY

CANYON

THE COCKSCOMB

CADS CROTCH

P 1440

P 1475

1753

BRIGHAM PLAINS

OLD PAHREAH 1440

P

YELLOW ROCK TRAIL

COTTONWOOD WASH

SAM POLLOCK ARCH

CG

MOVIE SET

THE BOX

HIGHWAY 89 MILE POSTS 30-31

NAVAJO SANDSTONE

KAYENTA F.

HIGHWAY 89 MILE POSTS 17-18

P 1435

LOWER HACKBERRY CANYON

NAVAJO SANDSTONE

KAYENTA FORMATION

MOENAVE F.

STREAM BED

CHINLE F.

SCALE
0 1 2 3 4 5 6   KMS

103

Hattie Green Mine Trail

Location and Access Perhaps the easiest hike featured in this book, and the one with the best access is the trail and hike to the Hattie Green Mine. The Hattie Green is an old copper mine which sits right on top of The Cockscomb, sometimes known as the East Kaibab Monocline. This mine consists of two tunnels, and three other pits, prospects or adits. The claim on the site was first filed in 1893. Get more information on this mine under *Mines and Mining History*. The location of this hike is about half way between Kanab and Page. It's also about 11 kms northwest of the Paria Ranger Station. Access is very easy. Park right on Highway 89, about 300 meters or so south of mile post 28. With a high clearance vehicle(HCV), you can get into the short canyon near the mine, but you can't go far, unless you've got a 4WD. It's best just to park on the highway, because you'll have to cross a narrow piece of private land, and it's better you walk across it rather than take a vehicle in. No one should mind if you walk to the mine.

Trail or Route Conditions From the highway, walk due east. Cross a fence, then a shallow drainage. In the middle of a meadow surrounded by sagebrush, look for a very faint 4WD track running east. Follow this as it curves to the south and around the southern end of a low and minor sub-ridge of The Cockscomb. Once around this, the road enters a short little valley within The Cockscomb. At about the point where the campsite is shown, the track then follows the dry creek bed north, which is very rough and sandy. Walk north from the campsite about a km, and notice on the left or west, a small man-made stone structure (a pile of rocks). About 40 meters or so north of the stone pile, look uphill to the east, and search for some stone cairns marking the lower part of the trail. Further up, you'll see the trail, which is an old wagon road. This first trail takes you to the top of The Cockscomb, where some of the mining activity took place. A second trail, this one running to the western tunnel, is located about another 30-40 meters north of where the first trail runs up the slope. The bottom of the trail is marked by cairns, but a bit further up, it turns into an old wagon road. Both of these trails can be seen as you walk up the canyon, but only if you know where to look.

Elevations The highway trailhead, 1500 meters; the ridge-top adit, about 1675 meters.

Hike Length and Time Needed The one-way distance is about 3 kms. The hike can be made in as little as 2-3 hours, round-trip; but it's recommended you take a lunch and water, and take at least half a day for the trip.

Water There's none on the hike, so take your own.

Map USGS or BLM map Smoky Mountain(1:100,000), or Paria(1:62,500).

Main Attraction A good look at The Cockscomb, some interesting tunnels and one copper ore heap. Old mine enthusiasts should take along a flashlight for exploring the tunnels.

Ideal Time to Hike Spring or fall, but can be done anytime.

Hiking Boots Any dry weather boots or shoes.

Author's Experience The author has been there twice, before and after doing research on the history of the mine.

Five Mile Ranch

Added to the Hattie Green Mine hike is a little about one of the local ranches. The Five Mile Ranch is one of the least known outposts written about in this book. It's also one of the very last places to have been homesteaded in the entire region. The ranch is located in what is called Five Mile Valley, about 8 kms(5 miles) due south of old Pahreah, thus the name Five Mile. At least one old timer from Tropic says the name was the Cottonwood Ranch, as it's near to Cottonwood Spring. It's just west of The Cockscomb and east of Highway 89. To get there, turn off Highway 89, between mile posts 28 and 29, and park at the gate where the road enters the electric sub-station.

The earliest written record the Kane County courthouse has on the Five Mile Ranch is dated May 11, 1913. That's when William J. Henderson filed a claim on the water rights to one or both of the springs involved with the Five Mile Ranch spread. To the north is the Five Mile Spring; to the south about one km is Cottonwood Spring. The old ranch house is at Cottonwood Spring.

The next recorded information about Five Mile was on June 17, 1937. This was when Herman Mangum got a patent on it from the government under the Homestead Act. To have gotten it under the Homestead Act, he would have had to live there awhile before getting title to the land, in 1937. Herman Mangum was the son of John Mangum.

The John Mangum family lived in or around Pahreah after it was mostly abandoned early in this century. Later on Herm Pollock, Wallace Ott, and Kay Clark remember the family when they lived in The Dugout, two or three kms north of Pahreah. That time period was the late 1920's and early 1930's.

In about 1930 an oil company outfit was drilling test holes in the northern end of the Rush Beds, in the area south and west of Grosvenor or Butler Valley Arch. That outfit pumped water to their camp from what has been called ever since, Pump House Spring and Canyon. When their hole came up dry, they sold parts and equipment to various local people. One of those people was John Mangum, who bought a wagon load of used lumber.

MAP 23, HATTIE GREEN MINE TRAIL

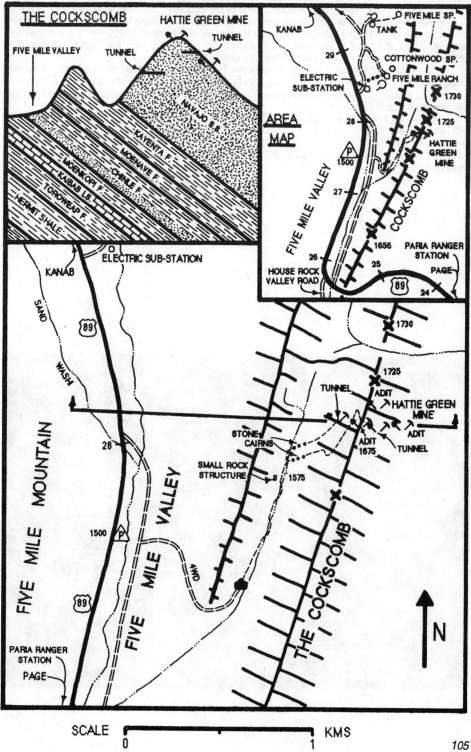

THE COCKSCOMB

HATTIE GREEN MINE

FIVE MILE VALLEY

TUNNEL

TUNNEL

NAVAJO S.S.

KAYENTA F.

MOENAVE F.

CHINLE F.

MOENKOPI F.

KAIBAB LS.

TOROWEAP F.

HERMIT SHALE

AREA MAP

KANAB

FIVE MILE SP.

TANK

COTTONWOOD SP.

ELECTRIC SUB-STATION

FIVE MILE RANCH

1730

29

28

1725

HATTIE GREEN MINE

P 1500

27

FIVE MILE VALLEY

26

1656

25

PARIA RANGER STATION

PAGE

HOUSE ROCK VALLEY ROAD

89

24

COCKSCOMB

ELECTRIC SUB-STATION

KANAB

89

SAND

WASH

1730

1725

TUNNEL

ADIT

HATTIE GREEN MINE

STONE CAIRNS

ADIT

1675

ADIT

TUNNEL

28

SMALL ROCK STRUCTURE

1575

FIVE MILE MOUNTAIN

1500 P

4WD

FIVE MILE VALLEY

THE COCKSCOMB

89

PARIA RANGER STATION

PAGE

N

SCALE

0

1

KMS

105

John and son Herman, along with Jim Ed Smith, and son Layton, hauled the lumber down Cottonwood Wash, before a road was built, and to Cottonwood Spring in the Five Mile Valley. That was sometime between 1932 and 1935. Just southwest of the Cottonwood Spring, they built a small house out of the used lumber. It's a two-room house; not too fancy, and without insulation. The back room wall was papered; not with wallpaper, but with the pages of the latest magazine. This homemade wallpaper job is still there today, and you can catch up on events from the 1930's. The author remembers one advertisement for new Dodge cars selling for $640.

Throughout the years the area around the Five Mile Homestead has been owned by two individuals. Apparently the Five Mile Spring was held by Henderson through 1945, but before that, Delmar G. Robinson of Kanab, bought out the Five Mile Ranch from the Mangums in May, 1942. The Mangums then headed for Idaho.

Later on in September, 1959, it was deeded over to Delmars son, Don R. Robinson. Finally in 1963, the Litchfield Company obtained a Quit Claim Deed on at least part the property around the spring and ranch house. Now in 1987, Jeff Johnson of Kanab leases the place and runs cows there. If you park at the sub-station, and walk in, no one should care. Just don't go in hunting for some kind of souvenirs!

The east tunnel at the Hattie Green Mine.

An ore heap, right on top of The Cockscomb at the Hattie Green Mine.

At Cottonwood Spring is the Five Mile Ranch House.

Buckskin Gulch

Location and Access Map 24 and Part 1, includes the upper part of what is traditionally known as the Paria River hike, and its best known tributary, the Buckskin Gulch. This map covers all the upper part of the Lower Paria River Gorge, and includes the Paria down to as far as The Confluence; that's where the Buckskin Gulch enters from the west.

Map 25 and Part 2, includes that part of the Paria from The Confluence down to Wrather Canyon. This is the best part of the Paria, because it has many springs, good narrows, excellent campsites, an old historic trail to the rim, and at least one good panel of petroglyphs.

Map 26 and Part 3, shows the Paria River from Wrather Canyon down to about Bush Head Canyon. This is the part of the gorge where it begins to open up a bit, and becomes wider. This is where it begins to look more like the Grand Canyon. This section has one of the best arches in the world, four routes to the rim for fine views of the canyon country, more good springs, water, campsites, and more petroglyphs.

The last map of the Paria is Map 27 and Part 4. It begins just below Bush Head Canyon and ends at Lee's Ferry on the Colorado River. The canyon in this section opens up wide, and it has old ranches, some abandoned uranium prospects or adits, and some of the best petroglyphs on boulders the author has seen. Each of these segments could be one days hike, but to see all the sites, side canyons, and do side trips, it's recommended you take it in 5 or 6 days.

In 1984, all of this Lower Paria River Canyon, and including the Vermilion Cliffs, were put aside as wilderness areas. Now this one large cresent shaped region is officially called the Paria Canyon--Vermilion Cliffs Wilderness Area. It includes all of the Paria from the power lines on down to Lee's Ferry.

There are four ways to get into this gorge, all of which are from Highway 89, which runs between Kanab and Page. The normal entry point, is the White House Trailhead. It's the easiest of access and can be used regardless of the weather conditions, as it's a graveled road. Reach this car-park and camp site by driving south from Highway 89, between mile posts 20 and 21. Just as you turn off the highway look due south, and you'll see the Paria Ranger Station.

Be sure and stop there before entering the canyon. You'll want to speak to Rod Schipper(Skip), the BLM ranger assigned to watching over the lower canyon. He has worked(and lived) there since 1980, and knows more about the canyon than anyone. He will answer any last minute questions, and can give you the latest weather report, the last minute water situation and a free permit for all those who intend to camp in the canyon.

If he's not there, the latest weather report will be posted on the bulletin board in front of the station. If he's not there, self register at the trailhead. All hikers are urged to sign in at the trail

The upper part of the Buckskin Gulch. It's just like this for 20 kms.

MAP 24, LOWER PARIA RIVER GORGE-- PART 1
THE BUCKSKIN GULCH

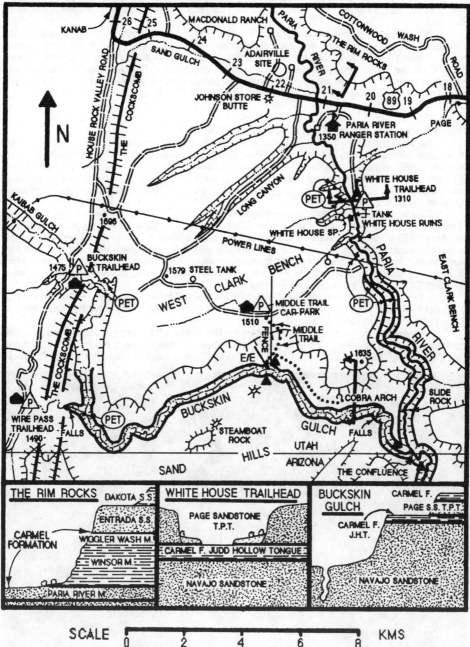

KANAB

MACDONALD RANCH

26 25 24

SAND GULCH

23

ADAIRVILLE SITE

22

21

20 89 19 18

THE RIM ROCKS

COTTONWOOD WASH

PARIA RIVER

PAGE

HOUSE ROCK VALLEY ROAD

THE COCKSCOMB

JOHNSON STORE BUTTE

N

Paria River Ranger Station
1350

WHITE HOUSE TRAILHEAD
1310

PET

P

TANK

WHITE HOUSE RUINS

KAIBAB GULCH

1696

LONG CANYON

WHITE HOUSE SP.

POWER LINES

BENCH

PARIA

RIVER

EAST CLARK BENCH

BUCKSKIN TRAILHEAD

1475 P

1579 STEEL TANK

CLARK

WEST

MIDDLE TRAIL CAR PARK
1510 P

MIDDLE TRAIL

PET

PET

THE COCKSCOMB

FENCE

E/E

1635

COBRA ARCH

SLIDE ROCK

WIRE PASS TRAILHEAD
1490

P

FALLS

PET

BUCKSKIN

STEAMBOAT ROCK

GULCH

FALLS

SAND

HILLS

UTAH

ARIZONA

THE CONFLUENCE

THE RIM ROCKS
DAKOTA S.S.
ENTRADA S.S.
CARMEL FORMATION
WIGGLER WASH M.
WINSOR M.
PARIA RIVER M.

WHITE HOUSE TRAILHEAD
PAGE SANDSTONE T.P.T.
CARMEL F. JUDD HOLLOW TONGUE
NAVAJO SANDSTONE

BUCKSKIN GULCH
CARMEL F.
PAGE S.S. T.P.T.
CARMEL F. J.H.T.
NAVAJO SANDSTONE

SCALE

0   2   4   6   8   KMS

register, whether they're going on an overnight trip, or just for a day-hike. The BLM wants to know how many people are visiting the canyon.

Skip is normally there in the morning hours, often times including his days off, which are Tuesdays and Wednesdays. If you need to fill water jugs, do it at the ranger station well, as all the trailheads are dry. From Skips place(resident and office), drive south about 3 kms to the White House Trailhead, the place where most people begin the hike to Lee's Ferry, and to the bottom end of the Buckskin.

White House Trailhead has picnic tables, fire pits, toilets, and can be used as a campsite, although it lacks a water supply. If you get there without water, you can go back to the ranger station, or walk across the river and down stream about 300 meters and up a small side canyon to the west, where the White House Spring is located. This water is very good and Skip sometimes gets his coffee water from there. If you have time you can visit some petroglyphs just across the river to the west and up two minor draws. The white rocks at this trailhead is the Thousand Pockets Tongue of the Page Sandstone.

The White House or Clark Cabin ruins

The story behind the White House Cabin and White House Spring was told to the author by Kay Clark, who now(1987) lives in Henrieville. The story begins in the Luna Valley of New Mexico. In February, 1887, Wilford Clark(Kay Clarks father) was born to the wife of Owen Washington Clark. Right after this child was born and the mother strong enough to travel, the small family moved from Luna Valley to southern Utah and set up a homestead on the Paria River, just down stream from where the White House Trailhead is today.

They arrived in June, 1887, and immediately built a small cabin. The family lived in the Clark Cabin only about one year, then in 1888, moved up river a ways to the Adairville site(Adairville existed only from 1873 until 1878, and was abandoned because of lack of summertime water). Largely because of water problems, that place didn't work out, and so in 1889 the family moved to Pahreah, which at that time was in the process of losing population. Remember, the first big floods, which caused many people to have second thoughts about living at Pahreah, roared down the canyon in 1883 and '84. A second big flood came in 1896.

In 1892, Kay Clarks grandfather, Owen W. Clark, moved the whole family once again, this time to a safer and more promising land, around the town of Cannonville. The family has been there in Bryce Valley most of the time since.

Back now to the name of White House. After the Clarks left the original cabin, sheep herders used the place as a camp and a supply depot, when they had their flocks to the southeast on top of East Clark Bench(both the East Clark and West Clark Benches are named after Owen W. Clark).

One of many pools you'll encounter in the Buckskin Gulch hike.

Sometime in the 1890's, the cabin burned down, apparently due to carelessness on the part of a sheepman.

It was the sheepmen who gave the place the name, White House Cabin and White House Spring. When they were out on the range for a long time, and had to drink any water they could get, they always enjoyed going back to the Clark Cabin, because of the good tasting water they could get out of the little year-round spring located just up stream and up a little draw to the west. As the story goes, someone commented that this water was so good, it could have come direct from the White House(in Washington DC). Thus the name stuck, on both the cabin and the spring.

To find the White House Ruins today, walk from the trailhead parking lot down canyon on an obvious trail on the east side of the river. Don't cross the stream. After about 300 meters you'll see an empty water tank at the mouth of White House Spring drainage west of the Paria. From this tank, the ruins are about 200 meters southeast. Stay on the trail as the river pushes it up against the east bank. Then as the trail comes to the open little bench, and where you'll see the little hikers sign pointing down canyon, look southeast and 10 meters from the sign is a pile of stones. This is the remains of the cabin fireplace. There were at one time some corrals just north of the ruins, but they have been washed away by floods.

The other three trailheads are for entry into the best narrows or slot canyon hike on the Colorado Plateau, the Buckskin Gulch. To reach the Buckskin Trailhead, drive west from the ranger station and through The Cockscomb. Just west of where the highway cuts through the monocline, and between mile posts 25 and 26, turn south on the House Rock Valley Road. This road is rather well maintained as far south as the Utah-Arizona line, but it seems to be less maintained on the Arizona side. If you drive this road south, you'll end up on Highway 89A in the House Rock Valley, at the western end of the Vermilion Cliffs. This House Rock Valley Road is fairly heavily traveled in the warmer months, and by all kinds of vehicles. From the highway to the first car-park, called the Buckskin Trailhead, is about 7 kms. It's where the Kaibab Gulch cuts through The Cockscomb.

From the Buckskin Trailhead, continue south for about another 6 or 7 kms, and you'll come to the Wire Pass Trailhead. This one is the more popular of the two trailheads at the head of the Buckskin Gulch, because it shortens the walk by an hour or two. You can camp at either trailhead, but take plenty of water with you. The Wire Pass Trailhead is located on the lower end of Coyote Wash, but for some reason, that part of the drainage below the trailhead is not called Coyote Wash. Instead it's the Wire Pass?

The fourth and last entry possibility into the Buckskin, is from the West Clark Bench and Middle Trail. Get there by driving south from Highway 89, on the first road running south on the west side of the Paria River Bridge, and between mile posts 21 and 22. This is a public access road, but

The entry point called the Middle Trail; the only entry/exit in the Buckskin.

you'll still have to pass through some private land and two gates(there are several homes and roads in the area west of the river and south of the highway). Leave the gates as you find them; sometimes open, but usually closed. Then drive up Long Canyon, on a maintained road, but which can be slick and muddy in wet weather. At the head of the canyon, stay on the most used road, the one which runs left at the two junctions, and continue on toward the steel tank(no water). Then drive down a shallow drainage towards the Middle Trail Car-park near the fence, as shown. When you first see the fence, stop quick! There's a big sand trap just before the fence. There are several sandy places in the last km or so before the fence, but the author made it OK in his VW Rabbit.

In June, the driest month, sandy roads tend to be their worst, so a shovel in the trunk should be standard equipment, just in case. Park just before the north-south running fence. This latter car-park and the Middle Trail are the least used, but it affords a different view of the country you'll be walking through, and the access road is generally good for all vehicles.

Trail or Route Conditions Most people just going into the Buckskin, usually begin at the White House Trailhead and walk down to The Confluence and up the Gulch a ways, then return the same way to their car. This part of the hike down the Paria is very easy, and normally there are no obstacles whatsoever. However, in September, 1980, a flood came down and created a deep hole just above The Confluence in the Paria. For much of one season, and until the river gradually filled it in, hikers had to ferry packs across on air mattresses or inner tubes(Skip still has some of these in his storage shed).

If you walk slowly and watch carefully along some of the canyon walls not far below the White House Trailhead, and on the west side, you may find several panels of petroglyphs. Just up canyon from the power lines(wilderness boundary) is one panel, and not far below the lines is a second. The third petroglyph shown on the map is near the one that's white man made, perhaps a survey marker, high on the west wall. About 15 meters upstream from that obvious marker is another hard-to-see panel. About one km above The Confluence, is Slide Rock(called an arch on BLM maps). This is a section of the Navajo wall which has broken off and slid down into the river. Presently, the river flows underneath it, making a short tunnel.

If you begin at the Buckskin Trailhead, then you also have an unobstructed walk into the Gulch. Just after you begin the walk, after maybe a km, and just after you walk through a gate-like narrow place, turn to the left, or north, and look for a good panel of big horn sheep petroglyphs on a wall on the bench above the creek bed. A little further, and on the right side somewhere, are more petroglyphs high on the wall. The author failed to find these, but if you're not in a hurry, you can surely locate them. After the petroglyphs, the canyon is open for the first part, but then begins to narrow as you near the confluence of the Buckskin and Wire Pass.

From Wire Pass Trailhead, you'll first pass through open country, then the wash narrows quickly. Soon you'll come to a minor obstacle, a chokestone which has created a dropoff of about 3

Just 3 kms or so from the Middle Trail is Cobra Arch.

meters. Have with you a short rope, or simple parachute cord, to lower your pack over this fall. Getting back up this dropoff might be a struggle for some, but it's not life threatening, and with a rope, no one should have a problem. If this dropoff is too much to handle, then skirt around it on the south side, and re-enter the wash further down. This by-pass makes things easier.

Below the obstacle, there are some very tight narrows in the Wire Pass just before you arrive at the Buckskin Gulch. Right at the Wire Pass--Buckskin Confluence, there are more big horn sheep petroglyphs.

From the Wire Pass--Buckskin Confluence, the real Buckskin Gulch begins, and doesn't end until The Confluence of the Paria. This part of the canyon is nearly 20 kms long, and averages 4-5 meters in width for it's entire length. At times the gorge may open a bit, to 8 or 10 meters, then narrow down to no more than a meter wide. The author recalls something like 40 to 50 places in the Buckskin where logs were seen wedged into the walls high above, mute evidence of nature on the rampage, and a grim reminder of the danger of walking this gorge. *One last reminder, have a good weather forecast before entering this canyon!* Normally the narrows depth is somewhere between 30 and 50 meters, but down canyon near the Paria, the walls are surely in the neighborhood of 100 meters in height. This is the deepest, darkest and narrowest of all the slot canyon hikes in the world.

For the most part the walk down the Buckskin is uneventful, but normally there are several small pools you must wade through. There is no running water in the Gulch, except of course in time of flood, but the bottom is so hidden from the sun, and the temperatures so cool, there is little evaporation; therefore the pools usually stay around a long time. One such pool, invariable having water almost the year-round, is called the Cesspool. It's about one km up canyon from the Middle Trail entry/exit point. At times you may have to float your pack across the Cesspool.

From the Middle Trail Car-park, you can also enter the Buckskin. This is near the middle of the Gulch. From the trailhead, you follow the fenceline right over the minor cliffs, and right to the Gulch; or better still, walk to the east of the fence a bit, to where there's a break in the top layer of the Navajo, which allows you to get down from the rim a little more easily. The point where you enter the gorge itself, is about a 100 meters due south of the end of the fence. Look for it. From the lip of the narrows it's a slow and careful scramble down the slickrock, but anyone should be able to enter or exit the narrows at this point, and get onto either the north or south rim.

For those taking this hike in two days, this is a good place to camp, as it allows you to take another look at the weather situation, half way through the gorge. This is obviously a hike you don't want to do in a monsoon weather pattern. It also allows one to exit, and take a 3 km side trip to Cobra Arch, a walk well worth while. From this exit point, you can find a high point nearby for some views of Steamboat Rock and other features atop the Sand Hills, sometimes known as the Paria Plateau.

Down canyon from the Middle Trail entry/exit point, is what could be called the only obstacle in the Buckskin. This is a falls, created by some large boulders which have broken off the canyon

This is the falls in the lower Buckskin Gulch. Someone has cut steps into one large boulder.

walls(it's about 2.5 kms up from The Confluence). The worst part is a 5 meter climb over one of these boulders. In recent years, someone has cut out several steps and handholds into one of the boulders, and hung two ropes over the falls. At last report, one rope was gone, probably cut by a hiker, who thought it had deteriorated to the point of being dangerous. To insure that you have no problems, take along a 10 meter long rope of some kind(a parachute cord is good enough), to allow you to lower your packs over this dropoff. Ordinarily, hikers could slide or jump down this fall if necessary, as there are several routes down it to choose from.

Near The Confluence(a km or so above the Paria), there are several campsites on some sandy benches high above the creek bed. This is a heavily used area, and at times in the past, has been closed to camping. The reason for closing it, is that it simply becomes overused and by closing it down, allows the vegetation to recover. If you're camping there, please tread lightly and stay on existing paths and tent sites. The last time the author was there, campers had reported seeing several rattlesnakes. How they got there is anyone's guess.

Elevations The White House Trailhead, 1310 meters; Buckskin Trailhead, 1475; Wire Pass Trailhead, 1490 meters; and the Middle Trail Car-park, about 1510 meters. The Confluence of the Buckskin and Paria, is near 1250 meters.

Hike Length and Time Needed The distance from the Buckskin Trailhead to the confluence of Wire Pass, is about 7 kms. From that point to The Confluence with the Paria, is another 20 kms. From The Confluence back up to the White House Trailhead is another 11 kms or so. This makes the total distance from the Buckskin to the White House Trailhead, about 38 kms. From the Wire Pass to White House, is about 33 kms. This can be done in one long day, but it's not recommended.

The author once saw a group of teenage boy scouts doing this one-day marathon, but they were dragging pretty slow as they were last seen trudging along in the direction of the White House Trailhead. Doing this in two, or maybe three days, is much more common, practical and enjoyable. On a two or three day trip you can camp at the Middle Trail entry/exit point, or just above The Confluence of the Paria(in the lower end of the Buckskin).

The major problem with doing this hike with a camp at the Middle Trail entry/exit point, is that you'd have to carry at least one 3.75 liter(one gallon) jug full of water; perhaps more in hot weather, less in cold or cooler conditions. Most people however, make it all the way through the Buckskin in one day, and end up camping near The Confluence.

Water The Buckskin is normally a bone-dry wash, but with an occasional pool of water to wade through. Since most people don't have the courage to drink this, count on it being a dry hike. Carry all the water you'll need. About two kms up the Buckskin from The Confluence, you'll begin to see pools of water, and about one km from the Paria and just above the campsites, it begins to flow pretty good(at least most of the time). This seep is considered a year-round water supply. But since this campsite area and the lower part of the Buckskin is so heavily used, and with people walking in the water all the time, especially in the spring and fall months, you'd better plan to filter or purify it first.

Another option for those camping at The Confluence, is to take empty jugs(always have plenty of empty jugs, as they weigh almost nothing) down the Paria a ways, and fill them up at Wall Spring or at the spring just above it(see the next map of the Paria, Part 2). This is about 3.5 kms below The Confluence. Still another alternative, is to purify or filter the water in the Paria River. Since most of this water seeps out of the bottom layers of the Navajo Sandstone in the Upper Paria River Gorge and below the town of Cannonville, it's not really that bad; it's just a little muddy looking at times, especially if there's any storm activity up canyon. The author hasn't had experience with filters, but it seems they would clog-up badly if used in muddy water. So a bottle of Iodine tablets might be handy in an emergency.

This part of the Paria flows year-round, except that the MacDonalds, who lease a ranch just north of Highway 89 and near the site of old Adairville, use a bulldozer and make a small temporary dam across the creek during part of the year, and use it for irrigation. This usually occurs in May and early June. However, in the heat of the summer, water in the Paria doesn't even reach their ranch. In July, and after the first storm or flood of the season, the Paria River then flows again, usually until the next summer. To check on the Paria water, just glance at the creek bed as you drive across the bridge on Highway 89. Also, it's important to check on the water situation at the ranger station, or ask other hikers of it's whereabouts.

Map BLM map Hikers Guide to Paria River(1:62,500). This is perhaps the best, because this one map covers the entire hike to Lee's Ferry, and it points out the major water holes and other sites of interest. You can buy it for $1.00 at the Paria Ranger Station, or the Kanab and St. George BLM offices. Also, the USGS or BLM maps Kanab and especially Smoky Mountain(for the Buckskin Gulch only), and to these two add Glen Canyon Dam, which shows the Paria River from the state line, or The Confluence, on down to Lee's Ferry(all at 1:100,000 scale). This last map also shows the Vermilion Cliffs. Or you might try the 1:62,500 scale maps Paria, Paria Plateau, and Lee's Ferry.

Another excellent map is one of the series of four field study maps which were prepared by the BLM, USGS, and others, covering the Paria Plateau(the Sand Hills). Each map is at scale 1:62,500,

Young hikers enjoying the narrows of Buckskin Gulch.

and very much the same, except each has a different emphasis; such as (A) geology, (B) geochemical data, (C) mines and prospects, and (D) mineral resource potential. Get these maps from any USGS outlet for $1.50 each. The maps are in the series MF-1475, and A, B, C, and D. Each of these covers the entire Lower Paria River Hike, and the Vermilion Cliffs and all of the House Rock Valley Road.

Main Attraction The best narrows or slot canyon hike in the world. Also with an exit at the Middle Trail, you can have a look at Cobra Arch, one of the most unique around. Even during the busy season(usually June in the Buckskin Gulch part), there is solitude, as this is an official wilderness area. Be sure you read the part on *Fotography* in the Introduction to this book, which will help you take home some good fotos of this very dark chasm.

Ideal Time to Hike Because of the cold temperature of the water in the pools of the Buckskin, June has become the popular time to visit this canyon. It's getting warm at that time of year, but once inside the narrows, it's very cool. You'll almost never see the sun; and it's that way for 20 kms! So the heat of the outside world(above the narrows) doesn't really matter, except for the walk back up the Paria to the White House Trailhead.

June is the driest month of the year, not only for this region, but for the state of Utah as a whole. Kanab receives about 31 cms(12 in.) of rainfall annually, part of it in winter. With the low temps and lack of sun in the gorge, the pools of water, especially the Cesspool, simply don't evaporate. Pools seem to stay in the Buckskin most of each winter, and often times until about June, then sometimes become totally dry for a time. Each year is different. If you were to go down it in winter, or right after a summer storm, you'd likely have to float your pack across one or more pools on an air mattress. See Skip at the Paria Ranger Station for the latest word on the Cesspool situation and hiking conditions in the Buckskin.

You can hike the Buckskin throughout the summer, but you'd want a good weather forecast. If you're there in a dry spell, then fine. But if you're there in a wet period, with showers around, think twice about this hike. Southern Utah has about two or three very wet monsoon periods each summer, each lasting a week of two. These periods usually occur from about mid-July to mid-September. This is the period you should be most cautious.

Actually, as narrow as the place is, there are still many high places you could get up to and away from raging flood waters. But when the floods do come, they usually come in a surge, and you won't have much time to look for a hide out. Always listen to the local radio stations for the latest weather forecasts as you drive into the area. Remember, the Buckskin Gulch is the worst place in the world to be in a flash flood!

Hiking Boots If the latest information says the Gulch is bone dry, then you could use dry weather boots or shoes. But you'll still have to wade in the lower Buckskin and usually the Paria as well, so best to take wading type boots or shoes for the whole hike.

Author's Experience The author has been into the Buckskin, at least part way, on five occasions, and from each trailhead. On one trip he made it from The Confluence campsite to the Wire Pass Trailhead, with large pack, in less than 6.5 hours. On his first trip to the Paria, he walked from the White House Trailhead, down the Paria, up the Buckskin to the falls, then back the same way in about 7 hours. Another time he left the Middle Trail Car-park, walked down to the bottom of the entry/exit point, back up and to Cobra Arch, then back to his car, all in about 3.5 hours. Most people will want much more time than that taken by the author. Some may want to almost double the author's times.

A wide angle view of the falls in the lower Buckskin Gulch.

Three or four kms downstream from The Confluence, is Wall Spring.

Lower Paria River Gorge--The Confluence to Lee's Ferry

Location and Access The Lower Paria River Gorge is so long and has so many interesting sites to see, it's been broken down into four parts, or at least four different maps. Part 1, covers mainly the Buckskin Gulch and the trailheads leading into it, and the upper part of the Lower Paria River Gorge or Canyon. The second, third and fourth maps, cover the canyon from The Confluence(of the Buckskin Gulch and the Paria River) all the way down to Lee's Ferry. This is where the Paria empties into the Colorado River.

Normally, the people who do the whole Paria River hike, start at the White House Trailhead. Get to this entry point by leaving Highway 89 between mile posts 20 and 21, and by driving south about 3 kms on an all-weather gravel road. Read more about this and the three other entry points under Part 1, the Buckskin Gulch.

Elevations The Whitehouse Trailhead is about 1310 meters; The Confluence, 1250; the Paria River at the bottom of Wrather Canyon, 1165; the mouth of Bush Head Canyon, about 1100; and Lee's Ferry, 950 meters.

Hike Length and Time Needed From the White House Trailhead to Lee's Ferry, is about 56 kms. From the Buckskin Trailhead to Lee's Ferry, about 72 kms. From Wire Pass Trailhead to Lee's Ferry, around 67 kms. A long hike anyway you look at it, but a fun one, and one which has several side canyons, or routes to the canyon rim, to explore.

A marathon-type walker could get through the canyon in 2 days, but some people would have trouble doing it in 3 or 4 days. Most do it in about 4, but this book introduces some new hikes out of the canyon and up to the rim, so 5 or 6 days would be more enjoyable, and recommended. If you're the type who likes to take it easy, do a lot of exploring, and one who likes to set up nice camps and relax, then a week isn't too long. However, the longer you plan to stay, the larger your pack will be!

Water From The Confluence to Lee's Ferry, you'll have a year-round flow in the Paria River all the way. You can drink this water only if you purify it with Iodine tablets or filter it first. During the irrigation season in the Bryce Valley(Tropic, Henrieville and Cannonville) which extends from about mid-April through the beginning of October, there is very little water flowing down the Paria below Cannonville. Most of the water you see entering this Lower Paria Gorge during this period of time, seeps out of the bottom layers of the Navajo Sandstone as the river cuts through the White Cliffs(that's below Cannonville). So it's pretty good water, but of course there are cows in the canyon, usually in the cooler 7 or 8 months of the year, so therein lies the danger.

In the heat of the summer, or at least in June and July, the water in the upper gorge(between The Box, where the Paria cuts through The Cockscomb, and Highway 89), disappears in the sands. Then it begins flowing again in the lower canyon at the bottom end of the Buckskin Gulch near The Confluence. It then flows year-round to Lee's Ferry.

The White House Trailhead, most popular entry to the Lower Paria River.

MAP 25, LOWER PARIA RIVER GORGE— PART 2

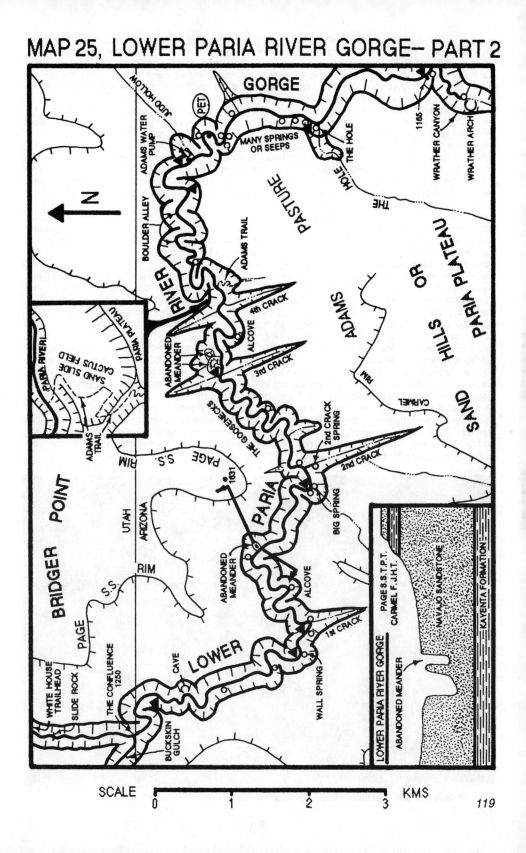

SCALE

0   1   2   3   KMS

For those who prefer to drink good spring water without filtration or chemicals, you can take water from Wall, Big, and Shower Springs, and from springs inside Wrather and Bush Head Canyons. However, between The Confluence and Bush Head, are a number of minor seeps, which likely will have water flowing from them most of the time. The author always carries a small $3 bottle of Iodine tablets in his pack, but in 17 years of climbing and hiking around the world, has only used them four times in the backcountry. But it's something you must have if you need it.

The alternative to chemicals, is filtration. The 1987 REI catalog shows four filters designed for hikers. They sell for $549, $165, $40, and $34. Some manufactures are making a fist full of dollars on the scare tactics of some people, especially some national park rangers(The BLM and the NPS are required to tell hikers to boil or treat all water--even *spring water,* to save their necks from possible law suits!). The author prefers spring water, and Iodine tablets as an emergency backup.

Another thing to remember, carry several water bottles or plastic jugs. They don't weigh much, and can be thrown away at the end of the trip. By having a couple of 3.75 liter(one gallon) jugs, you can increase the number of potential campsites to you, by allowing you to carry water from good springs to unoccupied sites.

Main Attractions A deep and narrow canyon, several places in which to climb or hike out to the rim, interesting side canyons, one of the best arches in the world, a chance to see desert big horn sheep, many good campsites, petroglyphs, and a total wilderness experience, even though these days the canyon is becoming very popular. It's a great trip for those who have time off work in the spring or fall. More later under *Trail and Route Conditions.*

Ideal Time to Hike If you're doing this hike, from the White House Trailhead straight down the Paria to Lee's Ferry, with just a quick look into the bottom of the Buckskin, then spring or fall are best. More specifically, the best time is from about the first of April through May; and again from about mid-September through October, or maybe just into November. The author prefers the spring months because the days are longer. Remember, March 21, has the same amount of daylight as does September 21.

By June first, the temperatures are getting up there to around 30 C(86 F) on average, and that's pretty warm when walking in the sun all day carrying a pack. You can count on temps of about 40 C all through July and into August, at Lee's Ferry. In the narrows parts, and when wading in the creek, the heat doesn't effect you so much; but in the lower end of the canyon near Lee's Ferry, the altitude is only about 950 meters, and you'll walking in the sun constantly.

Another reason to stay out of the area in about June, is that there are big horse flies which bite you on the back of the legs. They seem to congregate in the more open areas, with water and tamarisk bushes. You'll also be hindered by the very small gnats which get in your hair and bite. In the spring and fall, these two pests don't exist. Neither do they seem to exist in the narrow parts of the canyon at any time, just in the more open places.

Slide Rock(Arch), a major landmark not far below the White House Trailhead.

The Confluence, of the Buckskin and the Paria.

Hiking Boots You'll be walking in or through the Paria River(at least from The Confluence on down to Lee's Ferry) all the way. In the narrower places you'll be hiking right in the stream continually. The water is generally only ankle deep, but your footwear will be wet all the time. So some kind of wading boot or shoes is a must.

In the last few years, a number of new hiking boots or shoes have been on the market, designed especially for this type of hike. What you'll want is the kind which aren't affected by water. In other words, a shoe which doesn't have leather. There aren't many like this around, but you can find them if you look. The Converse All Star basketball shoes, which are made of rubber and canvas, are good, except they have a thin sole, and low heel. There are the plain ordinary running shoes too. They are very good, but they have leather parts, which will have to be oiled after the hike, or they'll shrink and crack.

Another tip, since this is such a long hike, take a pair of shoes in good condition. If you have an old pair, and are trying to put them out of their misery, it might pay to take along a newer and light weight pair as a back-up. This is an especially good suggestion, if you intend to use some of the trails or routes out of the canyon and up to the rim. It takes a lot out of footwear to be used under strenuous conditions when wet all the time.

Author's Experience The author has been down into the canyon from the White House Trailhead on three occasions, and up from Lee's Ferry on two other trips. On each trip, he went to somewhere in the middle of the canyon, and returned the same way to his car, thus avoiding a car shuttle or hitch hiking.

Trail and Route Conditions--from The Confluence to Lee's Ferry The first half of the way between The Confluence and Lee's Ferry is narrow, although it's not the slot-type canyon you find in the Buckskin Gulch. There are many springs, running water the year-round in the Paria River, and there are no obstacles. If you were caught in this section by a flashflood, you would have very little trouble finding a high place out of the way of the torrent. There are many good campsites, and always one site near each of the good springs. Taking fotos is in some ways easier than in the darker Buckskin, because here you will see the sun much of the time. There are several abandoned meanders, or abandoned stream channels to explore, and there are some petroglyphs, an historic pumping site, and several trails or routes to the rim.

If you arrive at The Confluence, and find the campsites just inside the lower Buckskin to be full or too crowded or noisy, then you could walk down stream about a km to find another place, high and dry and safe. Some might prefer this campsite to the Buckskin sites anyway, as it is closer to the springs located another two or three kms down the canyon. Just a couple of bends down river from this campsite is a large alcove type cave, which might prove interesting.

About 3.5 or 4 kms below The Confluence, is a nice campsite and a usually good spring the

A group of hikers near The Confluence. Their dogs carry their own food.

author is calling Wall Spring. It has put out a lot of good water each time the author has been there, but Skip, the Paria Ranger, recalls times where its flow was so low, it was hard to get a drink from it. But normally you can rely on this spring.

Just 300 meters below Wall Spring is yet another good campsite and spring (labeled #9 on the old BLM map, #7 on the new), which may in the long run be more reliable than its neighbor upstream. This spring is at or near a side canyon this author calls the 1st Crack. It's the result of a minor fault, as are all four of the Crack Canyons shown on Map 25.

From the Wall Spring area, the canyon tends to the northeast a bit. Along this section you'll see a large alcove or overhang, which may be one of the deepest in the Paria, and is similar to those found in the Coyote Gulch of the Escalante River. A km or so beyond this overhang or alcove, is another overhang where the river under-cuts the Navajo wall, and just beyond, is a feature known as an abandoned meander, or an abandoned stream channel(#10 on the old BLM map, #8 on the new one).

A few thousand years ago, the Paria River ran through this channel, but it slowly cut or undercut one of it's walls in the process of making a goose-neck curve. It finally abandoned the old loop for a new one. The former stream channel is 5 or 6 meters above the present level of the river bed. It'll be worth while to take a break from wading the river and check this one out. The access is easy and there are camping possibilities on the north side of the meander.

From the abandoned meander, the canyon tends to the southeast for about two kms. Just before you arrive at the 2nd Crack, you'll come to the best spring in the canyon. Some BLM rangers used to refer to this as Eleven Mile Spring(it's shown as #11 on the old BLM map, #9 on the new--which was about 11 miles or 18 kms down stream from the White House Trailhead), but previous kilomage may be in error. Later calculations set the distance at closer to 20 kms. The author has called it Big Spring on this map. Across the river is another good and very popular campsite. If the camp is full when you arrive, just go down stream a ways to find still more camping places and springs.

Right at the very bottom of what the author calls the 2nd Crack, is another seemingly good spring. It flows out of this little side canyon with a good discharge, at least when the author saw it. If you're a rock climber, it might be fun to look for a route out of the canyon to the south and up this 2nd Crack. Someone who is experienced with doing *chimney work* might be able to get out of or beyond the first set of ledges, and find a way south up this crack canyon to the rim. It looked promising, for a real tough guy(or gal?).

As you pass the 2nd Crack, the Paria then tends to the northeast, and you enter a section of the canyon where there are few if any springs. Between 2nd Crack and the Adams Pump count on it being dry, except for the river water. The author has placed several springs on the map in this section, but they are mostly just minor seeps, and don't have much discharge. This part of the canyon has some very tight turns, some very high walls and it's as narrow as any part of the Paria River below the

The first of several abandoned meanders.

area just above The Confluence. The author has labeled one section the *Goosenecks.* You'll be walking right in the stream throughout most of this narrows.

At or near the bottom of the Goosenecks is the 3rd Crack. It, like the other two upstream, is a little inconspicuous. It's hard at times to follow the river channel on the map; that's part of the reason these crack canyons are not easily seen. It's also a little difficult to keep your orientation(north-south) as you walk down this narrow gorge. A compass is helpful.

Just beyond the 3rd Crack, and on your left, is another abandoned stream channel. It's maybe 10-15 meters above the river level, and easy to get into. The author followed it for a ways, then returned the same way. But it appears on the Paria Plateau Map(1:62,500), to be a kind of double abandoned meander. It might be worth while to take the time to check this one out. It could also make an interesting campsite.

Less than two kms below the 3rd Crack you'll come to the 4th Crack. This one is more obvious than the previous three, partly because the canyon is beginning to open up and become wider. From the rim above, it appeared that a good climber could possibly make it out of the canyon to the north, using this very narrow slit in the wall, but the author didn't have the time to give it a try. In the 4th Crack running south, there are some ledges to skirt and a little climbing, but from the top of the Adams Trail, where the author looked down on it, it appeared to be climbable.

About half a km beyond the 4th Crack, and on the south side of the creek bed, is the beginning of the old Adams Trail. More interesting than the trail itself, is the hard-luck story behind it.

The Adams Trail

The area to the south of this middle part of the Lower Paria River Gorge is called the Sand Hills by all the local cattlemen; the Paria Plateau by geologists. The name Sand Hills is very fitting, as the top-most layer or formation is made up mostly of the Navajo Sandstone. When it weathers away, it forms very sandy conditions. Because of the sand, the only way one can get around the plateau, is to walk, ride a horse, drive a 4WD, or use the tracks in winter when the sand is either wet or frozen.

Despite the poor travel conditions, the area has been used for cattle, sheep and goat grazing since about the mid-1880's. It's fairly high, rising to 2043 meters on the southern edge at Powell's Monument. This means it has good pasturage, and it's surrounded on three sides by impassible cliffs or canyons. On the north is the Buckskin Gulch, the north and east by the Paria River Gorge, and on the south by the Vermilion Cliffs, which rise up 500 or 600 meters above the valley. The only easy way onto the plateau is from the west and the Coyote and House Rock Valleys.

Throughout the years cattlemen slowly but surely began to develop the water potential, as there is no running water on the plateau, not even one spring. They built small dams below exposed slickrock slopes, to catch what rainwater there was. They blasted holes in the slickrock to make

One of many "gooseneck" curves of the lower Paria.

Morning sun on the Navajo wall, streaked with desert varnish.

The biggest and best spring in the canyon, is what the author calls Big Spring.

The beginning of the Adams Trail.

stock tanks, and of course there were natural potholes or tanks in the slickrock. The number of cattle was always small, and limited by the available water. Things went well for 50 years or so. Then a long drought began in the 1930's, which coincided with the Great Depression.

During this drought period, which was complicated by the Depression, there were several different cattlemen who had stock on the Sand Hills range. The northeast quarter of the plateau was used by a man named Johnny Adams. As he began to see his cattle die of thirst, he began to take a hard look down into the Paria Canyon. He must have pondered long and hard as to how he might get his cattle down to the year-round flowing river, or how he might get some of that water up to his cows.

Finally he thought he had the problem solved. He had investigated pumping equipment and had come to the conclusion that with available technology and pumps, he could move water from the river to the rim, a vertical distance at that point of the canyon of about 215 meters. So in the winter of 1938-39 he made the decision to build a rough access trail to install pumping equipment. After searching the rim, he found a place, which with a little dynamite and work, could be used.

The Adams Trail was hacked out of the canyon wall in the spring of 1939, and the pump, gasoline engine, and 300 meters of 5 cm(2") pipe were trucked in over the Sand Hills access road. For the last part of the journey, pack animals were used to haul in the equipment.

According to P.T. Reilly, the man who researched the history of this pumping station(and which is written in the Utah Historical Quarterly), it was Dean Cutler who straw-bossed the job for Adams who was elderly. The remaining crew members were Lorin Broadbent, Eugene McAllister, and Lynn Ford. The country was very rough, and getting the equipment to the rim was a major undertaking. Water and food were packed in, and the most luxurious comfort was ones bedroll spread out on the ground, although rattlesnakes were numerous after the weather began to warm.

Their first job was to construct a rough trail to get the motor and pump down to the river. It was never intended to be a good trail, only good enough for men to scramble up and down. Horses were apparently never taken down the trail. The men lowered the pump and motor down the cliffs with ropes, one step at a time. Finally the pump and engine were in place, then pipe was carried down one section at a time, and attached.

It was well into summer when they installed the last section of pipe. They had intended to fill several potholes which were just above the rim. When the pipe was finally in place, they climbed down to the river to give it a try. But the river was very muddy, the result of storms up stream. They decided to abandon any pumping until the creek cleared. But that night it rained. It filled all the stock tanks and potholes. The drought was over, and the pump was never even tested. There it sat for two years.

In 1941, Adams sold it to another cattlemen, A. T. Spence. But Spence never used it. He ended up selling it to Merle Findlay in 1944. The pump continued to sit and gather dust and rust. Findlay owned the unused pump for four years, then sold it to Gerald Swapp in 1948.

The upper part of the Adams Trail. It angles up to the left making a dugway.

Gerald Swapps cattle range was the area north of the Paria, called the Flat Top and East Clark Bench. It was, and still is a good grazing country, but lack of a good water supply has always restricted the potential of the range. After mulling over the idea of pumping water from the Paria up to the benchland for 10 years, Swapp finally bought the unused and untested pumping rig to give it a try. His intention was to pump water into the lower end of Judd Hollow, which is about 3 kms down stream from where the pump was set up at the bottom of the Adams Trail.

To do the job, Swapp hired Eugene McAllister(who was one of the original members of the crew who put the pipe and pump in place) and Tony Woolley. In December, 1948, the three men walked down into the canyon along the trail, got the engine running and got a good flow of water out the upper end of the pipe.

Later, in January of 1949, under some rather cold conditions, Woolley rode a horse down the Paria Canyon, in similar fashion to the feat performed by John D. Lee in 1871. The pipe was all disconnected, and placed in bundles, which were tied together at one end. Then the rope was tied to the cross-tree of the saddle, and dragged down the partially frozen stream to Judd Hollow. The 4 cylinder, Fairbanks--Morris flathead engine and the pump, were carried by horseback downstream, one at a time.

To avoid damaging the pump by using it with muddy water, the crew dug a sump at the edge of the north bank of the stream(a hole, lined with rocks, which would allow water to filter in slowly, thus avoiding the muddy water when the stream was running high). Their intention was to run the pipe directly up to the bottom of Judd Hollow, a rise of 300 meters. Then they hoped to run it northeast for another 3 kms to a tank in the area where cattle were located. This would require much more pipe. So Woolley rode the horse down canyon to Lee's Ferry, while Swapp and McAllister hiked back up the trail to the truck, and drove back to Kanab, to get more pipe and a booster to the pump.

But things just didn't work out for Swapp. He had been ill throughout the ordeal of replacing the pump and pipe, so he decided to remain in Kanab until he felt better. However, he got worse instead. Finally he was taken to the hospital in Cedar City, where he died on March 28, 1949.

After this second effort to pump Paria River water upon the benchland surrounding the canyon, no one every tried the feat again. And there it sits today; the engine, pump and one length of pipe running into the ground where the sump was dug. You can see it on the north side of the stream on a low bench at the mouth of Judd Hollow.

To find the Adams Trail, walk down stream about 200 meters from where the south arm of 4th Crack drains into the canyon. On the south side of the creek, on a minor bench, and in an area which is rather broad, look for yet another rounded bench rising perhaps 10 to 15 meters above the embankment. You may first notice some hand or foot holds notched into the sandstone wall, which are likely old Indian made steps. They are very smooth and worn today. The author never did make it

Typical campsite along the middle part of the Paria.

Another shaded campsite along the river.

The old and rusting Adams Pump, now located at the mouth of Judd Hollow.

up the steep part using these steps. But just to the east or left(as you look at the rock face), is a broad vertical crack in the sandstone bench. You have to get down on all fours to make it up, but it's very easy climbing for anyone.

Once you arrive on this first bench, walk east along the top, gradually turning to the right or south. Almost immediately you begin to walk up a steep sandslide covered with cactus. To avoid damaging this pristine cactus field and the cryptogamic soil, veer to the right and walk west a ways, then turn south up the minor drainage. Further up you'll come to the base of a talus slope on the right.

Head up this slope which comes down from where a minor drainage comes off the wall in front of you. Once you arrive near the top of this talus slope, you begin to see the old trail. Near the top of the slope, and almost next to the canyon wall, you'll turn right or to the northwest, and walk along near the base of the cliff. After about 100 meters, you come to more cliffs and at a kind of dead-end place. At that point, look to the left, or south along the cliff face, and you'll just be able to make out a faint line indicating the trail angling up along the cliff face. Walk up this ramp, which is a little steep in a place or two, but which is easy walking. An unloaded burro could surely make it up, and a big horn sheep or deer would have no trouble at all.

Further along you come to a level section, then less than 100 meters away, you'll again come to what is obviously a constructed trail. It zig zags up one last steep place to the southwest, before running due south up the minor drainage you saw from below. At the top of this little draw, the trail vanishes on top of the plateau.

This is an easy walk, and it seems a pity no one took the time to finish the trail. Just a little more work, and it would be good enough for cattle to use. Once you get on the trail, anyone can make it to the top in about half an hour. From the top, you can walk along the rim in either direction, for some fine views of the canyon below.

Going down river again. Between the Adams Trail and the mouth of Judd Hollow, the river makes some tight bends and is again enclosed in high walls. After about 1.5 kms, you'll come to a half km section where large boulders have fallen off the canyon wall and landed in the stream channel. In this part the river meanders back and forth between rocks. In times of flood and high water, deep holes are scoured out next to some of these boulders. If you're there not long after a flood, you may encounter the deepest water of the entire hike.

This place called *Boulder Alley* by the author, may have been the place which inspired a story to be written about the Paria Canyon, by a member of the October, 1872, military expedition to the region. The author found this story, *An Episode of Military Explorations and Surveys,* in the October, 1881 issue of The United Service. It was written nearly a decade after the event, and for obvious reasons. The author is identified only as T. V. B., and it goes like this(edited slightly for this book).

[I know that the hero of the following narrative would rather lose he tongue than speak of a

One of many springs along the river, seeping from the sandstone walls.

noble deed performed by himself. Nevertheless, every noble action deserves to be known. I beg the Lieutenant's Pardon.]

In the month of October, 1872, the different field-parties composing "explorations and surveys west of the one hundredth meridian," rendezvoused near St. George, in Southern Utah, and after a week spent in preparations for the final work of the season again broke camp, the writer being assigned to the "party of the southeast," of which Lieutenant W. L. M., of the corps of engineers, had charge. The duty assigned to this "party" was the exploration of the "rim of the Great Basin" of Southern Utah, thence to go to the Colorado River, ascend and explore the Canyon of the Paria, and return.

After a couple of days' march the greater number of packers and escort were left in camp, as it was thought that a smaller party could do more effective work, and the number of explorers was reduced to ten,--Lieutenant M., topographer, a cook, two packers, two soldiers, a Mormon, a Pah-Ute, and myself. The Indian was to be our guide, but as he only knew enough of English to ask for whisky, the Mormon was taken along as interpreter.

In those high regions the nights were already disagreeably cold, so that after making camp we would pile up half a dozen dead pine-trees and start a fire that lit up the pine woods for miles, and sometimes even compelled us to shift camp, much to the disgust of our Pah-Ute, who was fearful of a visit from his dreaded foes, the Navajos, and did his best to convince us that one could warm himself better over a small fire than a large one, generally finishing the pantomime by telling us that "whitey man big fool!"

In due time we struck the "Great Navajo Trail," used by the Navajo Indians in their annual trading expeditions to the settlements of Southern Utah, and here our Indian became quite frantic with anxiety to go back to his own hunting-grounds, pleading that "his father never went farther;" but he had to stay with us, and every morning, without fail, he mysteriously showed us the footprints of savage enemies who had been lurking about the camp through the night,--though we failed to see an Indian during the entire trip, or had even a mule stolen.

The party derived considerable amusement from the repugnance of the mule ridden by Lieutenant M. for the Pah-Ute: neither did time do much towards reconciling the two. Whenever the Indian made his appearance unexpectedly before the lieutenant's charger, off came the lieutenant and away went the mule, a manoeuvre to which our chief at last became so accustomed that rather than be violently ejected from the saddle he would gracefully slide off when he saw "coming events cast their shadows before," and he owned, good-naturedly, that when that mule wanted him off he might as well come. So that the Indian was quite as much a trial to the lieutenant as to the mule.

We encamped on the Paria River two miles from its junction with the Colorado. I speak of the Paria as a river because it is honored with that rank on the maps, but feel as through I owed the reader an apology for deceiving him, for in a less arid country it would scarcely be dignified with the name of creek. But in this respect the pilgrim of the great trans-Rocky Southwest cannot afford to be fastidious. In those water-scarce regions everything having the appearance of running water is at least a creek, and the imagination delights in exalting a creek into a river. So on all the maps of New Mexico and Arizona the Rio Colorado Chiquito figures prominently, and would readily impose itself upon the unwary as a second Mississippi, yet memory vividly and lugubriously recalls the times when, not in one particular locality but in many, I boldly straddled it with my legs, and in that position washed my soiled undergarments; and worse, for too often it contained no water to wash with.

Two miles from our camp, at the junction of the Colorado and Paria, amid that weird scenery, isolated from all the world, was the ranch of John D. Lee, late bishop and major in the Mormon Church. The martial bishop was not often at home, and Mrs. Lee No. 17, with her nine children, garrisoned the ranch and battled with the elements for a livelihood.

In the mean time we had lost our Indian and his adjutant, the Mormon, much to the relief of Lieutenant M.'s charger. The two worthies had, from the beginning, overloaded their stomachs with ham and bacon, articles of diet to which the Indian and Mormon stomach is not accustomed, and had brought upon themselves severe bilious attacks.

The canyon of the Paria, which we were now to explore, was estimated to be about thirty two miles in length, and it was said that no human being had ever succeeded in getting through it. A flock of geese, the Mormons told us, had swam through the canyon, from the Mormon settlement of Paria to the Colorado River, and through we did not succeed in getting through it ourselves, our very failure, me-thinks proves that we were not geese.

Early on the morning of November 20 we started on the performance of what we all knew would be a difficult and dangerous task. At first the gorge was several hundred yards wide, the walls of the canyon sloping and not more than seven hundred feet in height; but with every mile the canyon narrowed and its walls became higher and more vertical, until at the end of five miles it did not average more than thirty yards in width, while the walls had attained a vertical height of fifteen hundred feet. The creek occupied the middle of the chasm, and often the entire space, from wall to wall, so that we were obliged continually to cross and recross it, as well as ride against the stream, a task which was rendered more difficult by oft-recurring patches of quicksand in which our animals became mired, obliging us to make frequent halts to dig them out. In this way we accomplished ten miles the first day, camping in a cotton-wood grove where the canyon had widened, and where enough grass grew to feed our animals.

The next day the difficulties increased. Occasionally the walls met overhead forming caverns dark as night, through which we waded and half swam, often compelled to bend over the saddle, so low was the rocky ceiling. Nor was the labor of urging the bewildered mules through these dark passages an easy one. That night we encamped, wet and chilled, on a peninsula of rocks large enough to accommodate ourselves and our animals.

The third day was bitter cold. Soon after starting the mule, ridden by the cook, Kittelman, a middle-aged German, whose duty on the march it was to lead the burdenless bell-horse, sank, belly-deep, in quicksand, and stuck fast, keeling over on his side and lying on Kittelman. We were occupied half an hour digging out the mule, during which time it required the strength of two men to keep the mule's head above water, and of one to perform a similar office for the poor cook. The mule, in his struggles, frequently struck Kittelman in the face, so that the latter, when extricated, was badly bruised and stupid from cold and excitement. No time was to be lost, however, and in his half-frozen condition the man had to mount the bell-horse and follow the party.

We now found ice formed in localities where the water was deeper and less rapid. This increased in thickness from one-eighth to one-half inch, when our mules refused to take to it farther, and we found ourselves compelled to dismount, wade up the icy stream, often to our armpits in water, and here and there break the crust of ice by means of our carbines, rocks, etc. This task was performed by Lieutenant M. and myself, for which purpose we kept a few hundred yards ahead of the party, leading our mules.

About 3 P.M. we came to a sharp bend in the canyon, where the water had cut into and undermined a portion of the wall. forming a large and deep pool, about fifty feet wide and forty long, which was also covered with a crust of ice, half an inch thick. This pool we must needs cross. After breaking up the ice with large rocks, I attempted to wade through it, but when about ten feet from the edge sunk knee-deep in quicksand and was fain to scramble back. I then mounted my mule and attempted to ride him in, but no amount of either urging or coaxing would induce the otherwise tractable animal to take to the water. Lieutenant M. then made the attempt with his mule, with the same result; the animals instinctively shrank back. By this time the remainder of the party had come up. The bell-horse had been ridden by the cook since the accident of the morning, and was saddled. I was about to mount him to ride him through the pool, knowing that he would obey under all circumstances, when Kittelman, though shivering with cold and scarcely more than half conscious, anticipated the movement, saying that he was not afraid to ride his horse where any other man was willing to go. The animal entered the pool without hesitation, and had gotten nearly half-way across when, as if sucked down, man and horse disappeared. In about twenty seconds the man's head again came to the surface, as well as that of the horse, Kittelman no longer on the horse but evidently still clutching the bridle,--his gaze vacant. After a few seconds, to our horror, man and horse again disappeared, and now it was that we began to realize that a human being, our companion and servitor during months of exploring, was about to perish before our eyes--almost within reach of our hands-- and we utterly powerless for help, for who would plunge into that ice-covered pool, occupied as it was by a horse struggling for life?

Among the party was a packer by name of Evans, a large, powerful man. He had passed most of his life in Oregon, and his swimming-feats on the Columbia River, as related by himself, surpassed those performed by Leander and Byron. To him all eyes were now turned and there he stood, the picture of sickening fear and cowardice. Lieutenant M. now called out in agonized tones, "My God! will nobody save that man?" and hearing no response, without waiting to disencumber himself of overcoat or boots, he plunged, head foremost, into the awful hole. After fifteen seconds of terrible suspense, during which the horse had regained the surface and crawled to the rocks on which we were assembled, Lieutenant M. reappeared, holding the body of Kittelman in his arms. The latter was still alive, but only drew breath four or five times after leaving the water. We at once placed him on a pile of blankets, and four of the party chafed him vigorously for an hour and used other means of resuscitation, but in vain--he was dead.

In the mean time one of our packers had scaled a crevice in the rocks, to a point where a lot of stunted cedars could be seen, of which he threw down a sufficient quantity to keep up a fire during the night. Through not unused to hardships and stirring scenes, I shall never forget that night's camp. We were upon a peninsula of rocks, just large enough to accommodate the party; beside us flowed the dark stream; over us rose to a vertical height of over three thousand feet the rocky walls of the chasm, but a few stars being visible. The body of Kittelman lay a few feet from the fire, covered by a blanket. The glare of the fire served only to intensify the weirdness of the scene. Added to this was the knowledge that should to-morrow be an unusually warm day the snow would melt in the mountains, *the stream would rise, and we should be drowned like rats in a cage before the end of the canyon could again be reached.*

So we waited anxiously for morning. The body of Kittelman was sewed up, sailor-fashion, in a piece of canvas and packed on a mule, the frozen bones cracking horribly during the process. We carried the body with us for about two hours, when we came upon a crevice in the rocks, some twelve feet above low water, and into that we laid the remains and covered them with rocks, assured that no human hands would ever disturb them.

And though we returned to the mouth of the canyon unsuccessful, and with a life less, we had gained a hero more.

T. V. B.

Portions of this military episode in the Paria Gorge are obviously exaggerated and were written to entertain. Never has this author heard of quicksand in the canyon, but horses could easily get quagmired. Their feet cover less area than peoples, but they might have 10 times the body weight. John D. Lee also took a herd of cows down this same canyon, almost exactly one year before this military expedition, and it took him 8 days to get from about Rock House to the Colorado River. For cattle, horses or mules, it's apparently a different set of circumstances than for hikers.

Not far below *Boulder Alley,* where the big rocks are in the stream channel, you'll come to the Adams Water Pump on the left, about 5 meters above the creek. Just behind the pump is another of many abandoned meanders in the canyon. About a km below the pump and on a sharp bend in the river, are several good campsites and one panel of petroglyphs.

Just below the petroglyphs, you'll normally begin to see seeps along the rivers edge. In the river section between the petroglyphs and The Hole, there are many places where you can camp and get water. The BLM publications don't mention these springs, so it's possible some could either dry up or have such a small discharge at times, as to make it difficult to obtain water from them. Each time the author visited this part of the canyon, it appeared they would flow year-round.

The next attraction is The Hole. The Hole perhaps refers to two places; first, the canyon which comes down from the Sand Hills and flows into the Paria; and second, the very bottom end of this same canyon, right next to the river. All you'll ever see is this lower end of The Hole Canyon. Because of the high vertical cliffs, it's impossible to reach the upper part of the drainage from the river. At the very bottom, and right next to the river, the seeping waters have eroded away the sandstone, making an alcove or cave-like feature shaped like an inverted key hole; thus the name The Hole.

You can walk into this dark recess about 40 meters, where you'll find a seep at the very back end, right where the water falls to when it rains and water comes off the slickrock areas above. Near

The Hole, a deep recess in the Navajo wall, not far north of Wrather Canyon.

the front end or entrance to The Hole, you can set up camp on a little bench, which is completely under a big overhang. This would be a good place to camp for those hardy souls who prefer to travel without a tent. The seep will likely have water when you arrive, although this seep isn't on anybody's "best springs list". Up stream about 50 meters or so, is another seep, which had a good flow upon each of the authors visits.

It's in the area below where the Adams Pump is situated that the canyon begins to widen, and from The Hole down, it continues to open up. Between The Hole and Wrather Canyon there isn't anything special to see, except there are many places with scattered cottonwood trees which could make good campsites. Only problem is, the author doesn't recall seeing many good seeps.

Wrather Canyon

is one of the real gems of the Lower Paria River Gorge. It's a short side canyon, only about a km long, but it has one of the best and most interesting arches in the world called Wrather Arch. It also has a spring not far below the arch, which provides water for a small year-round flowing stream in parts of the canyon.

As you approach this canyon from upstream, you'll be looking right into it. But as the stream inside Wrather comes near the Paria, it turns abruptly east, and parallels the Paria for maybe 150 meters. You'll have to reach the very mouth of Wrather Creek before you can enter the canyon. Inside the canyon is a hiker-made trail right up to and underneath the arch. Along the way is a good example of riparian vegetation. There are cottonwood and box elder trees, water cress, mosses, cat tails, and other plants this author can't describe. It's a little green paradise in the middle of the desert.

Because the bottom of Wrather Canyon is so narrow and fragile, the BLM asks that hikers don't camp in the canyon. There's not much space anyway. Instead, camp at the canyon mouth, across the river to the north, and in one of several groves of cottonwood trees. When you go up to the arch, take your empty water jugs to be filled. By not camping inside the canyon, you can also help preserve the good quality of water for those who follow in your footsteps.

Wrather Canyon Overlook Hike

For those with a little time, and those who like climbing and want a break from trudging along in this seemingly endless gorge, here's a diversion. Take a hike to the canyon rim right above Wrather Arch.

From the camp sites at the mouth of Wrather, head down canyon 700-800 meters. At about that point you'll be passing through an area of tall grasses, sort of like bullrushes. On the right will be a low bench which you can breech easily. Above this low bench, is a triangle-shaped sandslide

Looking down on the river from the North Rim Overlook.

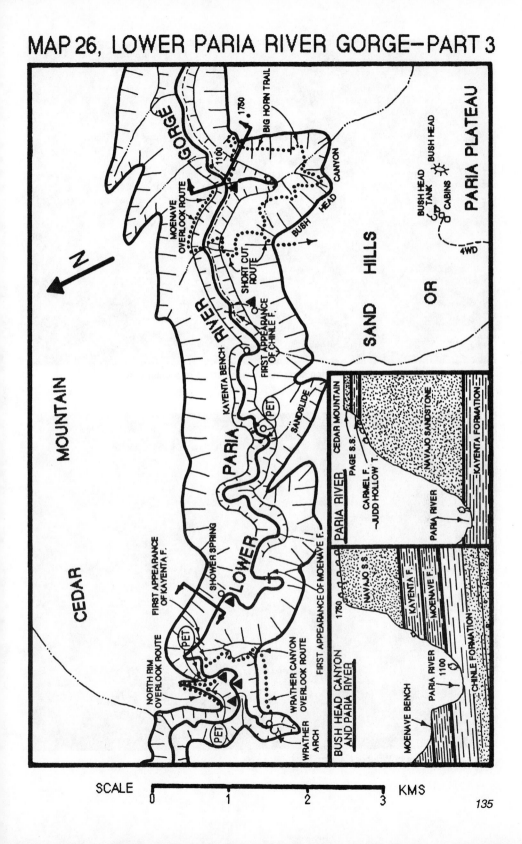

SCALE

0   1   2   3   KMS

Inside Wrather Canyon is a small spring and stream, with cattails and water cress.

The narrow bottom of Wrather Canyon.

Looking south east at the route up to the Wrather Arch Overlook(from the North Rim Overlook).

Wrather Arch, from underneath or inside.

coming down from the southeast. Walk upon the bench and head straight up the sandslide toward its apex. At the top is a short gully which comes down on the right(west) side of the slide. You'll climb right up this mini canyon or gully, which has several short and easy pitches.

At the very top of the gully is the most challenging part of the entire hike. There are two short cliffs or dropoffs you must scale. The height is only about three meters each, and there are plenty of hand and foot holds, but the sandstone is a little crumbly. Just take your time, and test each handhold. The author had no problem, but he's done a lot of this sort of thing. Others may want a short rope, perhaps just a piece of parachute cord, to add a touch of security. If only one member of a group can get up, then all others should be able to make it up safely.

From the top of the gully, make a hard right turn and head due west, contouring around the corner. You'll be just below some massive Navajo cliffs. Shortly, you'll turn south, still bench-walking or contouring towards another minor, but steep drainage. It comes down from the pass to your upper left. There are several routes up this final slope, so pick the one which suits you best.

Upon arriving at the top, rim-walk to the west and towards the edge of Wrather Canyon. You should reach the rim directly above the arch. It looks a lot smaller from above, than from below, indicating the great height of the wall you're on. When the author got to this rim, he spotted three desert big horn rams, but had the wrong lens on his camera to get a good foto. This hike may be one of the best side trips in the whole canyon. Take fotos of the arch from about mid-morning through mid-day.

North Rim Overlook Hike

If you're a natural bridge and arch watcher, then here's a hike that will place you high on the north rim of the Paria, and directly across from the mouth of Wrather Canyon. From this overlook, you can see right up the middle of Wrather, and have perhaps the best view of all of the arch itself.

Begin at the campsites at the mouth of Wrather Canyon, and walk down canyon about 300 meters. As you pass the last corner, look straight ahead to the north and to the left a bit, and you'll see a kind of crack canyon, similar to the fault-made cracks further up canyon. It's shape and geologic origin become very clear when viewed from the south rim.

Head straight for the crack, passing where you can, through the low cliff or bench made by one of the lower layers of Navajo Sandstone. Right as you're about to enter the bottom of the crack canyon, look to your right and at the corner, and you'll see a good panel of petroglyphs. In about the same area on your left, is still another panel. To the author and others, this tells of an old Indian passage, as they normally put up etchings on well traveled routes. This is perhaps the only place in the canyon where you can go from rim to rim, via the river in between. There is another panel on the

Wide angle look at Wrather Arch.

other side of the river, at about the place you begin the hike to the Wrather Canyon Overlook, lending more credibility to the idea that this is an old Indian trail.

As you get into the narrow chasm, you'll be walking or climbing due north. The way is easy at first, then it steepens and narrows. Near the top you'll see the bones of one deer and the antlers of yet another, just below the steepest part on the hike. These are the remains of deer which didn't quite make it to water, but don't worry, you are better equipped than the deer were. This last steep little pitch is almost vertical, but since it's right on the fault line, there's been a build-up of minerals in the crack, which is now exposed. This new rock, different from the Navajo Sandstone, is harder and has numerous good hand holds. So although it's nearly vertical, and somewhere between 12 and 14 meters high, it's an easy climb. Just at the very bottom of the pitch is a chokestone you must pass on the right, but anyone should be able to *chimney* or wedge their way up this very minor two-meter high obstacle.

After the steep pitch, it's just a scramble to the rim, where you'll then make a hard left turn, and walk southwest to a point overlooking the river and the mouth of Wrather Canyon. Late morning to mid-day is the best time for taking fotos of the arch.

Going down canyon again, and within about a km from Wrather, you'll find about 4 panels or sites with petroglyphs. The next important stop, is Shower Spring, about 2 full kms down canyon from the mouth of Wrather. Throughout the years this one has proved to be a good and reliable water hole. It's in such a position, as to enable you to get under it and have a shower, thus the name. This important spring comes out of the rock right at the contact point between the Navajo above, and the Kayenta below. This indicates the permeability of the Navajo, and the impermeability of the Kayenta. Across the river is a fine campsite.

Below Shower Spring, the canyon widens still further, but the Kayenta Bench becomes more prominently exposed. Between Wrather and Bush Head Canyons, there are several minor seeps or springs, including one which comes out of the rock on the south side of the river below a big sandslide. Skip, the Paria Ranger, pointed out two locations of petroglyphs near this spring, on the north side of the river, but the author didn't see them. About 1.5 kms below the sandslide is the last spring in the main canyon, before Lee's Ferry.

The next major stop is Bush Head Canyon. Like Wrather, this one is very short, maybe only 1.5 kms from its mouth to its headwall. At the mouth of this canyon are several campsites, and best of all, water. It may or may not be flowing down to the very mouth of the canyon when you arrive, but even if it does, it might be best to walk 700-800 meters up canyon to where a very good spring comes right out of the bottom of the Moenave Formation. The water in this little canyon is surely good to drink as-is, because cattle don't quite make it this far into the lower Paria. However, the water has a kind of

Wrather Arch, as seen from the North Rim Overlook.

swampy taste to it lower down near the river. This is caused by the decaying cottonwood and box elder leaves lying in the creek bed. At the spring itself, it's *puro agua dulce!*

Right at, and just above the spring is a falls and you can't go up any further in the bottom of the canyon.

The Big Horn Trail

For the adventurous hiker who enjoys a little climbing, here's a fun side trip. The author calls it the Big Horn Trail. Actually there are no trails involved, just a couple of routes to the rim-top which may be used by a herd of desert big horn sheep.

The story behind the desert big horns must first be told. As indicated by the hundreds of petroglyph panels in the region, almost all of which show etchings of big horn sheep, one can conclude this magnificent animal has long been a part of the scene in this canyon and mesa country. But in the period of a little more than a century since the white man first began exploring the region, their numbers have gradually shrunk. Local ranchers believe the big horns caught diseases from domestic sheep and were hunted to near extinction, and it appears they virtually disappeared in the Paria Canyon. So it was decided to re-introduce sheep to this canyon.

In July of 1984, the Arizona Game and Fish Department, in cooperation with the BLM, started to carry out their plan. Because of the over grazed desert big horn sheep range on the south shore of Lake Mead, which is part of the Lake Mead National Recreation Area, it was decided to capture some of those sheep and place them in other areas suitable for their existence. The places chosen were the Lower Kanab Creek(between Kanab and the Colorado River), the Paria River Canyon and the Vermilion Cliffs.

Altogether, 53 sheep were captured in July of 1984, sixteen of which were taken to the Kanab Creek area. The remaining 37 were taken to Lee's Ferry. Nineteen were taken to and released at Fisher Springs, not far to the west of Lee's Ferry, and up against the Vermilion Cliffs. The remaining 18 sheep were transported by helicopter to the Bush Head Canyon area and released.

In the Bush Head Canyon release, there were 11 females, and 7 males or rams. Of the 18, five females were equipped with radio-telemetry collars. These special radios have the ability to send out a signal, not only when the sheep is alive and well, but can also detect when the animal dies with a mortality sensor. The radio signals are then monitored periodically by aircraft.

In the weeks and months following the transplant, numerous flights were made over both release sites, to monitor their movements. Very little movement was detected at first, but in the time since, the herd of sheep at Fisher Springs has moved out along the base of the Vermilion Cliffs, and several into the Marble Canyon region. Those at Bush Head, seemed to stay nearer the release site.

Looking down canyon(southeast) from the route up to the Wrather Arch Overlook.

About 8 months after the release, two sensors noted fatalities in the Bush Head area. In late February, 1985, with the help of a helicopter, the two sheep were found dead, apparently having fallen from icy cliffs.

After about a years time, it was observed that the Bush Head sheep had started migrating, perhaps on a seasonal basis, to other locations along the Paria River and to the mesa top, or the Paria Plateau. But each time the Game and Fish people fly over the region, it's been found that the sheep stay pretty close to the initial release site, indicating that location is a good one. In November, 1984, a volunteer group from Arizona State University helped to build a slickrock catchment basin somewhere on the plateau above the Bush Head Canyon area.

The author made one special trip up from the bottom of the Paria, just to check out the ways these sheep were getting up and down the canyon wall from the river to the rim. On an earlier trip the author saw at close range, three big horns on the lip of Wrather Canyon, which sparked this curiosity. In the end, he found two routes from the river to the rim and to the Sand Hills rock feature called Bush Head.

Here is one of two routes to the canyon rim. From the very mouth of Bush Head Canyon, look southeast and up the steep slope. You'll see a talus slope, then a green spot with tall grasses and bullrushes, indicating a wet spot or minor seep, just below the first bench. Head that way, straight up to the southeast. From the first little ledge, make your way up through several more benches and minor cliffs. Remember, you're heading for the big bench, just below the massive Navajo wall. There's an easy way through each little bench, but you'll have to zig zag a bit, and route-find on your own, to find the easier places to pass through. As you near the big bench, bench-walk or contour to the left or east, and into a minor canyon. On the other side of this drainage is one last step or cliff to get through, which is again very easy. Once on top of this, then you bench-walk or contour around to the west, then south, heading toward the big south wall of the upper Bush Head Basin.

As you near the headwall, you'll have to walk down through a break in the top layer of the Kayenta, to the mini valley below, then route-find back up to and into the most western of the two alcoves at the headwall of the canyon. Go straight for some trees, which appear to be near a spring(but there is no spring or water there).

From the head of this second draw, walk due north, still contouring or bench-walking along the top of the Kayenta. In one little mini canyon, you'll come to a cliff where it appears that'll be the end of your hike; but from there simply walk uphill to the west, then head down a little ramp to the bottom, thence again to the north.

As you near the place southwest of the mouth of Bush Head Canyon, you'll see in front of you another small canyon coming down from the left, or west, and a sandslide. Head up this canyon, but just into it, veer to the right or northwest, and route-find up through some minor cliffs. This part is

Another good year-round water supply is Shower Spring.

nearly a walk-up all the way to the rim. This hike might be called the Grand Tour of Bush Head Canyon, as the route winds its way in and out of a spectacular slickrock canyon.

From the rim, you might choose to walk due south about two kms to Bush Head, or the Bush Head Stock Tank. At that old stockman's camp, are two old cabins, a stockade type corral, and a small concrete dam, located at the base of a little slickrock valley. If there's been rain in the region within the month or so, this stock tank will be full. But don't count on drinking this cow-pie water! Cattle graze this area during the winter months, making the water unfit for human consumption.

Back at the Big Horn Trail. The longer and more scenic route has been described. If you've come up this one, but want a shorter way down, take the Short-cut Route back down to the river. Begin this one at the very last part of the first route described. Walk straight down the cliffy slope, but when it becomes less steep, veer to the left or west, and make your way around some of the intertongued beds at the contact point of the Navajo and Kayenta. There is no way of describing the route, except to say you may have to zig zag a bit in reaching the river. At one place, the author *chimneyed down* a 10 meter high crack in one of the layers or benches. If he had walked still further west, he may have found an easier way, and walked down through this bench.

As you work your way down this slope, you'll see a minor drainage below. Head for it. But just as you think you've got it made, you'll come to one last little dropoff. The author jumped down this one, but you can walk through it if you'll veer to the right and bench-walk to the east, until you come to a mini-dugway, where you walk down to the north and to the river and trail.

Which ever route you go up or down, it'll involves a little route-finding. There are no serious obstacles, but you may have to do some zig zagging on either of these routes to find the easy way up or down through the Kayenta and Moenave Formations. Take all the water you'll need for the day, as there's none above Bush Head Spring, and you can't get to it the spring from either of the routes just described. Also, take a lunch, as you can spend a day on this one. The author lost time exploring around for the Grand Tour Route, then went all the way to Bush Head Tank, finally returning via the Short-cut Route, arriving back at camp in just under 9 hours. Without the side trip to Bush Head, it would have been an easy day-hike. Most people would be happy to just get to the rim and return directly to camp, taking most of a day.

While interviewing some of the old timers in the region about some of the early day history of the canyon, Mel Schoppman of Greene Haven(northwest of Page), told the author about a scheme by his father John, and Rubin Broadbent. It seems they were looking for ways to either get water up to their cattle on top of the Sand Hills, or take cattle down to the river below. They searched, and finally found a way off the plateau and down to the river at Bush Head Canyon. The route they made on *horseback* was along what has just been described as the Short-cut Route. They considered constructing a cattle trail there, but it turned out to be too big a job. Years later Mel Schoppman also

A look at upper Bush Head Canyon, from the top of the trail.

made it up through the cliffs on horseback. With a little scouting around, this is an easy walk-up route.

According to everyone the author talked to, there are no routes up through the Vermilion Cliffs to the Paria Plateau between Bush Head Canyon and the Sand Hill Crack, discussed under hike #29. Rock climbers could surely find a route, but it likely couldn't be climbed by ordinary hikers.

As you leave Bush Head Canyon on your way to Lee's Ferry, you'll be walking along the south side of the river. You'll walk on an old cattle trail and hiker-made path, which over the years has gradually gotten better and more distinct with the increase of hikers. Actually, from 3 or 4 kms above Bush Head, you can get on the south side of the river and stay there until you're in the area of the three prominent boulders with petroglyphs, as shown on the map. In this section of about 10-12 kms, you won't have to cross the stream once.

The reason for the trail winding its way up and above the river, is that in this part of the canyon, the softer beds of the Chinle Formation are beginning to be exposed. When this occurs, the canyon automatically widens, and the cliffs made of the Navajo, Kayenta and Moenave, begin to pull apart. As this happens, occasionally large boulders break off the walls and roll down into the stream channel. In this section, the stream channel itself is choked with these house-sized rocks, therefore it's been naturally easier to walk along the bench above, than right along the river.

Further down canyon and just past the place where you come off the bench and begin walking along the river flood plain, look for some large boulders beside the trail. On one, at the right(west) side of the trail, are some good petroglyphs right on top. This the author calls Flat Top Rock on the map. From about that point, look up and to the east side of the river, and you can see a couple of boulders standing alone on the sandy hillside. One of these also has petroglyphs.

Another km or two below Flat Top Rock, and as you first cross over the river to the east side, are at least three more very good panels of petroglyphs, all on large boulders. One is Scorpion Rock, because of a large scorpion-like figure on it. Another is Upside Down Rock, because half the glyphs are upside down; half are right side up. The rock must have rolled down the slope half way through an etching party. Just around the corner and up the slope a ways to your left, is another good one. This might be called 10 Sheep Rock. It has, among other glyphs, 10 big horn sheep in a line. These *boulderglyphs* are some of the best the author has seen, and up to date, there is no white man graffiti on them. There's a good campsite just across the river from these boulderglyphs, but you'd have to drink river water.

The Wilson Ranch

About two kms down stream from the petroglyphs, you may see, at a point where the river turns east, some old fence post, some minor seeps, and an old mine test hole, called the Lehneer

One of two old cowboy cabins at Bush Head Tank.

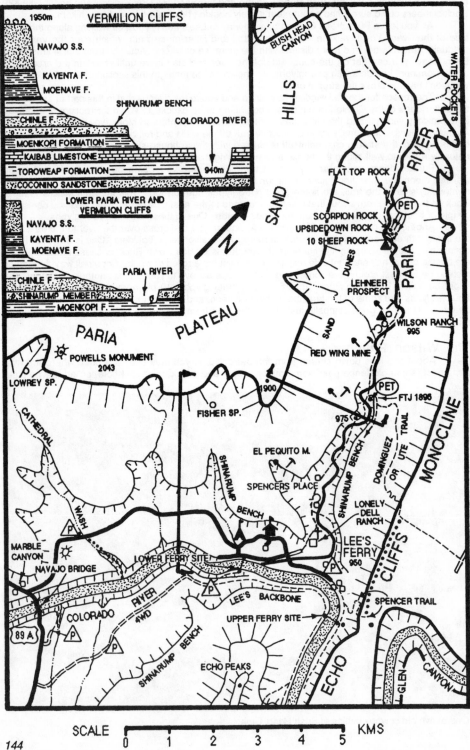

VERMILION CLIFFS

1950m

NAVAJO S.S.

KAYENTA F.
MOENAVE F.

CHINLE F.

SHINARUMP BENCH

MOENKOPI FORMATION
KAIBAB LIMESTONE
TOROWEAP FORMATION
COCONINO SANDSTONE

COLORADO RIVER

940m

LOWER PARIA RIVER AND VERMILION CLIFFS

NAVAJO S.S.

KAYENTA F.
MOENAVE F.

CHINLE F.

SHINARUMP MEMBER

MOENKOPI F.

PARIA RIVER

N

BUSH HEAD CANYON

HILLS

SAND

DUNES

PLATEAU

PARIA

RIVER

WATER POCKETS

FLAT TOP ROCK

PET

SCORPION ROCK
UPSIDEDOWN ROCK
10 SHEEP ROCK

LEHNEER PROSPECT

WILSON RANCH 995

RED WING MINE

PARIA

POWELLS MONUMENT 2043

LOWREY SP.

FISHER SP.

1900

PET

FTJ 1896

975

EL PEQUITO M.

SPENCERS PLACE

SHINARUMP BENCH

CATHEDRAL

WASH

P

SHINARUMP

BENCH

DOMINGUEZ

OR UTE TRAIL

LONELY DELL RANCH

MONOCLINE

MARBLE CANYON

NAVAJO BRIDGE

LOWER FERRY SITE

LEE'S FERRY 950

P

P

COLORADO

RIVER

4WD

89A

P

P

SHINARUMP BENCH

LEE'S BACKBONE

UPPER FERRY SITE

SPENCER TRAIL

ECHO PEAKS

ECHO

CLIFFS

GLEN CANYON

SCALE   KMS

0   1   2   3   4   5

Prospect. Another 100 or maybe 200 meters further on the right, is an old road going upon a bench. This is part of the old Wilson Ranch. Still further, you'll come to some large cottonwood trees, where the old Wilson Ranch house once stood. Its foundations can still be seen. At that point, and just behind you to the north, is a small wooden shack, built at the side of a large boulder.

The Wilson Ranch was first built by Owen Johnson and Sid Wilson in about 1918. They gathered lumber from a sawmill on the Kaibab near Jacob Lake and logs from Lee's Ferry, and hauled them in wagons about 8 kms up river to the site. With this material, they built a rather large two room cabin, in the shape of an "L". According to George W. Fisher, each room measured about 6 x 8 meters.

It was Sid Wilson who lived there and claimed the rights to the place. Throughout the years, no one ever actually owned the ranch, but each person who lived there was able to claim and sell his squatters rights. While at the ranch, Wilson ran some cattle, but worked at other jobs too. At one time he was the one who measured the water levels of the Paria and Colorado Rivers.

In 1927, Wilson left and sold his rights to Pete Nelson, but Nelson didn't actually live at the place until after about 1930. In 1933, George W. Fisher bought out Nelson, and lived there until he was drafted into the war in 1944. The BLM allowed Fisher to run about 200 head of cattle during his stay at the ranch.

It was the Fishers who installed a rough wooden floor to the house and covered it with Navajo rugs. They also built a windmill, and hooked it up to a small generator. The electricity first went to several batteries for storage, then was used for lights and a radio. They had a pump, which pumped water from the nearby spring to their house in a 10 mm(4") pipe. Water from the spring was also used to irrigate a small garden.

When the Fishers left in 1944, they sold it to a Navajo man by the name of Curly Tso, who lived mostly on the reservation. Curly had it for a number of years until his death, then his son sold it to the Graffs of Hurricane, Utah. Sometime when Curley owned the place, the house burned down. In 1974, the National Park Service bought out all the private holdings at Lee's Ferry, including the Lonely Dell Ranch. Since no one had any ownership papers on the Wilson Ranch, and it was part of the public domain, it just became part of the Paria Canyon--Vermilion Cliffs Wilderness Area.

Almost next to where the old ranch house stood is Wilson Spring. This spring has a good flow, but it seeps out of the hillside for about 30 meters, and hasn't been cared for in many years, so you can't expect to get a safe drink there. You'd do better to go to the river for water. At one time it was incased in pipe and fenced off so cattle couldn't pollute it, but now the spring is full of cow pies and its water undrinkable.

From Wilson Spring look south, and on a hill just to the west of the creek bed, can be seen a couple of tunnel entrances. This is the Red Wing Mine, which dates from the uranium boom days of the 1950's.

A km or two below the Red Wing, you'll see on your left, a faint track running up the hill to the east. This hill is actually the Shinarump Bench, and the track is the beginning of the Dominguez or Ute Trail. Actually the thing you see there is another 1950's uranium prospecting tracks, but it's in the same place as the old trail. Right where the trail begins to climb, you may see on a 1.5 meter high boulder, more petroglyphs, including a *"F.T.J. 1896"*. This glyph was etched by a member of the Johnson family who ran the ferry in the years after John D. Lee cashed in.

The Spencer Place

About 2 kms before you arrive at the Lonely Dell Ranch, is another old building, with the remains of a very old car(from the 1920's) lying there rusting away. This is what George W. Fisher calls the Spencer Place.

In the period between the two world wars, there were as many as 10 families living at Lee's Ferry, and mostly in the vicinity of the old Lonely Dell Ranch. Most of them were polygamists; some of whom had been/or were to be, excommunicated from the Mormon Church. One of these families belonged to Carling Spencer(no relation to Charles H. Spencer). It was from this man Spencer, that Fisher bought this old house or cabin in about 1940. Fisher put this house on skids, and dragged it up to the place it's at today. In those days it was simply called the Spencer Place.

Fisher fixed this place up to live in part time, when he wasn't up at the Wilson Ranch. Part of Fishers time in those days was spent working on constructing roads in the area, because he couldn't make it on ranching alone.

Less than a km below the Spencer Place is another wooden shack and corral, which are part of some of the later development of the Lonely Dell Ranch. This corral is used periodically today by cattlemen who still retain grazing rights in the area.

Just beyond this corral, and in the middle of a big flat, is the trail register, where hikers are encouraged to sign in or out of the canyon(to get a count on visitor use). From this point you can go straight ahead and visit the Lonely Dell Ranch, then walk to the car-park; or walk to the east, cross the creek for the last time, and end up at the car-park with the dozens of fishermens cars. If you take this direct route to the trailhead, you can then drive back to see the old ranch, museum and cemetery.

Scorpion Rock, with petroglyphs.

Small shelter or chicken coop at the Wilson Ranch.

The Spencer Place, and the remains of a very old car.

Part of the Lonely Dell Ranch built by Leo Weaver in about 1940. This stone building was used as part of his dude ranch operation.

Lonely Dell Ranch

The Lonely Dell Ranch really started on December 23, 1871, when John D. Lee and wives Emma and Rachel arrived at the place late in the afternoon. Early the next morning, Emma looked around and made a statement about how lonely the place was, thus the name. It was John D. Lee who was sent to the Paria to make and run a ferry for the Mormon Church. Read more of this man in *The Story of John D. Lee*.

After Lee was captured in November of 1874 in Panguitch, the church had to send help, because Emma Lee--wife #17, couldn't handle the job by herself. So they sent Warren M. Johnson in March, 1875, to take charge, and run the ferry service. At first Johnson took his first wife, then about a year later, brought his younger second wife to the ferry. After he arrived, he built a large two level house, which stood until 1926.

At the time Johnson arrived, Emma owned the ferry and had squatters rights to the Lonely Dell Ranch. So she and the Johnsons both profited from the ferry service. But in 1879, the Mormon Church bought the ferry rights from Emma for a reported $3000. She then moved south into Arizona and settled at Snowflake, where she lived until 1897.

Warren Johnson's family lived at the ranch and ran the ferry from 1875, until 1896. At that time the church decided he had completed his mission and released him. It had been a long struggle living at this desert outpost for so many years. Just one of the hardships he had to suffer through, was the loss of four of his younger children.

In May 1891, a family passing through the area traveling from Richfield, Utah, to Arizona, told Warren about a child of theirs which had gotten ill and died in Panguitch. No one thought about it then, but four days later, one of the Johnson children became ill and died. A few days later other children were struck with the same sickness. All together, four Johnson children died between May 19 and June 5, 1891. The disease was diphtheria, which three other children got, but recovered from. One large grave stone, with all their names on it, can be seen in the cemetery today just north of the Lonely Dell Ranch.

The church replaced Warren M. Johnson with a man named James Emett. Emett arrived in 1896, along with his two wives. While he ran the ferry he talked the church into building a cable across the river, to which the boat could be fastened. This made things much safer. Before that time there had been a number of accidents and drownings associated with the crossing.

While running the ferry, Emett also did a little farming and ran cattle, part of which was in the House Rock Valley to the west. Even though that area was mostly public domain and open to all, he had troubles with the Grand Canyon Cattle Company, which was run by B.F. Saunders and Charles

Lonely Dell Ranch, with Emma Lee's cabin on the right.

Dimmick. At one time in about 1907, Dimmick accused Emett of cattle stealing, and it went to court. Emett was found innocent.

But later, the GCCC got back at Emett, by buying the ferry service from the Mormon Church in August 1909. Shortly thereafter, Emett sold his land and property to this same company. At first the ferry was run by any GCCC cowboy who was staying at the Lonely Dell Ranch at the time. But things changed after less than a year, because the service was unreliable. In early 1910, the Grand Canyon Cattle Company hired the best men for the job, which were the sons of Warren M. Johnson.

Jerry Johnson arrived at the ferry in February, 1910, and was joined by brother Frank in July, and both ran the ferry. It was these men and their families who lived at the Lonely Dell Ranch and assumed responsibility for the ferry, until the Navajo Bridge opened across Marble Canyon, in January, 1929(Actually the last ferry crossing was on June 7, 1928. That's when two cars, and three men had trouble with the high waters, and the boat tipped over. All three men were drowned, and the boat floated down into Marble Canyon. Because the bridge was so near completion, the ferry wasn't replaced.)

Because of the way the ferry was handled in 1909-1910, the Coconino County became concerned about keeping this important link open. So the county bought the ferry service from the Grand Canyon Cattle Company in June 1910. They were the owners(but run by the Johnson's) until the bridge opened. In December of 1926, clothes drying near a stove caught on fire and burned down the two-story Johnson home at Lonely Dell. It had been built by Warren M Johnson in about 1877 and had stayed in the Johnson family until 1926.

When the bridge opened there wasn't so much traffic in or around Lee's Ferry, but several polygamist families lived there during the 1930's. The Church owned the ranch for a time, then the polygamist families of Lebaron, Spencer and Johnson bought it. At a later time the Church got it back, but then Leo and Hazel Weaver bought the Lonely Dell Ranch in the late 1930's and attempted, unsuccessfully, to run a dude ranch and raise Anglo-Arabian horses. While there, they constructed the long stone building which sits just to the northeast of the cabin refuted to have been built by John D. Lee himself, and which is now called Emma Lee's Cabin.

The Weavers stayed at Lonely Dell until the early 1940's, then moved out. Essy Bowers owned the ranch for a couple of years, then in 1943 sold it to a man name C. A. Griffin, a stockman from Flagstaff, who had a big herd of cattle on the Navajo Lands to the east. It was Griffin who first attempted to pump water out of the Paria onto farm land, rather than to build dams, which always washed out. In later years the LDS Church once again held title to the ranch.

In about 1963, Lee's Ferry was included into the Glen Canyon National Recreational Area, but the 65 hectares(160 acres) of private land remained private.

The grave stone of four Johnson children in the Lonely Dell Cemetery.

The Upper Ferry Terminal at Lee's Ferry. Beyond is the western side. You can still see some ruins there today (Arizona State Library).

Oxen pulling a wagon up the dugway to the Upper Ferry Terminal(Arizona State Library).

The home Warren Johnson built at Lonely Dell in 1877. It burned down in 1926(New Mexico State Archives).

The muddy Paria entering the clear and cold Colorado.

In 1974, the private property of the Lonely Dell Ranch was bought by the U. S. Government and National Park Service. Lonely Dell Ranch was put on the National Register of Historic Places in 1978.

For a lot more detailed information about Lee's Ferry, read *Desert River Crossing*, by Rusho and Crampton; *Lee's Ferry*, by Measeles; and *John D. Lee* and *Mountain Meadows Massacre*, both by Juanita Brooks.

Rusting hulks of old trucks at the Lonely Dell Ranch.

A cellar, the only cool place at Lonely Dell during the summer heat.

The Dugway road to the Upper Ferry Terminal.

Ruins at the Upper Ferry Terminal.

Dominguez and Spencer Trails

Location and Access Both trails featured on this map are at or near Lee's Ferry. The Dominguez Trail(sometimes called the Ute or Indian Trail), was used by Navajos and Utes in the early days, when they would cross the Colorado River to raid each others territory. In 1776, Spanish padres Dominguez and Escalante, used this same trail when searching out the Ute Ford(later called the Crossing of the Fathers) to cross the Colorado River on their historic journey. The Spencer Trail was built by the big-time promoter, Charles H. Spencer, partly as a short-cut from Lee's Ferry to coal fields to the north, and partly to impress investors who were given the grand tour of his mining operations at the Ferry. Park at one of two parking lots at or near the end of the road at Lee's Ferry.

Trail or Route Conditions To hike the Dominguez Trail, walk from the Paria R. Trailhead up stream along the lower Paria for about 5 kms. You'll see the trail running up a minor slope and through a break in the Shinarump to the right. It's where you see a small boulder with some petroglyphs. Once on the bench, you can see the approximate route, but not the trail. From that point you could walk straight up the steep slope to the top of the sand bench, and turn south; or you could follow an old mining track south a ways, then scramble up to the sand bench. Once on the sand bench, head south and to an obvious break in the steep cliffs. As you near the top of the sand bench next to the cliffy upper wall, you should pick up the real trail as it zig zags up the slope, then turns south, at or near the ridge crest. The Spencer Trail begins just east of Lee's Fort, an old boiler, and the sunken remains of the old steam boat, *Charles H. Spencer*. You'll have to look for it, but you can see the trail beginning as you near the site. Once on the trail, you can follow it easily as it zig zags up the steep cliffs. If you'd like to do both trails together on the same hike, then walk up the Dominguez, follow the ridge crest south, then head down the Spencer. It would be easier to locate the top of the Spencer when coming from the north, than to locate the top of the Dominguez coming from the south.

Elevations Lee's Ferry, 950 meters; top of Spencer, 1450; Dominguez Pass, 1500 meters.

Hike Length and Time Needed Spencer Trail is about 2.5 kms, one way, and will take about 2-3 hours round-trip. From the trailhead to Dominguez Pass is about 8 kms, one way. Most could do this in about half a day, returning the same way. If a loop-hike is made using both trails together, it's close to 16 kms. With the roughness of the ridge-top, it'll likely take the average person all of one day to make the hike.

Water Take it with you. There is water available at each trailhead.

Map USGS or BLM map Glen Canyon Dam(1:100,000), or Lee's Ferry(1:62,500).

Main Attraction Historic trails in an historic region, and fine views from the top.

Ideal Time to Hike Spring or fall. Summers are hot as hell, winters not too bad.

Hiking Boots Dry weather boots, except for the walk along the Paria R., to the Dominguez Trail.

Author's Experience He has climbed both trails, but has not made the full loop-hike.

One has a fine view of Lee's Ferry from the top of the Dominguez Trail.

154

MAP 28, DOMINGUEZ AND SPENCER TRAILS

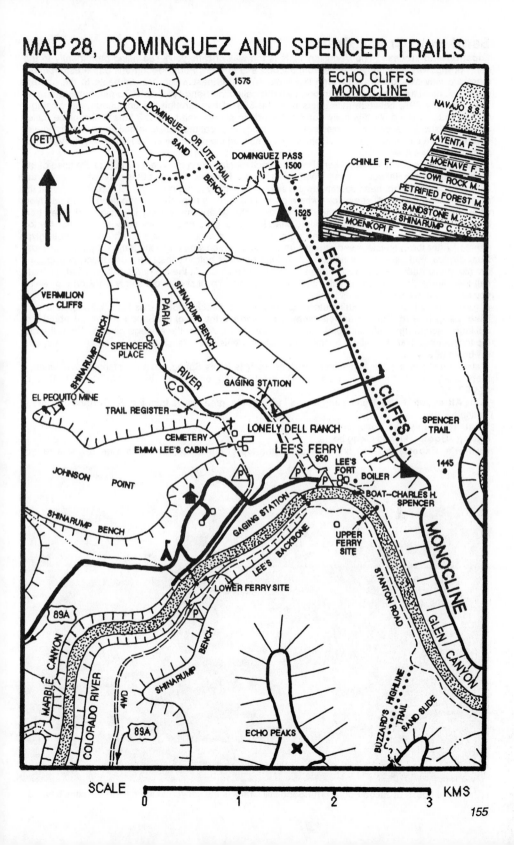

SCALE

0   1   2   3   KMS

Sand Hill Crack Trail

Location and Access The Vermilion Cliffs is the wall of cliffs you'll see rising prominently to the north of Highway 89A, as you drive from Jacob Lake to Lee's Ferry. Along this entire escarpment, there are only two routes up through the Navajo Wall, at least which are climbable to the average person. One of these routes is up through what is called the Sand Hill Crack. To get there, turn north from Highway 89A, between mile posts 557 and 558. Drive through the unlocked gate, closing it behind you. Then drive this fairly good(but sandy in places) road about 3 kms to the place called Jacob Pools(which is on a small piece of private land). Park at the old stone building or ranch house, which is on the old Honeymoon Trail, and which is now on the boundary to the Paria Canyon--Vermilion Cliffs Wilderness Area.

Trail or Route Conditions There is an old track running north from Jacob Pools to the base of the cliffs not far below Hancock Spring. Walk to very near Hancock Spring, but instead of turning to the left to reach the spring, head straight up the slope and slightly to the northeast. There is no trail at that point, but further up you'll see places where a lot of deer or big horn sheep have used the route. Now what you want to do is head for the cliffs on the right, where the walking is easier and away from dropoffs along the drainage bottom. Also, head for the single pinnacle near the wall and near the top of the route. At the pinnacle, you can go around it right or left, but to the left are two petroglyph panels. After the pinnacle, head straight up the gully, which was originally formed by a minor fault. Near the top, you see on your right, another long panel of petroglyphs. Because these petroglyphs are along this route, we can surmise this is an old Indian trail. At the top of the cliffs is what ranchers call the Sand Hills. Geologists call it the Paria Plateau. You'll see an old sandy track on top, which you can use to walk to the Jarvis Ranch and Pinnacle Valley.

Elevations Jacob Pools, 1589 meters; top of Sand Hill Crack, 2066; Jarvis Ranch, 2025 meters.

Hike Length and Time Needed From Jacob Pools to the top of the Sand Hill Crack is about 3 or 3.5 kms. Round-trip could be 3 or 4 hours, or about half a day for the average person. From the rim-top to the Jarvis Ranch is about 5 kms. From Jacob Pools to the ranch and back, about 17 kms, and will be an all day hike.

Water You can fill a water bottle at Hancock or Rachels Pools Spring, but none at the Jarvis Ranch.

Map USGS or BLM maps Glen Canyon Dam(1:100,000), or Emmett Wash or MF-1475 A, B, C or D(1:62,500).

Main Attraction Petroglyphs along an old Indian route, great views from the rim, historic Jacob and Rachels Pools.

Ideal Time to Hike Spring or fall.

Hiking Boots Rugged hiking boots.

Author's Experience His first trip, just to the top of the Crack, was less than 3 hours round-

The stone house at Jacob Pools. The Sand Hill Crack is the canyon to the right in the cliffs beyond.

MAP 29, SAND HILL CRACK TRAIL

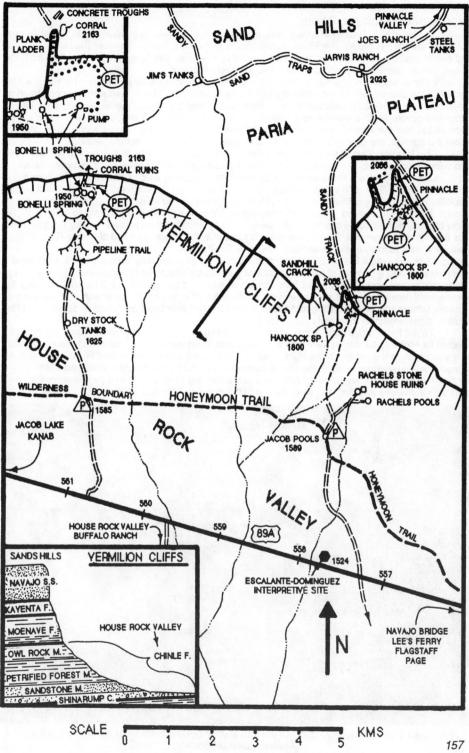

SAND HILLS

PINNACLE VALLEY

JOES RANCH

STEEL TANKS

JARVIS RANCH

2025

PLATEAU

PARIA

JIM'S TANKS

SAND TRAPS

SANDY

SAND

CONCRETE TROUGHS

CORRAL 2163

PLANK LADDER

PET

1950

PUMP

BONELLI SPRING

TROUGHS 2163

CORRAL RUINS

1950

BONELLI SPRING

PET

PIPELINE TRAIL

VERMILION

CLIFFS

DRY STOCK TANKS 1625

2088

PINNACLE

PET

HANCOCK SP. 1800

SANDY TRACK

SANDHILL CRACK

2088

PET

PINNACLE

HANCOCK SP. 1800

HOUSE

WILDERNESS BOUNDARY

P 1585

HONEYMOON TRAIL

RACHELS STONE HOUSE RUINS

RACHELS POOLS

JACOB LAKE KANAB

ROCK

JACOB POOLS 1589

P

561

560

559

89A

558

1524

557

VALLEY

HONEYMOON TRAIL

HOUSE ROCK VALLEY BUFFALO RANCH

ESCALANTE-DOMINGUEZ INTERPRETIVE SITE

N

NAVAJO BRIDGE LEE'S FERRY FLAGSTAFF PAGE

VERMILION CLIFFS

SANDS HILLS

NAVAJO S.S.

KAYENTA F.

MOENAVE F.

OWL ROCK M.

PETRIFIED FOREST M.

SANDSTONE M.

SHINARUMP C.

HOUSE ROCK VALLEY

CHINLE F.

SCALE

0 1 2 3 4 5 KMS

trip(which included lost time for route-finding). Second trip was to the steel tanks east of Jarvis Ranch, and back, in about 6.5 hours.

Jacob and Rachels Pools

In May, 1872, Rachel Woolsey, one of John D. Lee's wives, was moved into the area now called by various people as The Pools, Jacob Pools, or Rachels Pools. Her first shelter was a mud and willow shack, not much better than what the Indians lived in. On June 2, a group of men from the Powell Survey came through the area, and fotographed the scene.

Later in the fall of the same year, John D. started building a better house. He hired a man named Elisha Everett to help out, since the home was to be made of rock. It was mostly completed on Christmas Day of 1872. It measured 9 x 11 meters, and had two doors, two bedrooms, a kitchen, a parlor and covered with a wooden roof. Nearby was a cellar. The ruins of this rock house can still be seen just above the western-most spring called here Rachels Springs. In the same area, and just below the springs, are numerous rock walls, apparently used as fences to hold livestock.

This location was 32 kms from Lee's Ferry, and was set up to be a way-station for Mormons who were heading south to settle in Arizona. It was one days travel between these two water holes.

One day by wagon to the west, was another site of interest, which goes back to the spring and summer of 1873. This is the resting place or way-station along the Honeymoon Trail called *House Rock Spring*(the route got this name later, after many Mormons had settled in Arizona, and after the St. George Temple had opened. After that, that many young Mormon couples made the trip to southern Utah along this trail or road to be married in the temple. They usually return home in a very dreamy state, thus the name, *Honeymoon Trail*). This place is located in the upper west end of House Rock Valley. It was one days journey from House Rock Spring to The Pools.

At or just below House Rock Spring are a number of interesting sites. There's a grave of a young woman and a number of ruins of fences and old stone structures of some kind. If you walk up the drainage east about 400 meters from the grave site, and up against the cliffs and all along the lower cliffs themselves, you'll see dozens of *emigrantglyphs,* or signatures of some of the earliest Mormon settlers who were heading to Arizona in the very first year Lee's Ferry was in operation. Most of these signatures date from early June, 1873.

To get there, drive north from House Rock on Highway 89A, on the House Rock Valley Road heading for Highway 89. Using the *Fredonia* metric map, drive about 6 to 7 kms north from the highway until you come to the ranch on the right or east. This belongs to a man named Rich, but a woman named Adeline Halverson lives in the pickup camper there(1987), and runs the small operation. Seek her permission before going further. Adeline is just about the toughest old bird you'll ever meet. And don't step the wrong way with her, as she's one of the last *Pistol-Packen' Moma's* of the west!

Rachel Lee's shack, on June 2, 1872. In the foto is John D. Lee, two small sons and a daughter.

(Arizona Historical Society).

Once you talk to her, and get permission to drive right through her place, you'll be heading north about 1.5 kms to or near the end of the road. Those in cars can only drive part way, then they must walk the last little ways, as the upper part of this road is very rutted. Remember, you'll have to do some climbing to reach most of the pioneer signatures.

Back at The Pools. At the end of the sandy road coming up from the highway, is what is called Jacob Pools. It's about 1 or 1.5 kms southwest of Rachels Pools. At that location, are some corrals and a rather well build stone building. Information as to when this structure was built is scarce, but most of the old timers around believe it was built in the early part of this century when the Grand Canyon Cattle Company ran cows throughout the entire House Rock Valley. In those days, B. F. Saunders was running things. It was likely built just after the turn of the century, and may have been both a way-station and a ranch house, on the road running on to Lee's Ferry. Be aware that this place is privately owned, and is an active ranch, although no one lives there. The man who owns it now is a Mr. Graff from Hurricane, Utah.

History of the Sand Hills Ranches

Sandwiched in between two hikes to the top of the Vermilion Cliffs, is a short history of some of the ranching activity which has taken place over the last century on top of the Paria Plateau. Local stockmen have always known the place as the Sand Hills.

In the region between the Buckskin Gulch, the Lower Paria River Gorge, the Vermilion Cliffs, and The Cockscomb(sometimes known as East Kaibab Monocline), is the Paria Plateau. For the most part this is a moderately high and very isolated corner of the Colorado Plateau, which is extremely difficult to get to. The local name, the Sand Hills, tells the whole story.

The top layer of the Plateau, for the most part, is made up of sand, which has eroded away from the Navajo Sandstone Formation. This is primarily the reason it's almost a no mans land. It's not only difficult for a man to walk around on, but it's also difficult for horses; to say nothing of the problems people have in getting around in a 2WD car or pickup. This is 4WD county!

Actually, you can sometimes get around up there with a normal vehicle, but you have to do it when the sand is either wet or frozen, or both. Another method some of the old timers used, was to let about half the air out of their tires, which put more rubber to the road. As they left the sandy parts, they'd have to hand pump the tires back up again. For those without a 4WD vehicle, it's highly recommended you forego any visits to this little hideaway in the desert.

Joes Ranch

Joes Ranch was one of the first ranches to be settled in the country, but because of the difficulty in travel, the isolation, and the total lack of any live running water or permanent springs, it

The ruins of Rachels second stone house just above one of the springs, just north of Jacob Pools.

THE SAND HILLS—PARIA PLATEAU RANCHES

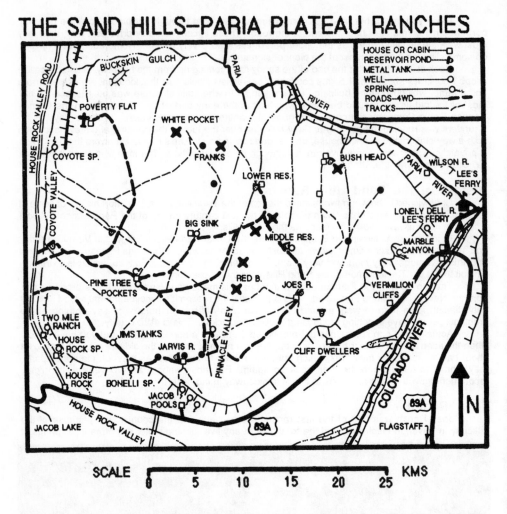

Legend (box):
HOUSE OR CABIN———□
RESERVOIR POND———◖
METAL TANK———●
WELL———○
SPRING———○ᵥᵥ
ROADS—4WD———
TRACKS———

BUCKSKIN GULCH
PARIA
RIVER
POVERTY FLAT
WHITE POCKET
COYOTE SP.
FRANKS
LOWER RES.
BUSH HEAD
WILSON R.
LEE'S FERRY
HOUSE ROCK VALLEY ROAD
COYOTE VALLEY
PARIA RIVER
LONELY DELL R.
LEE'S FERRY
BIG SINK
MIDDLE RES.
MARBLE CANYON
PINE TREE POCKETS
RED B.
JOES R.
VERMILION CLIFFS
TWO MILE RANCH
HOUSE ROCK SP.
JIMS TANKS
JARVIS R.
PINNACLE VALLEY
CLIFF DWELLERS
COLORADO RIVER
HOUSE ROCK
BONELLI SP.
JACOB POOLS
89A
JACOB LAKE
HOUSE ROCK VALLEY
89A
FLAGSTAFF
N

SCALE 0 5 10 15 20 25 KMS

has always been a kind of hardship post. The only real springs around are Two Mile and Coyote, located at the western edge of the Sand Hills, and in House Rock and Coyote Valleys.

The ranch get it's name from Joe Hamblin, one of three sons of Jacob Hamblin. Walt, Ben and Joe were their names. According to Dunk Findlay, Joe Hamblin had worked with John W. Powell on one or more of his surveying partys(but not the early river expeditions), had been in the area before, and returned later to build the ranch. The year he went there was 1884, and since it was the only ranch of any kind in the Sand Hills, it was always just called "The Ranch", by local cowboys and sheepmen. Joe Hamblin had cattle, as well as goats and sheep.

No one alive today knows how long the Hamblins had the ranch and the squatters rights, or in what year it was sold to Johnny Adams, the second owner. Dunk Findlay seems to think it was in 1926 Johnny Adams bought most of the squatters rights in the Sand Hills from Nephi, son of Joe Hamblin. Johnny Adams' herds grazed most of the Paria Plateau range for many years. He's the one who devised the scheme to pump Paria River water up onto the lower or northern end of the Sand Hills. It was in the winter, spring and summer of 1939, that he and his workers cut the trail, laid down the pipe and installed the pump. However, because the drought ended just at that time, he never used the pump. Read all about that scheme under the Lower Paria River Gorge, and the *Adams Trail*.

It was at the time Johnny Adams was at the Ranch in 1934, that the Taylor Grazing Act was passed. In the years after this legislation, the Sand Hills was broken up into two or more different grazing areas, much to the consternation of the old timers. Other cattlemen got in on the western part of the Plateau range, and fences were erected. This changed the whole setup. Just ask any old time cowpoke!

Quoting now from a letter written to the author by Dunk Findlay, *"The only water Adams had was at the Ranch, the Middle, and the Lower Reservoir. There was no other water on the Plateau. Other people had to graze when there was snow on the ground. That's when the sheep and goats were in there. Most times it served only as a winter range other than around the Ranch. That is why it was not over grazed"*.

After many years of riding the Sand Hills range, and after having developed many of the stock tanks and ponds seen there today, Adams finally sold out. According to Dunk Findlay, Adams was somehow forced out, partly because of the Depression. The man in the middle was Jim Jennings, who foreclosed on Adams, but then A.T. Spence, a cattleman from Phoenix, ended up with much of the Plateau range in 1941. Spence built cement cores to some of the little stock ponds and brought in several metal tanks, although he only had it a short time. In 1944, Dunks father, Merle Findlay bought out Spence.

Dunk remembers, *"The Ranch was a permanent ranch used year-round by Hamblin, Adams, Spence, and the Findlays. There were several times the cattle had to be moved away on account of lack of water, that's why we drilled a well. After the Taylor Grazing Act there was no place to move; before that cattle were moved any place there was water on the public domain. No one owned anything then."*

Once the Findlays had it, Dunk and his brother Lynn did most of the work around the range. After Merle died in 1960, these two brothers split up the range; Dunk to the west; Lynn to the east, and the area around Joes Ranch house. Actually, throughout the years each man or family who ran cattle or sheep on the range, did some work on it. One bit of work which had little to do with ranching was the building of an airstrip at Poverty Flat, located just east of the Coyote Buttes. The man who built that and the only one to ever use it was Rowd Sanders.

Developing a water system was of primary concern. As stated before, there was never any live running water on the whole plateau. The range itself was excellent, due to the altitude, which ranged up to about 2200 meters. But because of the water problem, it was virtually impossible to take or have enough livestock there to over graze the place.

In the early 1950's, the Findlays drilled a well in the lower northern end of Pinnacle Valley, with a drilling rig they had bought. A bit later they sold the drilling equipment to Fay Hamblin and Floyd Maddox, who drilled the second well at Poverty Flats. The third well was drilled by Roy Woolly at Pine Tree Pockets(locally it's just called *Pines*), which for many years was a kind of ranch headquarters for the western part of the Sand Hills range. Throughout the years, and since about 1950, eight wells in all have been drilled.

The Findlays were heavily involved with the development of a number of slickrock water basins

Emigrantglyphs, on the cliff face above House Rock Spring.

or rainwater stock tanks, and they installed a number of metal tanks for water storage, etc. Dunk and a man named John Rich also installed 4 or 5 pipelines, which ran water from several of the wells, down hill to the north(by gravity) to other water storage tanks, so the cattle could be spread out on the range more evenly.

In 1962, just after the Findlay brothers had divided the range, Lynn sold his part of the range to John Rich, who called his outfit the Vermilion Cliffs Cattle Company. This was the part with the old Joes Ranch house on it. Dunk held onto his part until March 1, 1980. That's when he sold his grazing rights to the Ramsay Cattle Company, along with about 500 head of cattle. Dunk recalls the times and said, *"We had 80 acres(about 30 hectares) of patented land at the Ranch. Adams got this after the survey; before that it was just a squatters claim. We had around 16 or 18 state sections leased, on the Ranch."*

Shortly thereafter and still in 1980, the Two Mile Corporation took over, and obtained all grazing rights to the entire Plateau. Actually, the name Two Mile Corp. came about after they bought out Dunk Findlay and the Vermilion Cliffs Cattle Co. Today, it's run by this one outfit, with about 1500 head of cattle. They run cattle on the Sand Hills year-round, with their winter range being in the north, just south of the Buckskin Gulch and the Lower Paria River Canyon; their summer range in the higher and cooler south half of the Plateau.

The ranch headquarters is located at Two Mile Spring, at the head of House Rock Valley. In 1987, the company had only three full-time employees. The ranch foreman J. R. Jones of Kanab, cowboy Mitch Kester, and the waterman LeRoy Rollins, who lives at Pines most of the time with his wife, and makes frequent sorties out to the various wells to pump water to storage tanks, and keeps a eye on the range and the facilities. In the spring and fall they hire part-time help.

Jarvis Ranch

The Jarvis Ranch came about and had something to do with the grazing rights changes back in the mid to late 1930's, as a result of the Taylor Grazing Act. Dunk Findlay says *"Jarvis never got a permit to run cattle--he was not there in the priority period. Jarvis was working for Walt Hamblin(Fay's dad) when the BLM finally gave him a small allotment of three or four sections."* According to Dunk Findlay, they never had many cows, maybe 15 or so, but they built a rather fine ranch house there anyway, which is just north of the Sand Hill Crack. That was in 1935.

The Jarvis house isn't just a line cabin or a bunk house, but instead a nice home. It's still used today by cowhands when they're in the area working cattle. It's painted white, has five good sized rooms and a propane gas lighting and cooking system. There's even a refrigerator, which is run on propane gas. Water was collected in the same way water is collected in most parts of Australia; by the use of roof rain gutters and down-pipes, which funnel rainwater down into a cistern below the house.

The ranch house at Pine Tree Pockets, in the western part of the Sand Hills.

There's water in the that tank today, but it may or may not be drinkable.

When A. T. Spence got a hold of the ranch in 1941, he(according to Dunk Findlay) used the *"house for his main headquarters. He had built the house at the lower reservoir, and it and the house at the Ranch were used as line cabins. Spence added two more rooms to the original Jarvis house. He said not to spoil a good thing he put hard wood floors in then too."*

After Dunk and his brother divided the range, Dunk made this house his headquarters.

It was Dunk Findlay who put the propane lights and refrigerator in the house, in or around 1962. He installed the metal tank next to the barn, and pumped water to it from the Pinnacle Valley Well. This was done by a small portable gasoline engine.

The Jarvis place also has a good barn which is still used today. Behind the barn are a couple of other metal water tanks, and just to the west, a dam which could catch a lot of water, if and when big storms ever occurred. Near the house is a fruit cellar for storage. The whole ranch site is situated in a part of the Sand Hills called the *Dark Forest*. It's a pinyon and cedar covered region, with very healthy and rather large trees.

Joes Ranch, a site used since 1884. Slickrock tank left, ranch house right.

Bonelli Spring Indian Trail

Location and Access The hike featured here is one of two going up through the Vermilion Cliffs to the top of the Sand Hills, or if you prefer, the Paria Plateau. To get to Bonelli Spring and an old Indian trail, drive along Highway 89A, the road running between Kanab and Jacob Lake, to Lee's Ferry and Navajo Bridge. Between mile posts 560 and 561, turn north. At first the road parallels the highway running along the fenceline to the west, then you open and close a gate. The road then turns east for a ways, again paralleling the fence. Finally it turns north as indicated on the map. After nearly two kms, you come to a junction. This is the old Honeymoon Trail and the wilderness boundary. Park there.

Trail or Route Conditions From the Honeymoon Trailhead, walk along the sandy track to and past some old and now dry stock tanks. Further along the road ends at the foothills of the Vermilion Cliffs, then you have to follow the plastic hose or pipeline which was installed years ago to bring water from Bonelli Spring down to the tanks. It's broken now, and the water comes only part way down, but you still use it as a trail guide. Remember, your target is Bonelli Spring straight ahead, about half way up the cliffs, where you can see some green and three trees(from far away it appears only as brush). At the base of the Navajo, you'll see the three parts to Bonelli Spring. From the eastern spring with the half-buried pump, go due north up the steep talus slope to the Navajo wall, with petroglyphs. Then turn west and make your way to the next wall, which is the bottom part of the Ladder Crack(author's name). Scramble up this narrow defile. Nearly at the top you'll pass a ladder made from a plank. Just above that is the rim, with several stone corrals and three cement water troughs.

Elevations From 1585 at the Honeymoon Trail to 2163 meters on top.

Hike Length and Time Needed It's about 6 kms from the trailhead to the rim-top, but in places it's steep and slow and go. It'll take about 4 or 5 hours for the average person to do the hike round-trip, or about half a day.

Water Take some with you, as it's always warm on the lower slope of the cliff face. There should always be good water to drink in the open square box part of Bonelli Spring(which cattle cannot get to).

Map USGS or BLM maps Glen Canyon Dam(1:100,000), or Emmett Wash or MF-1475 A, B, C, or D(1:62,500).

Main Attraction An invigorating climb, fine views from the top, an old pumping station by an early-day Basque sheepman, and a wall of petroglyphs, indicating this was an old Indian trail.

Ideal Time to Hike Spring or fall, but also in winter warm spells. Summers are very hot at the base of the cliffs.

Hiking Boots Rugged hiking boots.

Author's Experience The author climbed to the cement water troughs and returned, in about 3.5 hours.

Bonelli Spring

The spring which now carries the name Bonelli, was unknown and unused until this century. Sometime after about 1916, Alex Cram, who owned a large ranch in House Rock Valley, began to develop this minor seep. He blasted a square hole in the bottom of the Navajo cliff, in order to increase the flow and to better capture the water. Sometime later, he traded the squatters water rights to a man named W. J. Mackelprange for two horses.

Later, and in the early 1930's, this Basque sheepman named Bonelli from Flagstaff, Arizona, came into the country and bought the water rights to the spring. Prior to this time it may have been called Death Tanks, because they didn't put out much water(one source says the name Death Tanks referred to another little seep just down hill from Bonelli Spring?).

Bonelli brought sheep with him, but needed a water hole. After considering his options, he bought pumping equipment and pipe. He then set to work to construct a pumping station, pipeline, and troughs, in order to pump the water from the spring up to the rim-top and to several cement troughs. His operation was successful, and he had water on the rim for about four years. His sheep were on top of the Sand Hills during the summers, and down under the cliffs and in House Rock Valley during the winters.

But in 1936, the newly established BLM ran him out. Bonelli had apparently not been in the area long enough before the Taylor Grazing Act was passed in 1934, and wasn't eligible for a permit to run livestock in that part of the country. So after four apparently successful years, he had to abandon the operation.

At the site today, you will see a half buried pump, some hoses and an old rusty wheelbarrow at the most easterly of the three spring sites. The middle spring is the only one which has a flow large enough to get a drink out of today. It's shaped like a huge square tomb, which was blasted out of the lower Navajo. At the third seep or wet spot to the west, three cottonwood trees grow.

Just above the pump and next to the big wall, are odds and ends of the operation. On the rim-top, are three cement troughs, still in very good condition. Also right on the rim, are several stone

MAP 30, BONELLI SPRING INDIAN TRAIL

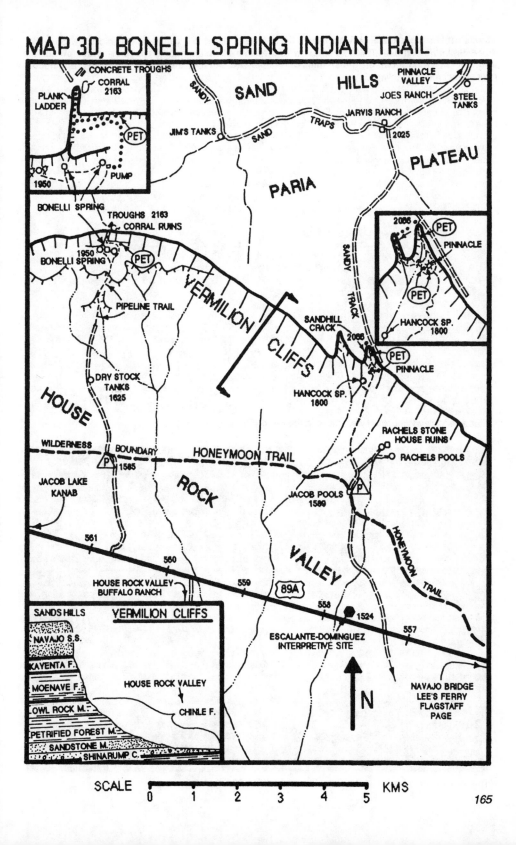

corrals--at least the author thought they were corrals. All the old timers said these were originally some kind of Indian ruins, but perhaps they had been modified to handle sheep or horses by Bonelli and others. There are many Indian ruins on the plateau, but they are mostly pit houses, and not as noticeable as cliff dwellings.

Pinnacle Valley Well. First well drilled in the Sand Hills.

The Jarvis Ranch house looks almost new. Built in 1935.

Bonelli Spring. Bonelli blasted out part of the wall to get at the water.

Bonelli's Pump sits half buried in sand.

The Story of John D. Lee and Mountain Meadows Massacre

A book on the Paria River cannot be written without including the life story of John D. Lee. Nearly all Utah and Arizona residents know of him, but people from other parts of the country or the world perhaps haven't. This chapter is a brief summery of the history of Lee's life, and is intended to let the reader understand events leading up to the Mountain Meadows Massacre and why John D. Lee was sent to the lower Paria to establish Lee's Ferry. The author used, with permission, a book by Juanita Brooks, *John Doyle Lee, Zealot-Pioneer Builder-Scapegoat*, as the primary source for this chapter.

John D. Lee was born on September 12, 1812, in Kaskaskia, the capital of the territory of Illinois. He lived in Illinois throughout his youth, and at age 16, left home to fend for himself. His first job was a mail rider, which lasted for 6 months. He had various jobs in the several years until he got married, which was on July 24, 1833, at age 21. He married Aggatha Ann Woolsey, the first of 19 women he was to marry during his lifetime.

It wasn't long after this that he became a convert to the Mormon Church. During the first 5 years of marriage, he was a missionary part of the time and had various jobs. It was in 1838, that he became part of the group of Mormons who left Nauvoo, Illinois, and migrated to Far West, Missouri. This according to Mormon doctrine was *Zion*. As you might imagine, when the Mormons rode into town, proclaiming this was their Zion, the reception wasn't too cheery. They had problems, and later had to leave.

Because Lee was a very religious man and totally devoted to the church, he became one of the leaders, and hob-nobbed with the big boys at the top. Because he was so good at things like farming, building homes, and working with machinery, he was called on throughout his life to go out and help settle new colonies. He was never a high ranking church authority, but was a major cog in the church settlement program for about 30 years.

From Far West, Missouri, the Mormons headed north in the direction of Council Bluffs, Iowa, and Winter Quarters near the present day Omaha, Nebraska. Since it was to take a couple of years to get all the Mormons to Utah, they needed to set up several temporary towns enroute, in preparation for the long haul to the Great Basin. John D. was much involved in building these temporary settlements.

While in Iowa, the Mormons were called upon to send a battalion of soldiers to California. This they did, but then President Brigham Young asked Lee to follow the group to Santa Fe, and collect the soldiers pay and bring it back to their families, who needed it a lot more than did the soldiers.

Because Lee was needed in the Winter Quarters area, he was not chosen to accompany the first Pioneer Party to Utah in 1847. He instead followed in June of 1848. Upon arriving in Utah and the Salt Lake Valley, he immediately began to built a home for his wives. At the time he had left Nauvoo, he had 10 wives; Brigham Young 17.

In one of the church meetings on December 2, 1850, in which Lee attended, Brigham Young mentioned they were going to send a group of volunteers south to what is now Cedar City, and establish an Iron Mission. There was a group of Englishmen who had the knowledge and skills to do the iron work, but they needed support in the venture After the meeting, Young told Lee, that when he had asked for volunteers, he meant Lee. Young said, *"If we are to establish an iron industry there, we must have a solid base of farming to help support it."*

The next thing Lee knew, he was leader of a small group heading for southern Utah in the dead of winter. On December 11, 1850, the wagons rolled out. Lee took two of his wives. As one can imagine, it wasn't an easy journey. There were no roads, just a trail, and snow was deep at times. They arrived at the present day site of Parowan, in February of 1851. Parowan was the first of several new settlements Lee was to set up in the next 20 years.

Things went well for Lee and the church for several years, but in 1857 things began to change. News of an impending crisis came to the leaders of the church on July 24, 1857. This was the 10th anniversary of the landing of the Pioneer Party in the Salt Lake Valley. They had a big celebration up Little Cottonwood Canyon, southeast of Salt Lake City. During the afternoon festival, two riders dragged into the canyon with news that, *"all mail routes to the east were counciled, and an army was enroute to put down the rebellion in Utah."* There of course was no rebellion, unless you consider it a rebellion for all the church big-wigs to have too many wives.

With this news, the church leaders and the people became a little hysterical, and there was a call to arms. Since the Mormons had been run out of several of the eastern states, they gradually became better prepared, in a military sense. The church in Utah was organized not only into wards and stakes(religious groupings), but also in the event of an emergence, such as trouble with the

JOHN D. LEE'S COUNTRY

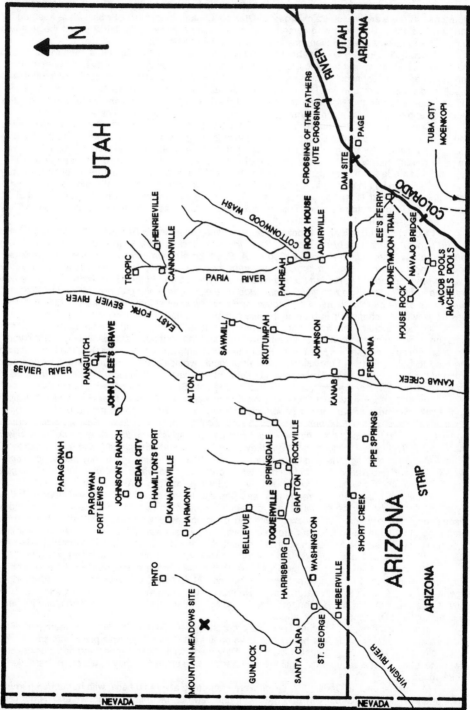

Adapted from Juanita Brooks book—JOHN DOYLE LEE—Zealot, Pioneer Builder, Scapegoat

Indians, they were organized into military companies and battalions as well. So preparations began, and in a way, Utah was almost in a state of marshal law.

In many ways things went on as normal. But there began to be a very deep distrust for all non-Mormons. There were wagon trains crossing Utah all summer long, most of which were heading for northern California. But those who came late in the season usually went to California via the southern route. This route was along present day Highway 91 and Interstate I5.

Since Salt Lake City was at about the half way point between the populated eastern states and the coast, it was an important place to stop, rest and restock supplies. However, because of the impending arrival of Johnson's Army, the leadership of the church issued orders to all settlements not to sell food stuffs to any gentiles. The church leaders also went to great pains to convince the various Indian leaders to join the Mormons to help repel the US Army. The Indians were told to join the Mormons and help fight Johnson's Army, or that army would kill all the Indians as well.

One can imagine the hardships this must have created for those unlucky travelers who were caught up in the middle of this Utah problem. One of these groups of wagons was called the *Fancher Train*. It was a loosely knit group of several independent elements who had joined forces in Utah to travel in greater safety. The leader was Charles Fancher. He had crossed the country in 1855, selected and made arrangements to buy a large tract of land, and returned in 1856 to bring his family and friends to join him in settling in California. They had a reported $4000 in gold coins, a large herd of cattle and horses and 11 well stocked wagons. There were 11 families, with 29 children; a total of 65 people. Traveling with the Fancher Train was a group of horsemen with their supply wagons. They called themselves the *"Missouri Wildcats."*

Quoting now from Juanita Brooks book, *"This group all arrived in Salt Lake City on August 3 and 4, and mindful of the fate of the Donner Party in 1846, decided to take the southern route. They followed a few days behind President George A. Smith on his journey south ordering the people to keep their grain and not to sell a kernel to any gentiles. The Fancher Train was well-to-do; they had cash to pay or goods to trade, but no one would sell. The attitude of the Mormons all along the way was one of belligerence and hostility, aggravated by the attitude of the group of "Missouri Wildcats", who spoke of the Mormon leaders with scorn, and boasted of what they had done in Missouri."* This was the way things shaped up in Utah, in the late summer and early fall of 1857.

As the Fancher Train moved south through the state, one thing after another aggravated the situation. The Mormons wouldn't sell them anything, and the emigrant train, especially the Wildcats, did or said things, to upset the Mormons. Finally the emigrants arrived in Cedar City, the last place on the road to California to get provisions. Since the locals wouldn't sell them anything, it's been said some of the Missourians helped themselves to some of the gardens. The local Mormon police tried to arrest some members of the party, but were just laughed at. So things continued to get worse.

"In the Sunday service at Cedar City on September 6, 1857, Stake President Isaac C. Haight spoke with bitterness of the coming of Johnston's Army, which he called an armed mob, and made pointed reference to the Fancher Train which had left only the day before. Following the regular service, a special pristhood meeting(men only) was called at which time the problems connected with the Fancher Train were discussed. Were they mice or men that they should take such treatment? Should they let such braggarts come into their midst and boast of the indignities they had heaped upon them in Missouri and Nauvoo? Should a man who would boast that he had the gun that "shot the guts out of Old Joe Smith" go unpunished?" Such was the feelings of the people in Cedar City.

Finally at the meeting a resolution was passed, to the effect that *"We will deal with this situation now, so that our hands will be free to meet the army when it comes."* But then there was more discussion. Some wanted to do away with the emigrants who were the chief offenders; others preferring to let them all go and prepare themselves for the real war with Johnson's Army. Another resolution was presented to the effect that they should send a rider to Brigham Young seeking his council. It was passed, and they sent a rider(who returned late, and after the big event was over).

Still later a third resolution was passed, that of sending a messenger to John D. Lee at Harmony asking him to come and manage the Indians. At that time, Lee was an "Indian Farmer", or agent, and was second in command. Jacob Hamblin was the agent, but since he was in Salt Lake City, it was Lee who was called upon for advice. Lee had gotten on well with the Indians, and it's been said he spoke at least some of their language.

In the meantime, the Fancher Train had proceeded to a high meadow in the northern part of the Pine Valley Mountains. This was barely one days drive from Cedar City. This place was called, and would always be known as, Mountain Meadows. They made camp near a spring and had plans to stay awhile to let their cattle recuperate, until the weather became cooler, so they could cross the desert in more comfort.

Meanwhile back in Cedar City, things were happening at a rapid pace, with horsemen hurrying back and forth between Cedar City and Parowan, and between Mountains Meadows and Cedar City. At that time, there were three men who were the most important leaders in the area. William H. Dame from Parowan, was appointed colonel commanding all the Iron County military. Isaac C. Haight was the Stake President, who lived in Cedar City. And John D. Lee, who was the acting Indian agent, in the absence of Jacob Hamblin.

The Mormons were successful in getting the Indians on their side at this time. It seems both groups had no need for these emigrants, but for different reasons. A band of Indians had followed the Fancher Train south from Holden in central Utah, and had hoped the Mormons would help them attack the wagon train, and steal the cattle and other needed items. This same band of Indians joined others in the area of Cedar City, and had asked Lee to join them for an attack at Mountain Meadows. It seems that Lee had gone back home at Harmony to set things in order, and promised the Indians he would return on Tuesday, September 8.

But the Indians were ready for action, and knowing they and the Mormons were on the same side, made a pre-dawn attack on the emigrant camp on the morning of September 8. The emigrants were caught by surprise, but were well equipped and repulsed the attack. Later, Lee stated that 7 white men were killed, along with several Indians.

When Lee joined the Indians on Wednesday the 9th, they were upset and excited. They insisted that the Mormons join forces and make another attack immediately. Lee wanted to go south and get help from the Santa Clara and Washington settlements, but about that time a group of whites from those communities came, and they decided to send a messager to Cedar City and to Haight. He left at 2 P.M..

In Cedar City, the bell rang out for the militia to gather. A statement was read that some of the emigrants had been killed, and they wanted volunteers to help bury them. But according to Brooks story, a Nephi Johnson indicated a deception on the part of Isaac C. Haight. Johnson suggested that Haight had said something to the effect that, *"Lee had suggested that they withdraw and let the emigrants go, and Haight sent word to Lee to clean up the dirty job he had started, and that he had sent out a company of men with shovels to bury the dead, but they would find something else to do when they got there."*

During the night of Wednesday the 9th, the military unit from Cedar City arrived at the Fancher camp. But at the same time, three emigrants had left camp under the cover of darkness and had gone to Cedar City to ask for help from the Mormons. As they neared their destination, and while watering their horses in a small stream, they were attacked by members of the Mormon Militia. One man was killed, and the other two scattered. It was later learned the remaining two men were killed by Indians at the Santa Clara crossing, and on down the Virgin River a ways. Again in Cedar City, the Mormon leaders gathered for council. It was decided to send John M. Higbee to Parowan in the night for advice from William. H. Dame.

Higbee returned the next day, Thursday the 10th, and delivered the message from Colonel Dame to Lee near the emigrant camp. The message indicated he should compromise with the Indians, allowing them to take all the cattle, then allow the emigrants to go. But then in the same message, he indicated if things couldn't be worked out, *"save women and children at all hazards"*. Lee was in a predicament, and with conflicting orders. What to do? Years later Lee insisted, *"that he had written orders to the effect that the emigrants must be decoyed from their shelter and all who were old enough to testify slain"*. Later in court, Klingensmith testified that *"Lee's instructions came through Higbee from Dame at Parowan"*. Klingensmith must have overheard the conversation between Higbee and Lee, *"Orders is from me to you that they are to be decoyed out and disarmed, in any manner, the best way you can."*

So there Lee was faced with a decision. The Indians and Mormons both wanted revenge. The Mormons felt they had rights to some kind of blood atonement, for the way the Missourians had treated them back in Far West. The Indians also wanted some of the cattle; and the Mormons knew the Fancher Party was a wealthy group and had all those wagons and household goods. Greed must have been a factor in what was to be the final decision.

Lee along with a William Bateman, carried a white flag into the emigrant camp and negotiations began. Lee told them that if those guilty men would come back to Cedar City and face charges, they would all be given protection. But to do this, they would all have to show good faith, and give up their arms. This the emigrants did, but ever since, people have wondered why they would give up their weapons? The day was Friday, September 11, 1857.

After the agreement was reached, all rifles and other weapons of the emigrants were loaded into one wagon, along with all children(17 in all) under the age of about 10 years. This wagon moved out in front. Then a second wagon was loaded up with the emigrants who had been wounded in the previous Indian attack. Some said there were two men and a women; others stated there were some older children in it as well.

Following the second wagon, were the women and older children walking in an unorganized group. Following them were the emigrant men, walking in single file, each escorted by an armed member of the Mormon Militia.

The idea was to save the small children, but have no witnesses. The first wagon went way out in front, so they could not see anything. Lee walked just in front of the second wagon, which was at least half a km behind the first. When the first wagon was just out of sight, somewhere near the marching men the signal was given, *"Do your duty. Instantly all the guns were fired, and at the same moment the Indians leaped from their ambush and fell upon the women and [older] children. The teamsters with Lee, and their assistants killed the ones in the second wagon and threw the bodies out into the brush beside the road."* The plan was carried out to perfection, and was over with in a hurry. It was estimated 120 people were murdered.

Just after the massacre, the Indians stripped the bodies for clothing and valuables. Then Lee issued the order to let the Indians have what they had, but no more. They were to return to their camp where some beef was ready for supper. The men of the Mormon Militia then heard several speeches by Higbee, Lee and others, to the effect that they had defended Zion and their families well, and that they had carried out *"Gods wishes"*. The men were then ordered to stay the night and bury the bodys before leaving for home the next morning.

The wagon with the rifles and children moved on up the valley to the Hamblin Ranch where Rachel(Mrs. Lee no. 6) was living. She cared for the children and put them to bed. Lee came later, and during the night, Haight and Dame came to the ranch. The next morning, they all went to the Meadows and saw the ghastly site. The bodies were still being buried, in the same holes the emigrants had dug previously to protect themselves from the Indians.

Then there was an argument between Haight and Dame about the orders given. The orders were confusing alright! This is the way Juanita Brooks stated part of the argument in her book.

"We must report this to President Young," Dame was saying.

"How will you report it?" Haight wanted to know.

"I will report it just as it is, a full report of everything."

"And will you say that it was done under your orders?"

"No"

Haight was furious with rage.

"You know that you issued the orders to wipe out this company, and you cannot deny it! You had better not try to deny it! If you think you can shift the blame for this onto me, you're fooled! You'll stand up to your orders like a man, or I'll send you to Hell cross lots."

About this time Lee interrupted to tell them it was done now and that we should go on from here. When the men finished with the burial, they gathered at the nearby spring and washed up. Then they all gathered around and Isaac C. Haight addressed the men. They were to say nothing to anyone and block it from their minds. Then they gathered in a circle, with Dame, Haight, Lee and Higbee at the four corners, and pledged they would never discuss it with anyone. Finally everybody left, including Lee, who wouldn't return to Mountain Meadows until the day he died.

A few days later they all met in Cedar City, and since John D. Lee was closest to Brigham Young, he was assigned to travel to Salt Lake City with the news of the killings. He left September 20, and arrived on the 29th. He reported the event to Brigham Young, which was written down by Wilford Woodruff. At that time John D. reported it as a job done by Indians.

The emigrant children were put into different homes, and cared for. As far as they were concerned, it was Lee and the other Mormons who had saved *them* from the Indians--the Indians being the ones who killed their parents. The wagons and other contraband were placed in the Bishops warehouse to be given out to needy Mormon families.

In the months and years after the massacre everything went about as normal, given the circumstances. Lee took wife number 17, a 22 year old girl from England, on January 7, 1858, when he was age 46. This was Emma Bachellor, the one who would accompany John D. to the bottom end of the Paria River in 1871, to set up a home at Lonely Dell, later to be known as Lee's Ferry.

Later on Lee was involved in setting up the Cotton Mission on the Santa Clara River, near present day St. George. While in the area, John D. stopped in Washington(just east of St. George), and bought some land, including a house in town, where he soon had two of his wives. And speaking of wives, still later in 1858, Lee seemed to be courting a young girl named Mary Ann. He apparently proposed to her, but she refused. She even wrote two letters of protest to Brigham Young. In January of 1859, he mentions in his diary, that she wanted instead to marry John D.'s oldest son, which she did.

It was in August of 1858, and after peace had finally been arranged between the Mormons, and Johnson's Army and the Federal Government, that a George A. Smith and James McKnight, both church officials, went to southern Utah, and made out two reports on the massacre. The reports didn't amount to much, because everyone remained silent.

In the mean time, Lee lived at the fort in Harmony most of the time, where he had about four of his wives. Since there were lots of travelers passing through Utah at that time, he took advantage of the times, and set up a *caravansary,* to accommodate the wagon trains. Harmony was in the right place. They got their business in the fall and early winter. For a couple of years after the massacre, things went well for John D., but then things gradually changed.

According to Juanita Brooks, in *"April [1859] word came that Judge Cradlebaugh was on his way to investigate the Mountain Meadows Massacre, accompanied by a force of two hundred soldiers. Jacob Forney, the new Indian agent, came ahead to gather up the surviving children that they might be returned to their relatives in the east. They took Charley Fancher from the Lee household, although he was reluctant to go, and in line with the policy followed by all who had kept any of the children, Lee made out a bill to the government for his care."* With this, the beginning of the federal investigation, John D. Lee went into hiding, and was on the run for most of the next 18 years.

Judge Cradlebaugh and his group arrived at Cedar City in May of 1859, and set up camp in a big field about 2.5 kms from town. His assignment was to *"collect and bury the bones of the slain emigrants, and to arrest as many participants in the massacre as he could catch.*

The judge brought warrants for the arrest of a half-dozen of the leaders, and he wanted information concerning others who were involved. He found the local people reluctant to talk, for none knew anything for a certainty, and if they did, they would not betray their brethren into the hands of the enemies of the church. A few did want to talk, but feared the consequences. At least one participant came to the judge secretly late at night and told the story of that tragic day, giving some names and details, and begging for protection and anonymity. The burden of the crime was more than he could bare."

Because many of the participants were either in hiding or had gone to different states, the judge was unable to make a single arrest. There was eventually a reward of $5000 offered for the arrests of Dame, Haight, Higbee, Klingensmith, or Lee. But no one ever turned any of them in. After spending a month in the area, the judge gave up the search, and returned to Salt Lake City.

In the years of 1860 and 1861, things went well for John D. He had two homes; one in Harmony, the other in Washington, and nearly all the wives he wanted. Both places were opened as caravansaries and taverns, and business was good.

Right at the end of 1861, there was a stormy period which lasted from December 25 until the beginning of February, 1862. This was a disaster for everyone in the region, and especially for John D. Lee and his families. The fort they had been living in at Harmony was made of mud, and it literally melted away. During the first part of February, they were all trying to move out of the Harmony Fort, and into some new dwellings at nearby New Harmony. But before they could all get moved, the roof of part of the building caved in, killing two of Lee's children.

Down at Washington, things were just as bad. John D. had just recently erected a molasses mill, which had earned him good money earlier the previous fall. It had been swept away, and the machinery buried in sand and mud. Because of this 40 day storm, it took Lee about four full years to get back to the financial position he had before the storm.

In 1866, John D. finally was on his feet again, and doing better. In that year he took his last wife, Ann Gordge, who was from Australia and just 18 years of age. Later in the same year, he lost his first bride, Aggatha, who died of a lingering illness. This was a sad occasion for Lee, and seemed to be a sort of beginning of the end for him.

It was about this time that the people of Harmony began giving him untold misery. *"Whisperings about the massacre continued; the stories became more numerous and highly colored. In many ways his neighbors showed their disapproval--by turning their cattle into his grain fields, interfering with his water ditches, and making snide remarks to his wives or children. He always attended church, he was first to fill the assignment made by Brigham Young to get out poles for the new telegraph line, he was prompt in paying his tithes. At Parowan and Cedar City, he was often called upon to speak at church, and at Kanarra he was held in high esteem. Perhaps his very industry, his driving use of his family and hired help, his shrewd trading, his ability to amass property and to live well made his neighbors all the more critical of him."*

In the fall of 1867, he made a trip to Salt Lake City, with a herd of goats belonging to Brigham Young, his adopted father. When he returned in December, he found his estate falling apart. Without Aggatha, and with his two oldest sons away on missions, there had not been the same enthusiasm as had been the case earlier.

It was in the late 1860's, that trouble began to brew for Brigham Young and the church leadership, and since John D. was always a strong supporter of the President, he began to feel the pinch as well. In 1868, there appeared in Salt Lake City a new publication, the *Utah Magazine*. This as it turned out, was a voice for those who were becoming discontented with the church leaders and their policies. Some of the unrest resulted in a number of excommunications in the northern part of the state. Many of these people wanted to be members of the church, but were simply critical of the leaders: thus they were booted from the church.

The original complaint against Young, was that he got too involved with their financial dealings, but later they condemned Young for condoning murder. During this period, there were some

A rare foto of John D. Lee, taken in 1875, at the age of 63.
(Arizona Historical Society).

mysterious deaths in Salt Lake City. Dr. K. Robinson was assassinated in 1866; John V. Long former secretary of Brigham Young, was found dead in a ditch in April, 1869; and Newton Brassfield was murdered on one of the main streets in April 1866. These men were part of the group generally known as the *Godbeites*, after it's chief spokesman, W. S. Godbe.

One of their worst complaints was that Brigham Young gave public recognition to men who had participated in the Mountain Meadows Massacre. The *Utah Reporter*, published in Corrine(in the middle of northern Utah's gentile country), *"ran a series of open letters addressed to Brigham Young, demanding that those guilty of that outrage be brought to justice. The articles were signed by "Argus," who claimed to have lived in Southern Utah and learned the facts from some of the participants."*

During the winter of 1869-70, Lee defended Brigham Young by visiting many communities in southern Utah, to as far north as Fillmore, and by making speeches in Youngs behalf.

In September of 1870, Brigham Young led a small group of men to explore areas east of the southern Utah settlements. Lee joined this group, and was assigned the jobs of locating the best route(as they were heading into new country without roads), and making camps along the way. William H. Dame was in charge of preparing meals.

Their route went through Panguitch, south to Roundy's Station(now called Alton), then down Johnson Canyon. At some point along the way, Brigham Young had a private talk with John D. He was urging Lee to move. Quoting again from Juanita Brooks book, Young said, *"I should like to see you enjoy peace for your remaining years. Gather your wives and children around you, select some fertile valley, and settle out here."*

Along the way they met, and were joined by John W. Powell. The party traveled east from the bottom of Johnson Canyon to the Paria River. They got to as far as the Peter Shurtz settlement of Rock House, and found a small patch of green corn and some squash. Lee was not impressed and made the statement, *"I wouldn't bring a wife of mine to such a place as this."* After the visit to the Paria River, they came to the conclusion there was little there to attract future settlements, and left. On their return, the party surveyed and laid out the site of Kanab, to be settled by some of those same men(one group had already tried to settle Kanab in about 1865, but had left on account of the Black Hawk War). After the lots were numbered, the settlers each drew a number from a hat to signify his home site.

Brigham Young wanted Levi Stewart to set up a sawmill, so as to make lumber to build Kanab. Levi stated he had worked with Lee before, and would like to have him as a partner again. John D. reluctantly said yes, out of sheer obedience to the church leader. The group then returned to the southwest Utah settlements, via Pipe Springs.

Lee immediately set to work to sell his property and settle accounts. He put up for sale and sold his holdings in Harmony, but kept the Washington property, leaving several of his wives there, until he could get back later. He started the trip to Kanab with wife Rachel and her children, 4 wagons, and 60 head of stock. The route taken was up through the canyon via Rockville, then over the plateau, and finally down to Kanab. It took 10 days to travel the very rough 150 kms.

From Kanab they moved on to the east to what is today Johnson, about 16 kms east of Kanab. They then went north up Johnson Canyon to a moderately high grassy valley now called Skutumpah. This was to be their new home, but they were to temporarily live a little above Skutumpah where the sawmill was to be located. It was about 15 kms to a site on Mill Creek where they built a camp. This was late October, 1870, that he first built a cabin for Rachel.

When the engineer and surveyor arrived, they quickly set up the sawmill, but almost immediately it broke down. Someone would have to return to Parowan for the repair. With Rachel safe in the new cabin, Lee left to get another part of his family. He met a second family group at Pipe Springs--it was one of his son-in-laws and several children, along with 3 wagons and 40 head of cattle. At that time, in mid-November, 1870, he was handed a letter which had to do with his excommunication from the Mormon Church! It was dated October 8, 1870. But at that time he mentioned it to no one.

The group went straight for Skutumpah, set up a tent for a temporary home, and went up canyon to Rachels cabin. Help from Kanab finally came in early December, and they worked fast and furious, because of the coming winter. They worked so fast the wagons coming and going from Kanab couldn't keep up. On December 13, news came of a disastrous fire in Kanab; the fort had burned to the ground, and 6 members of the bishops family were killed. That ended the winter logging operation in the upper Skutumpah.

John D. left Rachel and the others, and made a trip back to Washington, where he had a cold reception from his wives and children. The next morning he went on to St. George to speak about his excommunication to Brigham Young, who was in his usual winter home. He pleaded his case saying that he had been loyal to him and the church, and that now he was being singled out to bare the guilt of the massacre. He also stated that the decision to attack the Fancher Train was a mutual agreement between the highest church leaders in the area. After the meeting, Lee left and returned to Harmony, where he was invited to speak in church on Christmas Day, 1870.

Upon his return to Washington, he received a note from a high church official, stating, *"If you will consult your own safety & that of others, you will not press yourself nor an investigation on others at this time least you cause others to become accessory with you & thereby force them to inform upon you or to suffer. Our advice is, Trust no one. Make yourself scarce & keep out of the way."*

After these kind words, and on January 2, 1871, John D. set out once again for Skutumpah, this time with Caroline(Mrs. Lee no. 4), and her 8 children. It took them 15 days to reach Skutumpah this time, because of the heavy snows and poor travel conditions. Upon arriving, the whole family set to work cutting trees and sawing lumber, in order to build and finish a large home for Caroline. When that was completed, they dismantled Rachels cabin, and reconstructed it again down at Skutumpah. By the first of March, they began the third house, but about that time, Emma, wife 17, came up in an empty wagon. She was distressed, trying to decide which way to go--whether to stay with John D. or leave him for someone else. She decided to stay with her husband.

Soon after this and as the sawmill was roaring full blast, Lee sold his interest in the site. With all the lumber he needed, he continued to work at Skutumpah, until he had finished four homes, each with wood floors, shingle roofs, and glass windows. In June he made another quick trip back to St.

George to attend to business. While there he worked to sell out his Washington property, and bring the rest of his family to Skutumpah.

Enroute, and in Johnson Canyon, he met Isaac C. Haight, who was also in hiding. Together they went to Kanab, but waited outside town, while Jacob Hamblin and John Mangum brought them food, and more importantly, news. The news this time was that the federal authorities were clamping down on polygamists, and they were advised to transfer all their property to their wives. Lee set out to do this at once, naming Rachel Woolsey, Polly Young, Lavina Young, Sarah Caroline Williams, and Emma Bachellor as recipients. All of his other wives had deserted him by that time. But the real heart breaking news was that he was *ordered by the church* to take one or two of his wives, and move down to the Colorado River at the mouth of the Paria River. That was in August of 1871.

This was John D. Lee's greatest decision. But he would obey. He had 5 wives; which two would he take? He was heading for some wild country, and would end up in the middle of the desert and be in country controlled by Navajos. Problems would be immense, but even though he had been excommunicated, he still had the secret backing of Brigham Young. After all, it was Young who had ordered him to go.

The first wagons rolled out of Skutumpah in November of 1871. It consisted of 3 wagons, 57 head of loose stock, and Caroline and her family. At their first camp in lower Johnson Canyon, Jacob Hamblin joined them. He knew the country better than anyone, and he and Lee had a long visit on the best routes to take. It was decided to have the wagons head down what was to be called later the *Honeymoon Trail*, while John D. and 14 year old son Ralph, would take the cattle to the Paria, and drive them straight down the canyon.

At the Paria, and perhaps it was at Rock House, he met Tom Adair and John Mangum, and was happy to have these two men join him. The going down river was more difficult than anyone had anticipated. *"They spent 8 days on the trail, much of the time in water. Two days and one night they traveled without stopping because there was no place to camp When their provisions were gone, they shot a cow that had become hopelessly mired in quicksand and cut steaks from her, living for the next few days on a meat diet."*

Upon arriving at the mouth of the Paria, they found no wagons. Brigham Young had sent out a work crew to build a road, but neither the work crew nor Caroline had reached the Paria. Adair and Mangum return to Pahreah via the Ute, or Dominguez Trail, while Lee and Ralph headed around the Vermilion Cliffs in hoping to meet their wagons enroute. Because it was unfamiliar country, John D. got lost himself, and ended up returning all the way to Skutumpah.

The next day John D. and wives Emma and Rachel, and several wagons, headed out to find Caroline. Below Johnson, they found one broken down wagon, and knew she had gone on to Kanab instead. She had changed her mind, and had decided to go and stay there the winter and to give birth to another child, rather than go into the wilds alone.

Back on the road again, the new contingent made it to the Paria on December 23, 1871. The next morning, when they all had a chance to look around, Emma said, *"oh what a lonely dell"*. And for ever more the name of the small settlement or ranch at the mouth of the Paria is named Lonely Dell.

The first thing to do at the Paria River, was to build shelters. The first shelter was a dugout up against the hill, made of rock, and would later be a cellar. The second was a rock building with a door and two windows. When the two shelters were finished, John D. rode up canyon a ways to check on his cows. When he returned, he found Emma with a new baby, which was born on January 17, 1872. They named her Francis Dell Lee.

The very next day, January 18, they saw Navajos across the river. They wanted Lee to help them across. John D. and Rachel first had to work on one of Powells boats, which had been left there in 1869 on his first Colorado River Expedition. After repairs, Lee and Rachel made the first ferry crossings. It took three trips to get all the Navajos across. They later made some trades, Lee and the families ended up with blankets, cloth for making clothing, and other needed items. The Navajos got two horses, a mule and a colt.

In April, 1872, a group of miners came into camp, and the Lee family helped accommodate them. Emma cooked, in exchange for their help in building up the place, and for some needed tools. It was at about this time it was decided they would build two places; one at Lonely Dell, the other at the springs known as The Pools, or Jacob Pools. They were 32 kms apart, but the pools would be a welcome stop for travelers who were making the long journey from Utah to Arizona. It must be remembered that Lee was sent there to set up a ferry and provide food, shelter and accommodations for travelers. The church at that time was expanding into Arizona, and Lee, although officially excommunicated, was instrumental in this expansion.

By early May 1872, Rachel moved. The first shelter at Jacob Pools was of mud and willows, and didn't give much shelter. On June 2, a group of engineers of the Powell Survey, passed through the area and photographed Rachels first little willow shack. This was a different group than the river expedition.

In was on July 13, that Major Powell and his men landed at the Dell on their second Colorado River Expedition, and were out of about everything except coffee and flour. Emma cooked for them and both groups shared what they had; the expedition members enjoying Emmas vegetables.

John D. was in and out of Lonely Dell and the Pools. He had to help built shelters, and go north to get supplies from the settlements. This was all fine, because as long as he was on the move, it would be difficult for the authorities to track him down. At that time the federal people were always after the "cohabs", and a bit later they were after Lee especially for the Mountain Meadows Massacre.

On December 16, 1872, a man named Heath came with a load of lumber for the purpose of building a ferry boat. While he and a crew were in the process of building this boat, John D. was at Rachels place making a fine home. He had hired Elisha Everett to help do the rock work, for there was no other material there in which to build. This new home was mostly completed on Christmas Day. It measured about 9 x 11 meters, had two doors, two bedrooms, a kitchen, a parlor and covered with a wooden roof. Nearby was a cellar. If you're there today, you can still see the remains of this 1872 dwelling, just above one of the springs just north of Jacob Pools. Most people call this place at the springs Rachels Pools, as opposed to Jacob Pools, which is about a km to the south, southwest of her home site. At least the USGS maps put Jacob Pools out in the valley a ways, and on what was likely the actual route of the Honeymoon Trail. See the hiking *Map 29, Sand Hill Crack,* for the location.

The ferry boat was completed by January 11, 1873. Counting the Lee family and work crews, there were 22 people in all at the ferry site, and they all took a ride in the new boat, which they called *"The Colorado."* A little later, on February 1, a group of 12 men used the ferry for the first time. They were heading south to explore the Little Colorado River country for the church. From February 1873 until about November 1874, John D. Lee was the ferryman at what then and now is called Lee's Ferry. The first company of settlers on their way south arrived in April, 1873. They were charged $3.00 a wagon, and $.75 a horse for the service. For those who didn't have the money, payment was made in food or supplies, so things worked out well for the new ferryman.

In the summer of 1873, a message came from Kanab, that a unit of 600 soldiers were on their way to Lee's Ferry to set up a permanent camp. This spooked Lee pretty bad, so he swam a horse across the Colorado River, and headed south to Moenkopi. While at Moenkopi, John D. met Jacob Hamblin and later they made a deal for a swap. They agreed to trade places; Lee's or rather, Rachels home and holding at the Pools, for Jacob's claim at Moenave, near Moenkopi. In the fall, Jacob would help Rachel make the move down into Arizona. As it turned out, the story of the soldiers coming to Lee's Ferry wasn't true.

For about a year, things went well and uneventful. Then came the fall of 1874. A Sheriff W. Stokes had warrants for the arrest of eight men who were the leaders of, and had participated in, the Mountain Meadows Massacre. By then the name of John D. Lee was at the top of the list. The Sheriff was familiar with Lee's habits, and was aware of where his wives lived. At the time, Caroline lived in Panguitch. It was on a visit to this wife, that Lee was captured. This was in November of 1874. They took John D. to Beaver in a wagon. He was there in jail from November 10, until July 23, 1875, when the trial began.

At the trial the indictment included William H. Dame, Isaac C. Haight, John D. Lee, John M. Higbee, George Adair Jr., Elliot Wilden, Samuel Jukes, P.K. Smith, and William Stewart. Because all the participants had sworn to secrecy, no one would testify except Philip Klingensmith. As it turned out Klingensmiths testimony was rather accurate and precise. The defense made the point, *"that while Lee was present and might have participated, he was there by command of his superiors, both military and ecclesiastical, whose orders in this time of military rule would be death to disobey. While they admitted the facts of the massacre and all its unbelievable horror, they placed the responsibility upon the Mormon Church and its doctrine that men were justified in 'avenging the blood of the Prophets' as a part of their duty to God."*

In the end it was a hung jury. The eight Mormons being for acquittal, the four gentiles for conviction. This meant another trial. This time Lee would wait in Salt Lake City. But this meant hardship for his families. Rachel left Moenkopi for the settlements; Caroline is in Panguitch; Lavina and Polly remained at Skutumpah; and Emma stayed on at Lonely Dell. As for the ferry, the church sent Warren Johnson and his family to Lonely Dell to take charge of that operation.

John D. Lee left Beaver on August 9, 1875, and was taken to Salt Lake City. He was kept in the state penitentiary, which at that time was in the area of present day Trolley Square. As one might expect, Lee was a model prisoner, and ended up with many privileges. At various times he taught other inmates how to read, was a kind of doctor, and was even entrusted with some keys to the place. For some reason, he was released on May 11, 1876, on $15,000 bail. He was to appear in Beaver in about four months for the trial.

In the period before the second trial, John D. traveled around visiting his various wives and families. He was at Lonely Dell in August. His sons had tried to talk him in to going to Mexico to escape, but by doing so he had insisted, he would be admitting guilt. In late August of 1876, he left the ferry and headed for Skutumpah, via the Ute or Dominguez Trail. Just after he left, a messenger came via the Honeymoon Trail, with word from the church authorities counciling Lee to jump bond and leave the country. The church would assume the full responsibility to the bondsmen. But he missed the message.

In Beaver, the second trial began in September, 1876. For some reason the atmosphere of this trial was totally different. Twelve jurors were selected, all in good standing in the church. During the trial, seven witnesses were called, again all good members. They were all now willing to talk about the whole thing. The witnesses told of John D. Lee's participation, and that of Klingensmiths, but he had immunity since he had turned state's evidence. They also spoke of how Haight and Higbee were involved, but they were both dead at the time of the trial. It was very clear that something had been worked out so that everyone pointed the fickled finger at John D. Lee. To resolve the issue, perhaps it was necessary to have a scapegoat, so that life for the church could go on as normal? Lee never did take the stand or defend himself. He sat through the trial in silence.

At the end and when the jury came back, the statement read; *"Guilty of murder in the first degree."* Lee immediately wrote to Emma for more money, to take the case to a higher court. His attorney, W.W. Bishop felt he had been sold out. Meanwhile two petitions were circulated in southern Utah, asking that the Governor give him clemency. The Governor said he would consider the move, if Lee would speak up and tell all, and make an attempt to implicate those above him. But Lee remained silent, and there was no clemency.

So on March 23, 1877, John D. Lee was taken back to Mountain Meadows, the scene of the crime. There were a number of people there, including James Fennimore, the fotographer, who Lee had known and made friends with at Lonely Dell. A foto of the place shows John D. sitting on his coffin. Lee was blindfolded, but his hands were free, when the five shots were fired. He fell back in the coffin, and it was closed and loaded into a wagon. He was then carried to Panguitch and buried in the cemetery just east of town, and south of the highway.

To get to Mountain Meadows today, drive west out of Cedar City toward Beryl Junction and Enterprise, then south on the road toward St. George. About half way between Enterprise and Central, and off the paved road a ways to the west, is the monument. From St. George, drive north toward Veyo and Central, and in the direction of Enterprise. The monument reads:

Mountain Meadows
A FAVORITE RECRUITING PLACE ON THE OLD SPANISH TRAIL
In this vicinity, September 7-11, 1857, occurred one of the most lamentable tragedies in the annals of the West. A company of about 140 Arkansas and Missouri emigrants led by Captain Charles Fancher, enroute to California, was attacked by white men and Indians. All but 17, being small children, were killed. John D. Lee, who confessed participation as leader, was legally executed here March 23, 1877. Most of the emigrants were buried in their own defense pits.

Mountain Meadows, March 23, 1877. John D. Lee sits on his coffin awaiting execution by a firing squad(Library of Congress).

The grave of John D. Lee in Panguitch, Utah.

The monument to the Fancher Party at Mountain Meadows.

History of Ghost towns of the Paria River

One of the best sources for the history of the first settlements in the upper Paria River drainage, which today is called Bryce Valley, is *The Geology and Geography of the Paunsaugunt Region-Utah*, by Herbert E. Gregory. The following account is adapted from his early geologic explorations and travels throughout the region.

In the 1860's and 1870's, there were surveying parties traveling across parts of the upper Paria and Escalante Rivers, and they noted several large valleys which looked promising for settlement. One of the surveyors was A. H. Thompson, who said the upper valley of the Paria River was well watered, had good soil, and a good climate. He also noted there were coal beds near at hand and good range for grazing livestock.

Because of such reports, the first pioneer white settlers in the upper Paria Valley were the families of David O. Littlefield and Orley D. Bliss, who on December 24, 1874, laid out farms near the junction of the Paria River and Henrieville Creek. With the arrival of eight additional families in 1875, the original log houses at the base of the red cliffs grew into a small settlement called Cliff Town. Since those earliest days, the name gradually changed to **Clifton**. The old Clifton town site is located about 3 kms due south of Cannonville.

One of the new settlers, Ebenezer Bryce, who is said to have come to Clifton in 1875 or 1876, decided they needed more room and looked for another location to farm. He selected a site farther upstream in what was known then as Henderson Valley. This new settlement was first called **New Clifton**. Bryce, in association with a Daniel Goulding and others(1878-80), constructed an irrigation canal 11 kms long, planted orchards, and took up livestock raising.

It was during this time, and when Eb Bryce ran cattle into the canyons to the west, that Bryce Canyon received it's name. An early day saying around the region, which Bryce is given credit for, makes a statement about herding cattle into the area which is now called Bryce Canyon National Park. That statement was, *"It's a hell of a place to lose a cow".*

Bryce left New Clifton in 1880, and Goulding in 1883, selling their holdings to Isaac H. Losee, Orville S. Cox, and Ephraim Cottall, who renamed the site **Losee**. The Losee town site is located about 3 kms due east of the present day town of Tropic, in what is now called East Valley.

Three years after settlement, the people in the little town of Clifton, found themselves too closely hemmed in between the cliffs and the bank of the Paria, and their farm lands in the process of destruction by flood water. So in 1877 Clifton was abandoned, with most of its settlers going to a new site about 3 kms north. This new town was named **Cannonville,** after a high dignitary of the Mormon Church, George Q. Cannon.

Only seven graves are in the Losee Cemetery.

BRYCE VALLEY GHOST TOWNS—MINES
GEORGETOWN, CLIFTON, LOSEE

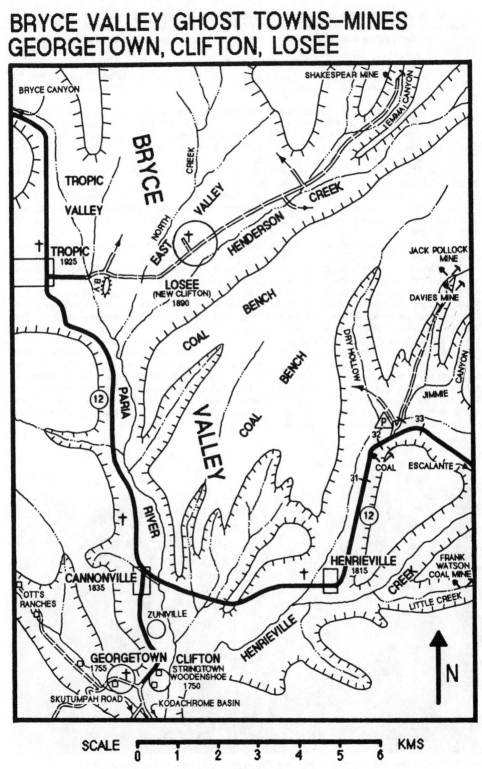

SHAKESPEAR MINE

BRYCE CANYON

BRYCE

TROPIC

VALLEY

NORTH CREEK

EAST VALLEY

HENDERSON CREEK

EMMA CANYON

TROPIC
1925

B.V.

LOSEE
(NEW CLIFTON)
1890

BENCH

COAL BENCH

JACK POLLOCK MINE

DAVIES MINE

DRY HOLLOW

CANYON

JIMMIE

P
33
32

12

PARIA

COAL BENCH

VALLEY

COAL

31

COAL

ESCALANTE

RIVER

HENRIEVILLE
1815

FRANK WATSON COAL MINE

12

CANNONVILLE
1835

HENRIEVILLE

CREEK

LITTLE CREEK

OTT'S RANCHES

ZUNIVILLE

N

GEORGETOWN
1755

CLIFTON
STRINGTOWN
WOODENSHOE
1750

SKUTUMPAH ROAD

KODACHROME BASIN

SCALE 0 1 2 3 4 5 6 KMS

While some of those who abandoned Clifton went to and settled Cannonville, three families headed east instead, and settled on Henrieville Creek, about 8 kms east of Cannonville. This is present day **Henrieville**, named in honor of James Henrie, president of the Panguitch Stake of the LDS Church.

In 1886, Seth Johnson, Joseph and Eleazer Asay, Richard C. Pinney, and other stockmen took up lands on lower Yellow Creek about 5 kms southwest of Cannonville and thus became the pioneer settlers of **Georgetown.** Like Cannonville, this new ranching community, was named after George Q. Cannon.

It was during the early 1880's, Cannonville became center of prosperity for the entire valley. That's where the Mormon Church Ward was set up, and it's where the most prosperous cattlemen lived. Later on, in the early 1890's, people were beginning to move out of Georgetown on account of the lack of water. Shortly after 1894, the town was so small, it became part of the Cannonville Ward of the LDS church. A year or two later, it was all but deserted except for a ranch or two.

About the same time Georgetown was thriving, there were some families who moved back into the areas left abandoned in the former Clifton settlement. Perhaps it wasn't totally deserted in the first place. In the late 1880's and/or early 1890's, this small area recieved the nick-name of **Stringtown**. It seems there were a number of separate ranches strung out along the road between Cannonville and Georgetown, thus the name Stringtown. It was never incorparated into a town, or an organized LDS ward or congregation.

If you talk to old timers in the Bryce Valley about early day settlements, they will always mention the name Woodenshoe. The man who knows a little more about it than anyone else, is Kay Clark of Henrieville. He recalls stories and history of his grandfather, Owen W. Clark. After the Clarks had moved into, then out of, the White House Cabin on the lower Paria, then had attemted to resettle Adairville, they moved to Pahreah for several years. That place wasn't as promising as they had hoped, so again they moved, this time north to what was then Stringtown, which was actually part of Cannonville at the time. They lived there until 1896, then sold the farm to some Dutch people. This family was poor and often wore wooden shoes; thus the name **Woodenshoe** was attached to the area of the original settlement of Clifton.

Another interesting story about early Bryce Valley settlement comes from Wallace Ott of Tropic. When he was a wee small boy of just two or three years of age, he remembered an event and place just south of Cannonville, in the same general area as Clifton, Stringtown and Woodenshoe. It seems that in about 1914 or 1915, there came into the valley a wagon train of Mormons who had fled Mexico. It was in August of 1912, that the Mormons of Chihuahua and Sonora had to leave, because of the Mexican Revolution and Poncho Villa. It must have taken them a couple of years to make it north to the Paria Valley, otherwise Wallace wouldn't have remembered the time.

In the Georgetown area, is an old ranch with these rusting hulks lying in the sagebrush.

They came in the fall of the year and asked if it was OK to make a temporary camp about one km south of Cannonville. Permission was granted and they simply made a half circle with their wagons and camped for the one winter. They were the poorest people Wallace had ever seen. Many were of large polygamist families, and the church had to help out for a time. In the spring, they all set out in different directions looking for new homes. In the meantime, their camp had gotten the local nickname of **Zuniville**.

By 1886 the increasing population was using about all the fields the available water would irrigate, but north of Cannonville there remained a large fertile valley of unirrigated land that was otherwise suitable for cultivation. To increase the arable area, the people of Cannonville in 1889, revived an old scheme outlined by Ebenezer Bryce back in 1880. That plan was to divert water from the East Fork of the Sevier River on top of the Paunsaugunt Plateau(top of Bryce Canyon)through a ditch or canal that would pass over the Pink Cliffs to the land in the upper Bryce Valley.

At the instigation of William Lewman the locally financed Cannonville & East Fork Irrigation Co. was organized, a reservoir site selected, and a survey made for a feeder canal about 16 kms long. Maurice Cope was made boss of the project, and work begun May 15, 1890. Anticipating the successful completion of the project James Ahlstrom, C. W. Snyder, and others began building houses on land that the proposed ditch was intended to water. In 1891 a town site was laid out and called **Tropic**, allegedly after it's fine climate. On May 23, 1892, the new-found water was flowing through the town site and onto the adjoining fields. This date marks almost a century of continuous habitation of Tropic, which is truly a man-made oasis.

This canal, known locally as the Tropic Ditch, is still used today, as it is the life blood of the town. It took two years of voluntary labor and hard work by 50 men, women and boys from Cannonville and the neighboring communities, to finish the project. It was mostly hand work with pick and shovel. The only payment received was a reliable water supply and a better place to make a home. The canal can be seen about 100 meters south of Ruby's Inn as you drive toward the entrance to the national park; or in the middle part of Tropic Canyon, as it crosses under the highway.

Today in the area of Georgetown, one can find the cemetery which is just north of the road. It's still used today by some people who reside in Cannonville. It has some old graves dating from the last century. A little further down the road to the west, you'll see the remains of an old ranch, but this one dates from this century, and isn't an historic site. However there are a couple of old 1920's cars hidden in the sagebrush out back. Just across the road from this old homestead(to the northwest), are the foundations of an even older home, complete with the remains of a wooden pipeline.

There's nothing remaining of anything historic in the area of Clifton, Stringtown or Woodenshoe, however there are two very old cabins near the end of the paved road(east side) as you drive south out of Cannonville. They are out in the fields a ways and are clearly visible from the road.

In the same area which was Clifton, Stringtown and Woodenshoe, is this old cabin which may be from the Woodenshoe era.

These may date from the later days of the Woodenshoe era, and are still used today as barns or shelters for livestock.

If you drive due east out of Tropic and past the "B.V." on the hillside, you'll be in the general area of New Clifton or Losee. There's nothing there today except the old Losee Cemetery. The author counted seven tombstones, only three of which could still be read. Two belonged to young children, the other an older woman. They all had died in 1889 or 1890.

To get to the cemetery, drive to about the middle of East Valley, and locate a narrow lane running north from the main graveled road. To the left of this lane is a line of cottonwood trees. About 200 meters along this narrow road and to the right, is the small cemetery site with a one-meter high fence around it. If you park on the road, walk to the site, and disturb nothing, no one should care if you cross their private land. The local farmers occasionally find stones or other debris in the Losee area, but this graveyard is really the only thing to see.

Pahreah

It was in December of 1869, Jacob Hamblin was sent out by the Mormon Church to head a group in organizing an Indian farm somewhere on the Paria River. These first settlers did well and they built a guard house and a small corral, where men could cook and have safe lodging. By March, 1870, they had 2.5 kms of ditches and 800 meters of fence built, and had 8 Indians there helping and learning about agriculture. Some of the first information about this settlement comes in the form of a letter from Jacob Hamblin to Erastus Snow of the LDS church. It was dated March 27, 1870. Trouble is, the letter doesn't state whether they settled at the site of Pahreah, or at Rock House, where Peter Shurtz had his homestead.

Gregory thinks they went to Rock House, 8 or 9 kms below the later town site of Pahreah, and settled there. Then three years later they were driven out by floods, and couldn't get water in their ditches. At that time, in 1873-1874, they relocated; some went down stream as did Thomas Adair, to settle at what was to be known as Adairville, while others went up through The Box of the Paria and founded the settlement of Pahreah.

Everyone seems to agree that a William Meeks was the leader and first bishop at Pahreah in the early years. The community did very well at first. They grew nut orchards, vineyards, vegetable farms, and raised cattle and sheep. In 1877, Pahreah was large enough to have organized an LDS ward by itself, and be a part of the Kanab Stake. According to most accounts, by the spring of 1884, the number of people reached an all time high. At that time, there were 107 members of the Mormon church, plus a number of other cattlemen and about 20 Piute Indians.

There were a series of floods, the first of which was in 1883. It was followed by a sevier winter of 1883-84, then more flooding in 1884, which washed away farm houses and fields and converted the

The only cabin left at old Pahreah. It was recently moved back from the river.

LOWER PARIA RIVER GHOST TOWNS
PAHREAH, ROCK HOUSE, ADAIRVILLE

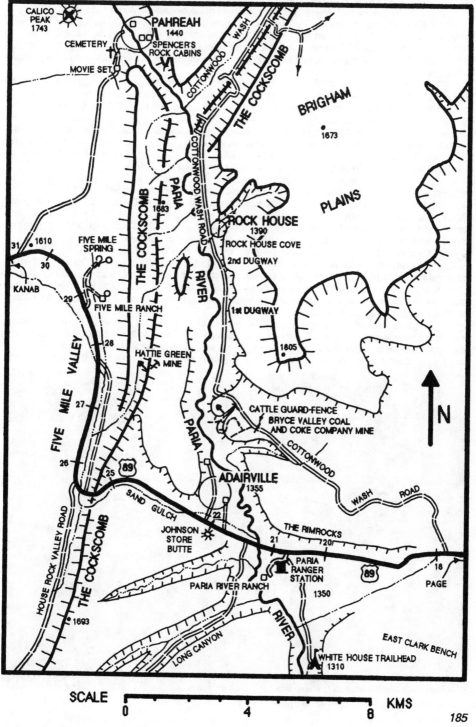

CALICO PEAK 1743

PAHREAH 1440

CEMETERY

SPENCER'S ROCK CABINS

MOVIE SET

COTTONWOOD WASH

THE COCKSCOMB

BRIGHAM 1673

PLAINS

COTTONWOOD WASH ROAD

PARIA 1683

THE COCKSCOMB

ROCK HOUSE 1390

ROCK HOUSE COVE

2nd DUGWAY

FIVE MILE SPRING

31 1610

30

KANAB

29

FIVE MILE RANCH

1st DUGWAY

1805

28

PARIA RIVER

FIVE MILE VALLEY

HATTIE GREEN MINE

27

CATTLE GUARD-FENCE

BRYCE VALLEY COAL AND COKE COMPANY MINE

26

25 89

COTTONWOOD

PARIA

SAND GULCH

ADAIRVILLE 1355

WASH ROAD

HOUSE ROCK VALLEY ROAD

THE COCKSCOMB

22

JOHNSON STORE BUTTE

THE RIMROCKS

21 720

N

1693

PARIA RANGER STATION

89 18

PAGE

PARIA RIVER RANCH

1350

LONG CANYON

RIVER

EAST CLARK BENCH

WHITE HOUSE TRAILHEAD 1310

SCALE

0   4   8   KMS

185

narrow stream channel into a wash that extended in places from canyon wall to canyon wall. This spelled doom for Pahreah. People started leaving. By September of 1884, only 48 people remained. The next year, 1885, the church ward was disorganized.

In the following years, people came and went, but mostly left. However, even in its declining years, Pahreah received a post office on July 26, 1893, and Emily P. Adair became the first postmaster. Finally things got even worse, and the post office closed on March 1, 1915.

In 1912, promoter Charles H. Spencer brought his miners up from Lee's Ferry, and tried unsuccessfully to extract gold from the Chinle clays. This after the gold mining failure at the ferry. In 1921, Spencer once again returned to Pahreah, this time to do some surveys for a proposed dam, to be located in The Box of the Paria, just downstream from Pahreah. Add this to the long list of failures for Spencer.

Throughout the years of this century, there were only one or two families living in or around the town. Their source of income was from farming and ranching, and to supply sheepmen who had large flocks in the region. One of the last settlers was a John Mangum. He lived in the area until about the mid-1930's, finally leaving for Idaho. In the same time period as the Mangums, was a Jack Seaton who ranched and was the sheep supplier for awhile. According to Leola Schoenfeld of Kanab, Jack lived in a dugout just southwest of Pahreah for several years. Then on April 2, 1932, Jack Seaton traded his holdings at Pahreah, for a home and land in Henrieville. This trade was with Jim Ed Smith. For three years, the family of Jim Ed Smith, including his son Layton, lived in Pahreah.

Layton recalls the family then sold Pahreah to Roy Twitchell in March of 1935, after living there for only three years. Roy was old then and most of the work was done by his son Cecil. The Twitchells stayed on for several years, but it was a tough life. Finally, after a long winter in the early 1940's, the Twitchells moved out. In 1942, at least some of the land around old Pahreah was purchased by a man named Burge, but he never did live there. It was Cecil Twitchell and Herman Mangum who spent the last winter there. After that, no one lived in Pahreah.

At Pahreah today, there is but one log cabin. This one was sitting on the very brink of the river, until a group of the Sons of the Utah Pioneers and BLM people went out to the rescue. They relocated the cabin back from the river about 50 meters. In the same area is another tumbled down cabin, a corral, and a couple of cellars. Just to the south less than half a km, are several old rock structures and some remains of the sluicing operation, dating from the time of Spencer. One of these rock buildings is in very good condition.

To get to Pahreah today, drive along Highway 89 to about half way between Kanab and Page. From between mile posts 30 and 31, turn north and drive about 8 kms to the old 1963 movie set and a small campground with toilets and picnic tables(but no water). After another km or so, you'll come to the Pahreah Cemetery on the left. The one large tombstone lists 13 people buried there. The original

Some corrals and trees about to be undercut by the river at Pahreah.

From the steep dugway on the road to Pahreah, you can see the movie set, and in the far background, old Pahreah.

From the top of the Carlo Ridge, one has a fine view of the Pahreah Valley.

grave markers are unreadable. Another km beyond the cemetery, is the end of the road at the edge of the river. Park at the sign, and walk across the river to the sites. Wear an old pair of shoes, or remove shoes, to wade in the usually ankle deep water of the Paria.

Rock House--Peter Shurtz Homestead
 The very first white settler to make a home in the Paria River drainage was a man by the name of Peter Shurtz(sometimes spelled Shirts). Shurtz migrated to the region in the spring of 1865 with his family, a wife and two children. One old timer in the area stated Shurtz had been a part of the Mountain Meadows Massacre and was also a polygamist; therefore was on the run at that time. The presumed site is about 8 or 9 kms down stream from Pahreah town site, and on the east side of the river.

 His first task was to build a ditch from the river into a little cove, surrounded on three sides by steep cliffs. The ditch ran from up stream, into this cove, then drained back into the river. In the back side of the cove he built his home. He made it from rocks, partly because rocks were so abundant, and logs weren't; and partly it's been said, so the Indians couldn't burn him out. The roof of the home was covered with flat slabs of shale type rock, called flagstone, of which there is an abundant supply in the area.

 He built his house right over the ditch, so he could have water if under attack. But surely any one attacking the place could, and surely would, cut off the water from up stream. Apparently he raised crops that first year, but then the Black Hawk War broke out, and hostilities erupted between Indians and white settlers all over the region.

 On November 12, 1865, Erastus Snow, one of the leaders of the Mormon Church, wrote all settlers in the region reminding them of the impending crisis, and to obey their church military leaders. One of the main events which signaled the beginning of the Black Hawk War(which lasted for about 5 years), was the killing of a Dr. Whitmore and Robert McIntyre by Indians at Pipe Springs, located south west of Kanab. This happened in January of 1866. At the time of that attack, Peter Shurtz was already besieged by Piute Indians. A militia force stationed in St. George, under the command of Col. MaArthur, attempted to rescue Shurtz, but deep snows prevented a speedy march.

 The military never got to the region until late March, but in the mean time Shurtz had outlasted the Indians, and by winters end, was apparently in better condition than the attackers, who were half starved. He talked to the Indians, explaining that since they had run off and killed one of his oxen, he could no longer plow his ground. On the promise that all who helped could share in the food, Shurtz got behind the plow, which was pulled by the Piutes, and started a new garden. However, in late March, Kanab was abandoned, and Shurtz and family were removed unwillingly(according to one account) to one of the larger settlements further west.

The Pahreah Movie Set is now a tourist stop. A waterless campground is nearby.

According to one story of the history of this settlement, March 1866, was the last time anyone lived at the Shurtz Homestead. Later, on December 7, 1869, Jacob Hamblin headed a small group of settlers to organize an Indian farm of some kind on the Paria River.

There's a different story about Rock House, as told by Herbert E. Gregory, who was a geologist and who did a lot of exploring in the 1920's in this part of the country. He claims that Shurtz stayed right on the land for three full years, instead of being marched out by the military in 1866. He then picked up and left the country for San Juan River. Gregory also states that Rock House was relocated in 1871, by six families, who did well for a short time. In 1872, 11 more families came in and grew corn and sorghum. He quoted someone as stating, *"In 1874, trouble with the ditches, caused the 15 families at Rock House to relocate above the hogback, at the present site of Pahreah."*

To reach Rock House, or the Rock House Cove as it's now called, drive north from Highway 89, from between mile posts 17 and 18. This is the Cottonwood Wash Road. Drive about 15 kms. As you near the cove, you will pass along part of the road which is pushed up against the hillside by the river. After you pass this first dugway, and after another 1.5 kms, you'll pass another dugway, which is again pushed up against the hill on the east by the river. Just after this second dugway(less than one km), on the right or east, is the Rock House Cove. It's in the western part of Section 4, T42S, R1W, on any of the USGS maps.

You'll know you're there when you see one single cottonwood tree just east and next to the road, which is at the northern end of a large flat area. That tree is also near the north end of a 200 meter long line of tamarisks. In this case they are so large, they're almost like trees. No one can say for sure if this is the Shurtz Homestead, but those tamarisks are the biggest this author has seen and in a line too straight for it have occurred by accident. The author, has never found any sign of the rock house, but most people who have seen the cove are convinced this is indeed the place. Kay Clark once stated he remembered a pile of rocks towards the south end of the line of tamarisks, but they're covered by sand now.

Adairville

Adairville is another of the once prosperous communities along the Paria River. The site of this little town is just north of mile post 22, on present day Highway 89, and about half way between Kanab and Page. This place is just east of The Cockscomb, whereas Pahreah is just to the west of The Cockscomb.

All sources agree that the year Adairville was first settled was in 1873, by a group of cattlemen, led by Thomas Adair. Some of these settlers came down from Rock House, where Adair had originally settled. In the beginning it too was prosperous, as they farmed the land, planted

Rock House Cove, and the very straight line of tamarisks.

gardens and raised livestock. According to Gregory, there were 8 families at Adairville in 1878, but they had some of the same problems as the earlier settlers had upstream at Rock House. They had had some minor floods, and couldn't get water to their fields, and the water in the river in the heat of summer didn't reach their settlement. Water in the Paria is reliable down to where it crosses The Cockscomb, but below The Box, it gradually seeps into the sands and disappears during early summer. So in 1878, those 8 families left, most of whom went upstream to Pahreah.

In the years after 1878, there was nearly always a rancher or two in the area. Kay Clark of Henrieville, says his grandfather built the cabin which was later known as the White House, in 1887. This is down stream a ways from where the trailhead to the Lower Paria is today. After a year or two there, they moved upstream to the area of Adairville and lived there for a couple of years. After that, the family moved up stream to Pahreah for a while, then on up to Bryce Valley in the early 1890's.

After the Clarks left Adairville, it's not certain just what happened to the place for a number of years, but Elbert(Farmer) Swapp of Kanab, remembers some of the later history. Elbert believes the land around Adairville was abandoned from the 1890's until the 1930's. However, the Cross Bar Land and Cattle Company filed on water rights in the area in 1912.

Finally the Adairville area was homesteaded by Charley Cram and Charley Mace in the 1930's, but they sold out to Elbert and Orson Swapp in the early 1940's. From that point on, the Swapps have owned most of the land south of Highway 89. The Swapps built the brick and cement ranch house just to the southwest of the Paria River Ranger Station in the 1940's. Most people refer to this as the Paria River Ranch.

Some of the land just north of the highway, and right where Adairville was founded, was homesteaded in the late 1930's by a Sandall Findlay. He later sold out to Fay Hamblin and Floyd Maddox. Finally, the Frosts bought them out, and have actually owned that land ever since, leasing it to the MacDonald family in recent years.

Just south of the MacDonalds farm buildings, is the Hepworth Place. It's the corrals and trailer house you see just north of the shaded rest area along the highway and northeast of the Johnson Store Butte.

Today, there's nothing left of the original Adairville, except perhaps for some of the old trees, just west of the Hepworth place, and just north of mile post 22 and Johnson Store Butte. There is one grave in there somewhere, but it's private land, and permission would have to be granted before entry can be made.

The Paria River Ranch, just south of the old Adairville site.

Geology of the Paria River Basin

While most people aren't really interested in geology, it's only a matter of time and one or more trips to the Colorado Plateau, before many begin to be hooked. All you have to do is look at a map of the lower 48 states, and you can see that many of our national parks and monuments are found on the Plateau.

The Colorado Plateau is a vast physiographic region covering the southeastern half of Utah, the northern half of Arizona, the northwestern corner of New Mexico, and the western fifth of Colorado. In other words, it covers the middle third of the Colorado River drainage system.

The thing that makes the Colorado Plateau so unique, is the flat lying rocks or strata. During millions of years, while the sediments were being laid down, the land remained relatively flat. Some times it was below sea level or was under the waters of a fresh water sea or lake. But always it remained relatively flat, even during this last time period when the entire region was uplifted to create what we have today. And what we have today, is a colorful and majestic canyon country unequalled anywhere.

Because much of the Plateau is dry, and has very little vegetation, the rocks are laid bare, and can be examined by all. This is why so many people become interested in geology when visiting this part of the country.

In the authors world travels, which began in 1970, and which have taken him to 129 countries and island groups, he has never seen anything to compare to this Plateau. The only land which remotely resembles it, is in southwestern Jordan, and in the canyons leading to the Petra ruins. Petra is in a sandstone canyon which is similar to the Navajo Sandstone, where peoples around 2000 years ago, carved homes and monuments into the sides of the sandstone canyon walls. But that area is very small; the Colorado Plateau very extensive.

The Paria River drainage is nearly in the middle of the Plateau, and has at least its share of unique geologic wonders. It starts out at Bryce Canyon National Park and Table Cliff Plateau. Then there are canyons like Bull Valley Gorge, Round Valley Draw, the Buckskin Gulch, and the Lower Paria River Canyon. Perhaps the most interesting geologic feature of all is The Cockscomb. All these areas combine to make a fascinating geology field trip.

Geologic Formations and Where They are Exposed

If we follow a line from the top of the Table Cliff Plateau, south to Lee's Ferry on the Colorado River, we will pass along all, or most, of the formations which are exposed in the drainage. Let's begin at the top of the Table Cliff and run down through the different formations, and where they are prominently seen. At the end of this list are three formations which are exposed in Kaibab Gulch, just west of the Buckskin Trailhead. Two of these are not exposed along the lower Paria River.

Tuff of Osiris It's found just on top of Table Cliff and to the north of Powell Point. It's of volcanic origin, as is the top of the Aquarius Plateau.

Variegated Sandstone Member--Wasatch Formation This is usually considered the top of the Wasatch Formation, and seen only in a few places on the rim of Bryce Canyon N.P. and on top of Table Cliff. It's more weather resistant; therefore a capstone.

White Limestone Member--Wasatch Formation This is prominently seen all along the rim of the Pink Cliffs in Bryce Canyon, the Sunset Cliffs on the west side of the Paunsaugunt Plateau, and along the top part of Table Cliff Plateau. This and the Pink Limestone below, look nothing like ordinary limestone.

Pink Limestone Member--Wasatch Formation Seen on the lower slopes of Table Cliff and on Canaan Peak, as well as in Bryce Canyon. In this member are found the famous *Hoodoos*, for which Bryce Canyon is famous. It's the same member as is seen in all the Pink Cliffs, the Sunset Cliffs, and in Cedar Breaks National Monument. Also seen on Canaan Peak. This is a crumbly limestone formation full of iron, which gives it it's color.

Pine Hollow Formation An indistinct mudstone strata immediately below the Pink Cliffs of Bryce and Table Cliff.

Canaan Peak Formation Another indistinct formation below the Pinks at the bottom of the Table Cliff. Made up of cobble-pebble, and sandstone conglomerate.

Kaiparowits Formation A slope maker, made of sandstone, limestone, siltstone, and clays, and is seen most prominently to the east of The Cockscomb, or between Henrieville and the pass between Table Cliff and Canaan Peak.

Wahweap Formation This is a cliff-making formation, most prominently exposed as the east side ridge of Cads Crotch, one of the features of the upper end of The Cockscomb. It's a brownish-yellowish sandstone, mudstone, siltstone and shale.

Straight Cliffs Formation This formation is another cliff-maker. It's best seen as the highest ridge of The Cockscomb. It also forms the western ridge of Cads Crotch, which is a prominent valley within the larger structure called The Cockscomb.

Tropic Shale The name tells the tale; it's mostly the gray clay beds you see around the town of Tropic, the type section location. It's also the grays you see above Henrieville on the way to Escalante. Another location is in one of the valleys of The Cockscomb. You'll be driving along this gray clay area in the bottom 16 to 18 kms of the Cottonwood Wash Road. It begins just north of Highway 89, and is slick as hell when wet.

Dakota Sandstone This one is made mostly of a light brown sandstone, which makes a prominent cliff, but it also has siltstone and some shale. You'll see this as one of the prominent and intermediate ridges within The Cockscomb. Remember, it's the first and very prominent ridge just west of the Tropic Shale Valley along The Cockscomb Valley, which in this case is called Cottonwood Wash.

Henrieville Sandstone The type section for this one is near the town of Henrieville. But it's seen in only a few areas, from the head or northern end of The Cockscomb, up through Butler Valley and at the head of Round Valley Draw. It's a yellow and cliff making massive sandstone. It's best seen at the Butler Valley Arch, more commonly known as Grosvenor Arch. It's that part of the wall from the top of the arch down to ground level.

There's a question on whether or not the *Morrison Formation* is exposed in this area, especially along The Cockscomb. In the lower end of The Cockscomb, the author sees no gap between the Dakota and the top of the Entrada, but there may be a thin layer of Morrison in there somewhere. Some reports place it in, but those are not detailed reports. Thompson and Stokes leave it out in their report.

Escalante Member--Entrada Sandstone An indistinct, and mostly sandstone member of the Entrada seen in the upper slopes of Kodachrome Basin.

Cannonville Member--Entrada Sandstone This is a mostly fine grain white sandstone, but looks nothing like the real thing, the Navajo Sandstone. It's type section are the slopes around Cannonville, but the best place to see this one is in Kodachrome Basin. It's the white upper slopes and cliffs you see above the more scenic red sandstone in the park.

Gunsight Butte Member--Entrada Sandstone This is the reddish brown sandstone layer you see in Kodachrome Basin. In this member, are found most of the *sand pipes* in the park. Another good place to see this one is in The Rimrocks, which are seen just north of Highway 89 in the vicinity of the Paria Ranger Station. It is the white capstone which forms the top of The Rimrocks, which is just above the colorful Winsor Member of the Carmel F. In this location, it's pure white. You can also see this member in the bottom part of the Cottonwood Wash and just east of the road. It's the white sandstone monoliths you see standing up alone like icebergs.

Wiggler Wash Member--Carmel Formation The type section for this strata is in the southern part of Kodachrome Basin where it's a thin gypsum layer, just below the red Gunsight Butte Member.

Winsor Member--Carmel Formation This is a mostly sandstone layer you can see just north of the Cottonwood Wash Road in the southern part of Kodachrome Basin. It's largely indistinct there, but the author believes this is the very colorful beds of clayish-looking deposits you see just north of Highway 89, between the eastern side of The Cockscomb and to just east of the Paria Ranger Station. These are the purple and white banded layers forming the lower part of The Rimrocks.

Paria River Member--Carmel Formation These are indistinct beds of mostly sandstone, mixed with thin layers of siltstone, as well as some limestone and gypsum. This one may be seen between the Paria Ranger Station and the White House Trailhead.

Thousand Pockets Tongue--Page Sandstone This is a massive sandstone layer, once considered a part of the Navajo. It's type section is in the area just east of the top of the Dominguez Trail or Pass, in the lower end of the Paria. It's the smooth white sandstone you see at the White House Trailhead and around the town of Page. White House Spring comes out of the bottom of this tongue.

Judd Hollow Tongue--Carmel Formation This tongue separates the the Page Sandstone from the Navajo below, and is easily seen all along the Cottonwood Wash. It's the first layer above the massive white and yellowish Navajo in that canyon. You'll also see it as you walk down stream from the White House Trailhead and into the Lower Paria River Gorge. The type section for this member is in Judd Hollow, which is just above where the old Adams Pump still sits in the middle part of the Lower Paria.

Navajo Sandstone This formation is probably the most famous and most seen of any formation on the Colorado Plateau. This is the one in which most of the fantastically narrow slot-type canyons are made. It is a very thick massive sandstone, up to 600 meters thick, and is considered by many to be one large fossil sand dune. It was created by wind-blown sand, therefore it has lots of crossbedding.

192

The Navajo is seen as the White Cliffs between Highway 89 and Cannonville, and in the narrows of Bull Valley Gorge, Round Valley Draw, the Buckskin Gulch, and the Lower Paria Canyon. It's also seen as the top most part of the big cliff making up the Vermilion Cliffs just south of the Sand Hills or Paria Plateau. Elsewhere, you see the Navajo in the big walls of Zion N. P., all the canyons of the Escalante, throughout the San Rafael Swell, in the Moab area, and all across the Navajo Nation, the type section location.

Kayenta Formation Where ever you see the Navajo, you'll see this one just below. And the author can't remember seeing a geology cross section without these two together. It's usually a deep reddish brown formation made of mudstone, sandstone and siltstone layers. It usually forms the bench just below the Navajo. Sometimes it intertongues with the Navajo, as it *appears* to do in the slopes above and to the southeast of the mouth of Bush Head Canyon in the lower end of the Paria. But one geologist says that is part of the lower Navajo, and was caused by fresh water ponding?

Moenave Formation This is the red cliff maker just below the Kayenta, and above the Chinle. To the east of the Echo Cliffs Monocline, this one turns into, and is called the Wingate Sandstone. But between the Paria and Zion, it's the Moenave. This formation forms the lower cliffs just above the talus slopes along the Vermilion Cliffs.

Owl Rock Member--Chinle Formation An indistinct, mostly sandstone layer just below the Moenave Cliffs along the base of the Vermilion Cliffs and just above the colorful variegated banded slopes around old Pahreah.

Petrified Forest Member--Chinle Formation This is the same formation where all the petrified wood is found in northern Arizona. It's also full of petrified wood in Utah. This is the very colorful banded layers of clay you see around the old town of Pahreah. It's this red, purple, green, pink and white layered formation which have attracted movie makers to old Pahreah throughout the years.

Lower Sandstone Member--Chinle Formation Another indistinct sandstone bed in the lower part of the Chinle. Probably best seen in the lower end of the Paria around Lee's Ferry and just above the prominent Shinarump Bench.

Shinarump Conglomerate Member--Chinle Formation A white and very course sandstone and pebblestone conglomerate, which forms a very prominent ridge, cliff or bench throughout Utah and northern Arizona. It's white only when disturbed, otherwise it's covered with desert varnish and very black looking. In other parts it's called the *Black Ledge*. It's best seen around Lee's Ferry, where it forms what is called Lee's Backbone, which is on the south side of the Colorado River. The original wagon route south from the ferry, went upon this layer, which made a very rough road. This member is also full of petrified wood.

Moenkopi Formation This is the chocolate brown strata you'll see all across Utah and Arizona, wherever the Shinarump is found. It makes up the slope below the Shinarump and is composed of claybeds along with sandstone and siltstones. You drive upon it as you make the side trip to old Pahreah. It's also seen along the road running between the Navajo Bridge and Marble Canyon, and Lee's Ferry. It's the brown layers just below the Shinarump Bench.

Kaibab Limestone This formation is seen at the land surface just west of the Buckskin and Wire Pass Trailheads, and on Buckskin and Five Mile Mountains. It's the capstone along the rim of Kaibab Gulch(that part of the gulch, wash or canyon just above the Buckskin Trailhead). It's this limestone which forms the top layer throughout the House Rock Valley. You are driving atop the Kaibab as you approach Lee's Ferry along Highway 89A from either direction. It forms the top layer in Marble Canyon, as seen at the rest stop at Navajo Bridge. You can also see the *Toroweap* and *Coconino Formations* in Marble Canyon if you stop at the Navajo Bridge on your way to Lee's Ferry.

Toroweap Formation In the Paria drainage, this formation is only seen in Kaibab Gulch, just up stream from the Buckskin Trailhead, and where the channel cuts deep into Buckskin Mountain.

Hermit Shale This is the lowest or oldest of all formations found in the Paria River system. It's the red rock seen only in the very bottom of the Kaibab Gulch, just up canyon above the Buckskin Trailhead. Normally the Coconino Sandstone is in that slot, but it's missing in Kaibab Gulch. However, the Coconino is seen just emerging in Marble Canyon below the bridge.

GEOLOGY CROSS SECTION
TABLE CLIFF PLATEAU TO LEE'S FERRY

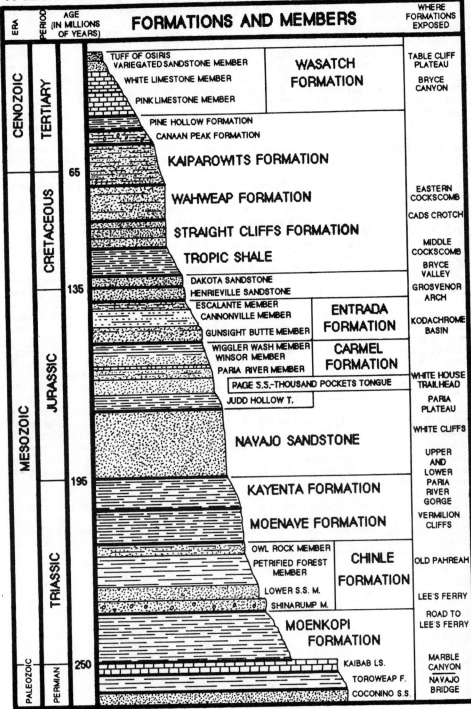

ERA	PERIOD	AGE (IN MILLIONS OF YEARS)	FORMATIONS AND MEMBERS	WHERE FORMATIONS EXPOSED
CENOZOIC	TERTIARY		TUFF OF OSIRIS / VARIEGATED SANDSTONE MEMBER / WHITE LIMESTONE MEMBER / PINK LIMESTONE MEMBER — WASATCH FORMATION	TABLE CLIFF PLATEAU / BRYCE CANYON
			PINE HOLLOW FORMATION	
			CANAAN PEAK FORMATION	
		65	KAIPAROWITS FORMATION	
MESOZOIC	CRETACEOUS		WAHWEAP FORMATION	EASTERN COCKSCOMB / CADS CROTCH
			STRAIGHT CLIFFS FORMATION	MIDDLE COCKSCOMB
			TROPIC SHALE	BRYCE VALLEY
		135	DAKOTA SANDSTONE	GROSVENOR ARCH
			HENRIEVILLE SANDSTONE	
	JURASSIC		ESCALANTE MEMBER / CANNONVILLE MEMBER / GUNSIGHT BUTTE MEMBER — ENTRADA FORMATION	KODACHROME BASIN
			WIGGLER WASH MEMBER / WINSOR MEMBER / PARIA RIVER MEMBER — CARMEL FORMATION	
			PAGE S.S.-THOUSAND POCKETS TONGUE	WHITE HOUSE TRAILHEAD
			JUDD HOLLOW T.	PARIA PLATEAU
			NAVAJO SANDSTONE	WHITE CLIFFS / UPPER AND LOWER PARIA RIVER GORGE
		195	KAYENTA FORMATION	
			MOENAVE FORMATION	VERMILION CLIFFS
	TRIASSIC		OWL ROCK MEMBER / PETRIFIED FOREST MEMBER / LOWER S.S. M. / SHINARUMP M. — CHINLE FORMATION	OLD PAHREAH / LEE'S FERRY
			MOENKOPI FORMATION	ROAD TO LEE'S FERRY / MARBLE CANYON
PALEOZOIC	PERMIAN	250	KAIBAB LS. / TOROWEAP F. / COCONINO S.S.	NAVAJO BRIDGE

Mining in the Paria River Drainage

Coal

Very little mining has occurred in the drainage of the Paria, but in the early days of settlement, coal was mined and used mostly in the blacksmith trade. If you look at the maps of Bryce Valley, and the Lower Paria River Ghosts Towns, you'll see coal mines near each of the former or present town sites. Most of the coal mining has occurred in the upper reaches of the Paria to the northeast of Tropic and north of Henrieville.

The coal mined in Bryce Valley comes from the bottom part of the Straight Cliffs Formation, while that coming from the mine above Adairville, comes from the Dakota Sandstone. There are also coal beds in the Tropic Shale, but they're so thin it was uneconomical to mine.

The most northerly coal mine in the valley is usually called the *Shakespear Mine*, but sometimes is referred to as the *Emma Canyon Mine.* It's located about 11 kms northeast of Tropic, in a little side drainage of Henderson Valley, called Emma Canyon.

Herm Pollock believes it was his grandfather William W. Pollock and his brother Jack, who may have been the first to dig coal out of this mine, and perhaps others in the valley. They were among the earliest settlers to the valley and were both blacksmiths. They needed coal to do their work. Obe Shakespear, long time Tropic resident, told the author he never knew coal in his life, until an uncle started mining it not too many years ago. Bryce Valley families always used cedar wood in their stoves, even though coal was there to be taken.

After the earlier blacksmith days, nothing happen in the mining business, until the late 1930's. This is when Lewis and Vern Ray(father and son) came into the valley from Orderville, and filed on the mineral rights to the coal in Emma Canyon. They mined coal for 5 or 6 years, and until about the mid-1940's, then sold it to Alton and Vernal Shakespear. They are the ones who did more mining than anyone. They shipped it to as far away as St. George and Panguitch, but most of it stayed in the valley. The mine was active until perhaps the late 1950's, then mining slowed down and was not used after about 1960. One person thought the state closed it down because of water and safety problems?

Finally in 1964, Alton Shakespear sold it for a reported $75,000 to a man from Denver. This new owner was hoping to invest more money into the business, and make big profits, but nothing ever happen to the scheme, and coal hasn't been mined there since.

The Shakespear Mine is located in the bottom part of the Straight Cliffs Formation, where there's a total of nearly 4 meters of coal in four separate beds. Today, it appears there are two

The two entrances to the Shakespear Mine in Emma Canyon.

tunnels, the openings of which are protected by the installation of large galvanized steel pipes which prevent cave ins.

To get to this site(in the NW corner of section 22, T36S, R2W), drive east out of Tropic toward the old townsite of Losee and into East Valley. There are several side roads, but continue in a northeast direction and straight into Emma Canyon. Just stay on this main road, which is rather good all the way, and for any vehicle.

In the area north of Henrieville, are the Pollock and Davies Mines. Both of these are also in the Straight Cliffs Formation, and presumably across the narrow canyon from each other. Everyone in Henrieville calls the one place the *Jack Pollock Mine*. He was one of the earliest settlers in Henrieville and he used the coal for blacksmithing. Today there is little or no evidence this old mine ever existed, but the one just across the canyon did operate for awhile. This was the Davis or *Davies Mine*.

Wallace Ott recalls a time he took Byron Davies up Coal Canyon and showed him the veins of coal. That was in the early 1940's, and after Davis had tried, apparently unsuccessfully, to mine coal from a mine down canyon around Adairville. It was Davies who did some mining there in the 1940's. He ran a shaft into the beds for 30 to 50 meters, but didn't have the money to go into mining big. The Davies Mine has one vein nearly 3 meters in thickness, another about 2 meters. The mining that was done was more for a promotional than anything else.

Davies and Ott and others, including Alfred Foster, organized the Garfield Coal Company in about 1960, but as yet nothing has happened. Selling it is still a possibility, and they still have money invested in the project

To get to these two old mines, which are nearly side by side, drive north out of Henrieville on Highway 12 in the direction of Escalante. After about 5 kms, turn left, or north, from between mile posts 32 and 33. The mines are almost due north of that point and in Coal Canyon, which is in between Jammie and Dry Hollow. From the highway, to the mines, is about 3 kms(located in the N half of section 36, T36S, R2W).

But you can't take a vehicle past the first wash and gate. So you might as well park on the highway and walk, as the road just into the mouth of the canyon is totally washed out anyway. Walking will take about 45 minutes, but you have to jump or climb around some deep gullies. The Davies Mine is on the south side of the canyon, and there is still a pile of coal and an chute at the site. Across the canyon north, one can just barely make out a faint line indicating some activity there many years ago.

Not far south of the Pollock and Davies Mines is another old coal mine one old timer called the *Jack Pollock Mine?* Maybe Jack Pollock had several mines, one for each town. It's right on Highway 12, between mile post 31 and 32, and about 4 kms north of Henrieville. No one in Henrieville today knows much about the history of this mine, except that one cold winter day, two boys from Henrieville,

The Davies Mine in Coal Canyon, north of Henrieville.

MINE LOCATIONS OF THE PARIA RIVER

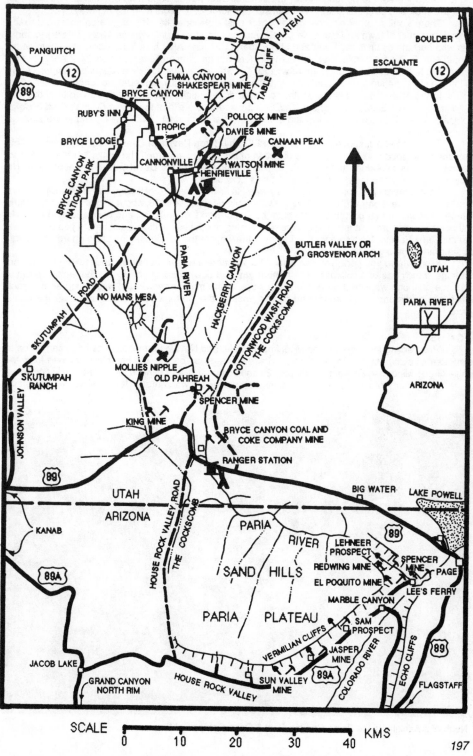

SCALE

0   10   20   30   40   KMS

went into the mine and started a fire to get warm. When they left, they failed to put out the fire properly and it started the coal to burning. Later the state of Utah had to send men and equipment down to cover the shaft and put out the fire. You can still see some of the coal from the highway.

There's still another old coal mine not far east of Henrieville. If you hike on some old roads about 5 kms east of town and into Little Creek, you may see the *Frank Watson Mine*. This is the same man who built the cabin in the lower end of Hackberry Canyon. After he left the Hackberry Country, he went to Henrieville for awhile, then ran a small store out on Watson Ridge, just south of Kodachrome Basin. His hottest selling item out there was rot-gut whiskey known locally as *Jamaica Ginger*. After he left the store, he started this coal mine in Little Creek, but he only worked there for one winter.

In the Adairville area is still another old abandoned mine. About 2.5 kms due north of the site of Adairville, and 1.5 kms north of the MacDonald place, is the site of the *Bryce Canyon Coal & Coke Company Mine*. This old mine is located in the center of section 21, T42S, R1W, and in the Dakota Sandstone.

This mine was first opened in the late 1930's by Byron Davies of Cannonville. It's been said he took out some good coal by truck in the direction of Kanab, but apparently he couldn't find a market for the coal. It was mined for just a couple of years, then was sold to David Quilter in about 1940. No mining ever took place there after that, and it was abandoned.

To get there, you could walk up the Paria River bed from the highway, but you can also drive almost to it. Drive along Highway 89 to between mile posts 17 and 18, about 5 kms east of the Paria Ranger Station. At that point turn north onto the Cottonwood Wash Road, and drive about 10 kms. At that point you will cross a minor drainage which runs southwest, which is just before you drop down into the Paria Valley. It's also about half a km to the west of the one fence and cattle guard. Park right on the road in the dry creek bed.

From where you park, you can walk 30 or 40 meters to the southwest, and look right down on the mine, which has one collapsed shaft and a tumbled-down loading chute. On the east side of the drainage, you can walk right down the steep slope to the mine, or you could walk along an old track which circles around to the south and comes back to the Cottonwood Wash Road near the cattle guard.

Copper

Prospecting for copper in the Moenkopi, Chinle, and Navajo Formations has been carried on at a number of places in the Paria Valley, and some low-grade copper ore has been shipped from the Hattie Green Mine, one km east of mile post 28 on Highway 89, and right on top of The Cockscomb.

The history of the Hattie Green Mine goes back nearly a century. It was March 8, 1893, that

North of Adairville, is the Bryce Canyon Coal & Coke Company Mine.

George J. Simonds filed a claim or notice of location on what was called the Hattie Green. Just a few days later, there were several other locations registered in the area just to the north They were the Silver Queen and Gold King claims which are about one km north of the Hattie Green and evidently on top of The Cockscomb. These were filed by several members of the Ahlstrom family. In the same time period, Tom Levy, Oren Twitchell and Murphy Alexander filed on what was called the Red Bird Claim. This was just south of The Box of the Paria. Of all these claims, only the Hattie Green produced.

According to Kay Clark of Henrieville, two brothers named Clint and Pat Willis, worked this mine in the late 1910's and early 1920's. They are the ones who did most of the work on the tunnels and adits, and who lugged out most of the copper ore. Kay Clark did some poking around the place and filed on the old claims in the 1960's, but nothing came of that.

To get to the Hattie Green(in section 18, T42S, R1W), stop on Highway 89, just south of mile post 28. Then walk due east across the gully, and locate a very faint track first running east, then south, then north inside a minor draw within The Cockscomb. From where you turn north, it's about one km to the mine, which sits atop The Cockscomb on the right. Read more on route details under the hiking section and *Map 23, the Hattie Green Mine.*

At the mine there are two tunnels, one coming in from the east side, the other from the west. The west side tunnel has wooden tracks which supported small ore cars within the mine. Right on top of the ridge is an ore heap with the blue-green stained rocks still lying there. There are also three other adits or test prospects in the area.

Manganese

Another mining operation took place not far south of Kitchen Corral Point and along the Nipple Ranch Road. This is the King Mine and it's primary mineral was manganese.

According to Calvin C. Johnson of Kanab, this operation first began sometime in the late 1930's. It was on November 15, 1939, that John H. Brown, filed a claim, and started mining. It was soon found they couldn't separate the manganese from the bentonite clays of the Petrified Forest Member of the Chinle Formation. After Brown gave up, several Johnson brothers from Short Creek, Arizona, worked it for 6 or 8 months. This was in the early 1940's. Then it was abandoned for about a decade.

In 1954 or 1955, a bigger outfit came in with a guy named Bennett in charge. In the year or two they worked the area, they spent upwards of $250,000 to develop it. They made five small dams in the one little canyon where most of the mining took place. They then built another dam across Kitchen Corral Wash, and caught flood water, and water from some nearby springs. They then pumped this water up the canyon to the five reservoirs, and used the water in the attempt to separate manganese

The northern part of the King Manganese Mine.

from the clays. At the height of the operation, 20 to 25 local men worked there. But they also had troubles with separation, and soon closed down.

   To see this old abandoned mine operation, drive along Highway 89 about 45 kms east of Kanab. Right at mile post 37, turn north onto the Nipple Ranch Road, and drive about 5 or 6 kms. At that point look for a couple of faintly visible roads running northeast into a minor canyon. Drive about half a km, and park under a large cedar tree. From there you can walk up canyon on an old and partly washed out road about 200 meters to the old ponds, one mine tunnel, and some loading chutes(it's in the middle of section 2, T42S, R3W). When you return to the Nipple Ranch Road, turn north, and drive about one km, and on your right or to the east, you'll see on a low hillside, some mining scars and an old loading chute.

Uranium

   In the very bottom or lower end of the Paria River Canyon in the vicinity of Lee's Ferry, and along Highway 89A just under the Vermilion Cliffs, are a number of uranium mines and prospects. These all go back to the 1950's boom days.

   In you're coming down canyon out of the Lower Gorge, you'll pass the *Red Wing Mine*, about 6.5 kms up from Lee's Ferry, and about half a km south of the Wilson Ranch site(in the N side of section 3, T40N, R7E). This mine has two adits, 13 and 17 meters long. The adits were tunneled into the Shinarump Member of the Chinle Formation, but the vegital trash heaps, where the uranium is concentrated, are right at the contact point of the Shinarump and the Moenkopi. About half a km up canyon from the Wilson Ranch is another adit, called the *Lehneer Prospect.* Not much happened there.

   Down near Lee's Ferry is the *El Pequito Mine*. It's found about 2 kms west of the Lonely Dell Ranch, at the head of a minor canyon just north of Johnson Point. El Pequito is in the Shinarump, and at the contact of the Moenkopi. Mineralization occurs in an old stream channel in the Shinarump. This mine is found in the NW corner of section 14, T40N, R7E.

   Going southwest from Lee's Ferry, you'll find the *Sam Prospect* in the SE corner of section 2, T39N, R6E. It's about 3 kms west of Vermilion Cliffs Lodge, along Highway 89A, and in the south side of Badger Creek. This adit is in the upper part of the Petrified Forest Member of the Chinle Formation. Not much went on there.

   Further along to the southwest, is the *Jasper Mine* in the SW corner of section 27, T39N, R6E. It's about half a km to the northeast of Cliff Dwellers Lodge, and about 100 meters from the highway. It too was located at or near the contact point of the Shinarump and the Moenkopi. They found small amounts of many minerals, including copper staining, but not much else.

The entrance to the Red Wing Uranium Mine, just south of the Wilson Ranch.

The only real uranium mine in these parts, was the *Sun Valley Mine*. It's 5 kms southwest of Cliff Dweller Lodge, and in the south half of section 6, T38N, R6E. At the time it was studied by Lane and Bush, this mine was owned and operated by Intermountain Exploration Co. The mine was started in 1954 during a period of intense uranium exploration in the area. An inclined shaft was sunk on a Shinarump outcropping, with the ore being on the contact with the Moenkopi. Several hundred tons of high grade uranium ore was shipped before the shaft was filled with mud from a flash flood. Later, a vertical shaft was sunk, and a drift was driven to connect with the old, sand-filled workings, but there was no further production. The Sun Valley Mine has been worked in recent years on a sporadic basis. Today all of these old mines and prospects are included in the Paria Canyon--Vermilion Cliffs Wilderness Area.

Gold

The story of gold mining along the Paria River, is also the story of Charles H. Spencer. As one writer has put it, *he seemed to enjoy the pursuit more than the gold itself, especially when it meant spending other peoples money looking for it.*

Spencer first arrived in the canyon country in 1909, where he set up an operation on the lower San Juan River, upstream from Lee's Ferry. There he was trying to separate gold from the Wingate Sandstone. During that stay, a couple of prospectors told about the possibilities of the Chinle Formation at Lee's Ferry, and that coal existed north of the Colorado River a ways. With that tip, he made tracks for Lee's Ferry, arriving there in April, 1910.

On arriving at the Ferry, Spencer looked things over and decided the Chinle clays 300 meters from the river could be a possibility. He speculated that a boiler could power a high pressure hose, which could wash the clays and shales down to the river, where gold could then be recovered with the help of an amalgamator. But his first job was to send his men out to look for the promised coal field. It was found in a side drainage about 45 kms up stream in Glen Canyon. The site was is Warm Creek.

While the hunt for coal went on, Spencer began experimenting with power dredging at the Ferry. At first he used wood to power the boiler. He then set up power hoses to wash the gold bearing clays down to a sluice and amalgamator at the river. Gold is indeed in the Chinle, but it's in the form of very fine dust. The method used, was to run the muddy water over the amalgamator which had mercury in the bottom. The mercury was supposed to absorb and trap the gold, allowing other materials to pass over. But instead, the operation merely clogged the amalgamator, and the mercury did not absorb the gold. While chemists worked on the problem, Spencer was thinking about how to get the coal from Warm Creek to the Ferry.

At first it was thought coal could be brought in by mule, using an old trail called the Ute or

Lee's Fort, once used by Charles H. Spencer and his mining crew.

The boiler used by Spencer's crew to power a water hose, which washed the Chinle clays down to a sluice box.

The steamboat *Charles H. Spencer* as it appeared in August, 1915.

Charles H. Spencer's stone house at Pahreah.

The very colorful Chinle clay beds, seen at old Pahreah.

Dominguez Trail, which was about 5 kms up canyon from the Ferry. Because of that extra distance, it was decided to make a shortcut route directly above the operation on the Colorado. So in the fall of 1910, Spencer and his men constructed the Spencer Trail from the river to the top of the cliffs. From there it was hoped they could head out to the northeast with mules for the Warm Creek coal fields. But the trail was never used to bring in coal, instead it was more of a promotional scheme than anything else.

The next job was to build a wagon road right down the dry creek bed of Warm Creek to the Colorado River. While workers were building the road, others were building a barge on the banks of the river. This all went well--they brought coal down the canyon, loaded it onto the barge, then floated it down to the Ferry. But then the problem was to get the barge back up stream again.

This problem, it was thought, could be solved by a tugboat of some kind. So with more investors money, a 9 meter long tug boat called the *Violet Louise*, was purchased and brought to the Ferry. As it turned out, it was far underpowered to push a large barge upstream against the current. The current wasn't that fast, but pushing a barge wasn't easy.

While Spencer worked on problems at the Ferry, the managers of the Chicago company he worked for, ordered a steam powered boat from San Francisco. The boat was built in 1911, dismantled, and shipped by train to Marysvale, Utah, the end of the railway line. It was then put onto large wagons for the rest of the 320 km trip to the mouth of Warm Creek. There it was reassembled in the spring of 1912. It was the biggest thing to sail the Colorado River above the Grand Canyon. It measured 28 x 8 meters, was powered by a coal boiler, and had a 4 meter wide stern paddlewheel. Even though this part of the project wasn't one of Spencers ideas, the boat was named the *Charles H. Spencer*.

The next problem was to find a crew for the boat. This wasn't easy in the middle of the desert, but they found a crew anyway, with a fellow by the name of Pete Hanna at the helm, the only crew member who had any experience with boats. They loaded the deck full of coal for the trial run. But almost immediately, they hit a sandbar. Then another. Finally Hanna turned the boat around and allowed it to sail down the river backwards, which gave it better maneuverability. They spent one night in the canyon, then next morning finished the 45 km run to the Ferry.

They then had to figure out how to get the *Spencer* back up stream against the current, which was stronger than anyone had expected. Hanna decided to keep most of the coal which had been brought down on board, to insure passage back up to Warm Creek. This was a good move, because they barely made it back up stream. They again loaded the boat as full as possible, and returned to the Ferry, where it sat for a couple of months. All this, while the chemists and the workers figured out what to do about separating the gold from the Chinle clays.

Finally it was decided to try something different. They ended up towing the original barge upstream with the *Spencer*. This worked fine. They then loaded up both the barge and the steamer with coal. The barge was then allowed to drift down stream with several workers guiding it around the sandbars, with the *Spencer* following. This worked fine too, and it appeared they had this part of the gold mining problem solved. The only thing left to do, was to find a successful way to get the gold out of the clay. This Spencer was never able to do, and the steamboat had made its last run.

Spencer left the Ferry later in 1912, bound for the nearly abandoned settlement of Pahreah. Meanwhile, the steamship *Charles H. Spencer* sat on the river tied to the bank. In 1915 the combination of high water and piles of drift wood, put the boat on its side, and it sank in a meter of water. Later, parts were stripped off and taken away, and some of the lumber from its decks was used for various projects. Today, you can just barely see the sunken remains of the boat just up stream from Lee's Fort and at the bottom end of the Spencer Trail. Near the old fort is the boiler and parts of the stern paddlewheel. Just north of the boiler one can still see scars where they operated the power sluicing machinery. Perhaps the best source of information about all the subjects of Lee's Ferry is found in the books, *Desert River Crossing* and *Lee's Ferry*.

From the Ferry, Spencer moved his operations to Pahreah. He was accompanied by Herbert A. Parkyn. The new dream was to extract gold from the same Chinle clays at Pahreah, but they failed at that as well. They did however set up some stone buildings at Pahreah, and tried some sluicing. These sites are still there at Pahreah today. Several attempts were made to refinance new schemes, including building a dam across The Box of the Paria River just below Pahreah townsite, but that too failed to bring in more money. Charles H. Spencer was in and out of Pahreah and Lee's Ferry all his life, but he never made a cent from any of his big-time promotional schemes.

BRYCE VALLEY & SKUTUMPAH ROAD RANCHES

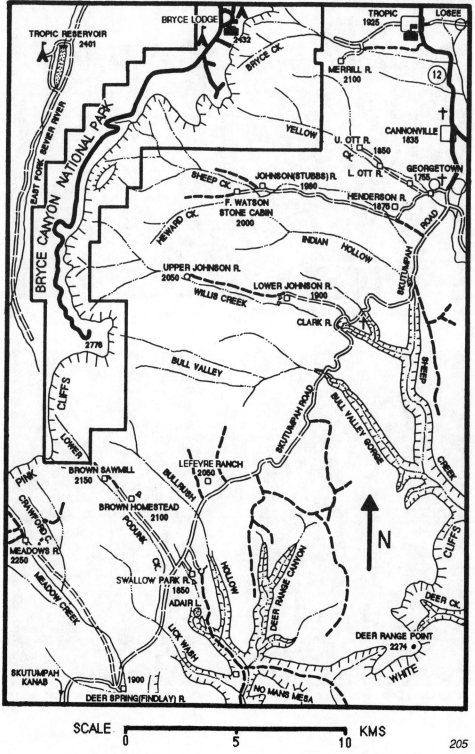

TROPIC RESERVOIR
2401

BRYCE LODGE

2432

BRYCE CK.

TROPIC
1925

LOSEE

MERRILL R.
2100

12

YELLOW

CANNONVILLE
1635

U. OTT R.

1850

L OTT R.

GEORGETOWN
1755

BRYCE CANYON NATIONAL PARK

EAST FORK SEVER RIVER

SHEEP CK.

JOHNSON (STUBBS) R.
1900

HENDERSON R.
1878

F. WATSON
STONE CABIN
2000

HEWARD CK.

INDIAN   HOLLOW

UPPER JOHNSON R.
2050

LOWER JOHNSON R.   1900

WILLIS CREEK

SKUTUMPAH   ROAD

CLARK R.

2776

BULL VALLEY

CLIFFS

SHEEP   CREEK

LOWER

SKUTUMPAH ROAD

BULL VALLEY GORGE

PINK

BROWN SAWMILL
2150

BULLRUSH

LEFEVRE RANCH
2050

N

CRAWFORD C.

BROWN HOMESTEAD
2100

PODUNK   CK.

CLIFFS

MEADOWS R.
2250

DEER RANGE CANYON

DEER CK.

MEADOW CREEK

SWALLOW PARK R.
1850

HOLLOW

ADAIR L.

DEER RANGE POINT
2274

SKUTUMPAH
KANAB

LICK   WASH

1900

WHITE

DEER SPRING (FINDLAY) R.

NO MANS MESA

SCALE

0   5   10   KMS

Deer Spring Ranch, along the Skutumpah Road.

Not far above Deer Spring Ranch is the Meadows, and this old cabin, part of which was built about the turn of the century.

This is the oldest structure on the upper Ott Ranch, and still used today for storage.

From high above, one can see Adair Lake, the fault line, and the old corral.

Further Reading

Desert River Crossing, Historic Lee's Ferry on the Colorado River, Rusho-Crampton, Peregrine Smith, Inc.

Lee's Ferry, A Crossing of the Colorado River, Measeles, Pruett Publishing.

Lees Ferry and Lonely Dell Ranch Historic Districts, Grand Canyon Natural History Association, South Rim-Grand Canyon, Arizona.

Golden Nuggets of Pioneer Days--A History of Garfield County, Daughters of Utah Pioneers, Panguitch, Utah.

History of Kane County, Daughters of Utah Pioneers, Kanab, Utah.

John Doyle Lee, Zealot-Pioneer Builder-Scapegoat, Juanita Brooks, A.H. Clark Co.

Mountain Meadows Massacre, Juanita Brooks, University of Oklahoma Press.

Some Dreams Die, Utah's Ghost Towns, George A. Thompson, Dream Garden Press.

Utah Ghost Towns, Stephen L. Carr, Western Epics.

Chinle Formation of the Paria Plateau, J. P. Akers, Masters Thesis, U. of Arizona, 1960.

Geology of Bryce Canyon National Park, Lindquist, Bryce Canyon Natural History Association.

Sandstone and Conglomerate-Breccia Pipes and Dikes of the Kodachrome Basin Area, Kane County, Utah, Cheryl Hannum, *Masters Thesis,* Brigham Young U, 1979.

Professional Paper #226, USGS, *The Geology and Geography of the Paunsaugunt Region Utah,* Gregory.

Professional Paper #164, USGS, *The Kaiparowits Region,* Gregory and Moore.

Bulletin #1331-B, USGS, 1972, *Geology of Table Cliff Region, Utah,* Bowers.

Bulletin #87, UGMS, October 1970, *Stratigraphy of the San Rafael Group, Southwest and South Central Utah,* Thompson and Stokes.

Bulletin #19, Utah Geological Survey, 1965, *Stratigraphy of the Dakota and Tropic Formations,* Lawrence.

USGS Map MF-1475-D, *Mine and Prospect Map, Vermilion Cliffs,* Miscellaneous Field Studies.

USGS Map I-1033-K, *Map-Geology of the Kaiparowits Plateau,* Carter and Sargent.

Biography of John G. Kitchen (unpublished manuscript), J. G. Kitchen Jr., 1964.

History of Deer Spring Ranch (unpublished manuscript), Graden Robinson, Kanab, Utah.

Journal of Range Management, *Vegetation and Soils of No Man's Mesa , Utah,* Mason and others, January, 1967.

National Geographic Magazine, *First Motor Sortie into Escalante Land,* Breed, September, 1949.

The United Service, *An Episode of Military Exploration and Surveys,* Vol. 5, #119, October 1881.

Utah Historical Quarterly, *Historic Utilization of Paria River,* Reilly, Vol. 45, #2, 1977.

Utah Historical Quarterly, *Lee's Ferry at Lonely Dell,* Juanita Brooks, Vol. 25, 1957.

Wildlife Surveys and Investigations-*Desert Bighorn Sheep Restocking,* 1984, Arizona Game and Fish Department.

Other Guide Books by the Author

Climbers and Hikers Guide to the Worlds Mountains(2nd Ed.), Kelsey, 800 pages, 377 maps, 380 fotos, waterproof cover, 14cm x 21cm(5 1/2" x 8" x 1 1/2"), ISBN 0-9605824-2-8. **US $19.95** (Mail orders US $20.95).

Utah Mountaineering Guide, and the Best Canyon Hikes(2nd Ed.), Kelsey, 192 pages, 105 fotos, waterproof cover, 15cm x 23cm(6" x 9"), ISBN 0-9605824-5-2. **US $7.95** (Mail orders US $8.95).

Canyon Hiking Guide to the Colorado Plateau, Kelsey, 256 pages, 117 hikes and maps, 130 fotos, waterproof cover, 15cm x 23cm(6" x 9"), ISBN 0-9605824-1-5. **US $9.95** (Mail orders US $10.95).

Hiking Utah's San Rafael Swell, Kelsey, 144 pages, 30 mapped hikes, plus lots of history, 104 fotos, waterproof cover, 15cm x 23 cm(6" x 9"), ISBN 0-9605824-4-4. **US $7.95** (Mail orders US $8.95).

Hiking and Exploring Utah's Henry Mountains and Robbers Roost, Kelsey, 224 pages, 38 hikes or climbs, 163 fotos, including The Life and Legend of Butch Cassidy, waterproof cover, 15cm x 23cm(6" x 9"), ISBN 0-9605824-6-0. **US $8.95** (Mail orders US $9.95).

China on Your Own, and The Hiking Guide to China's Nine Sacred Mountains(3rd and Revised Ed.), Jennings/Kelsey, 240 pages, 110 maps, 16 hikes or climbs, waterproof cover, 14cm 21cm(5 1/2" x 8 1/2"), ISBN 0-9691363-1-5. **US $9.95** (Please order this book from **Milestone Publications, P.O. Box 35548, Station E, Vancouver, B.C., Canada, V6M 4G8).**